A
TEMPERAMENT THEORY
OF
PERSONALITY DEVELOPMENT

WILEY SERIES IN BEHAVIOR

KENNETH MacCORQUODALE, Editor
University of Minnesota

A Temperament Theory of Personality Development
ARNOLD H. BUSS AND ROBERT PLOMIN

Serial Learning and Paralearning
E. RAE HARCUM

A
TEMPERAMENT THEORY
OF
PERSONALITY DEVELOPMENT

ARNOLD H. BUSS
University of Texas

ROBERT PLOMIN
University of Colorado

A WILEY-INTERSCIENCE PUBLICATION

JOHN WILEY & SONS, New York • London • Sydney • Toronto

Copyright © 1975 by John Wiley & Sons, Inc.

All rights reserved. Published simultaneously in Canada.

Library of Congress Cataloging in Publication Data:

Buss, Arnold Herbert, 1924–
 A temperament theory of personality development.

 (Wiley series in behavior)
 "A Wiley-Interscience publication."
 Bibliography: p.
 Includes index.
 1. Temperament. I. Plomin, Robert, 1948–
joint author. II. Title. [DNLM: 1. Personality
development. BF698 B981t]

BF798.B87   155.2′34   74-32442
ISBN 0-471-12649-7

Printed in the United States of America

10 9 8 7 6 5 4 3 2 1

SERIES PREFACE

Psychology is one of the lively sciences. Its foci of research and theoretical concentration are diverse among us, and always on the move, sometimes into unexploited areas of scholarship, sometimes back for second thoughts about familiar problems, often into other disciplines for problems and for problem-solving techniques. We are always trying to apply what we have learned, and we have had some great successes at it. The Wiley Series in Behavior reflects this liveliness.

The series can accommodate monographic publication of purely theoretical advances, purely empirical ones, or any mixture in between. It welcomes books that span the interfaces within the behavioral sciences and between the behavioral sciences and their neighboring disciplines. The series is, then, a forum for the discussion of those advanced, technical, and innovative developments in the behavioral sciences that keep its frontiers flexible and explanding.

KENNETH MACCORQUODALE

Minneapolis, Minnesota
December 1974

ACKNOWLEDGMENTS

In developing our theory and in writing this book we received considerable help and feedback from colleagues and friends. Lee Willerman was a source of both information and positive criticism. So was Michael Scheier. Joseph Horn and David Cohen helped us sharpen our ideas. Kenneth MacCorquodale, the editor of this series, performed his editorial functions with skill and dispatch. Valerie Foster typed the entire manuscript and helped in many ways to clean up the exposition. Above all, our wives understood what we were doing and helped by allowing us to do it; we dedicate this book to them.

A. H. B.

R. P.

CONTENTS

A
TEMPERAMENT THEORY
OF
PERSONALITY DEVELOPMENT

CHAPTER

1

INTRODUCTION

Temperament has a long history and a short scientific past. For centuries, most scholars believed in the humoral theory of personality. This theory linked four bodily fluids to distinctive personality attributes. For example, an excess of bile would cause a person to be chronically angry, hence the word *choleric* (angry), which literally means *bile*. Similarly, an excess of black bile would cause a person to be chronically sad, hence the term *melancholy*, which literally means *black bile*. The humoral theory of personality has been put to rest, along with other medieval, prescientific notions.

More recent theories of temperament have been more compatible with modern science. Traditional scholarship suggests that we review these theories before advancing our own. We shall reverse this sequence and discuss these theories at the end of the book, in Chapter 10. This tactic will allow us to compare our theory with previous ones, and this comparison should enhance understanding of all the theories. Whatever the differences among theories of temperament, all are based on a model that relates temperament to personality.

MODELS OF TEMPERAMENT AND PERSONALITY

Tabula Rasa

To aid understanding, we shall start with a nontemperament model of personality. This model assumes that each person starts life as a blank slate

1

(tabula rasa) that will be written on by experience. It assumes that man's nature is that he has no nature. It flatly rejects the possibility of inborn tendencies that determine individual differences in personality. Environment is all. If there are stable individual differences, they are learned during childhood, during adulthood, or both.

We have no quarrel with this model if it is restricted to *some* aspects of personality. There is presently no basis for assuming that differences among persons in self-esteem, guilt, or authoritarianism are derived from inborn dispositions. These and many other aspects of personality would seem to be wholly acquired during the course of living. But we cannot accept this model for *all* aspects of personality. Some behavioral tendencies—we would argue, some of the most basic personality tendencies—originate in inherited dispositions.

One-Way Temperament Model

For purposes of exposition, let us start with the simplest model of temperament. Such a model would make three assumptions. The first is that children start life with a small number of inherited personality dispositions. These innate tendencies are broad, and they ostensibly underlie a variety of personality traits. The second assumption is that the inborn dispositions determine many individual differences in personality. That is, some of the most important ways in which we differ from one another are determined mainly by inheritance. The third assumption is that the broad, inherited tendencies are modifiable by the environment. Presumably, what is inherited is a *reaction range* rather than a precise place on a personality dimension.

To make these points concrete, we shall use intelligence as an example. There is wide acceptance of an inherited component in intelligence, and there is a factual basis for this consensus. What is inherited? Presumably a broad disposition that is reflected in the notion of a *general intelligence* (*g*). One person is predisposed to be bright, another average, and another below average in intelligence. Their intelligence in adulthood, as measured by an intelligence test, reflects both the original disposition and the impact of the environment. Consider the score on one of the best subtests of intelligence, vocabulary. Those with a better inherited disposition have a higher vocabulary level, but those who have been exposed to a wider range of words also have a higher vocabulary level. In terms of the model, the original intellectual inheritance is modified by the environment.

The last sentence is the core of the model. It specifies two aspects, an inborn disposition and an environment that modifies this disposition. Note the direction of the effect: the environment alters the temperament. This is why we have called it the *one-way* temperament model. Our position is that this model is clearly better than a nontemperament model of personality, but it still does not suffice. We believe that temperament and environment *interact*: each affects the other.

Interaction Temperament Model

Our model of temperament is somewhat more complex. It includes everything in the one-way model *plus* one other assumption: that temperament can affect the environment. And the environment that is being influenced is mainly *social*, that is, other persons. There are three ways in which the environment can be changed.

SETTING THE TONE

Each of us is a complex of stimulus properties that impinge on others. Even before a social interaction starts, we can set the tone for the other person's initial behavior. Consider two persons waiting for a third to appear. One person might be calm, composed, and unmoving; the other might be upset, disorganized, and restless. So each one establishes a very different ambiance for the forthcoming interaction with the third person. We believe that individual differences in restlessness and composure have a temperamental basis, and such differences partially determine the way others behave initially, so a person can make his own environment in the general way he presents himself to others. The effect is indirect and diffuse.

INITIATING BEHAVIOR

Here the emphasis is on *instrumental* behavior: responses that have a direct impact on the environment. Compare two persons who differ in sociability. The highly sociable person tends to seek out others and initiate contact. He is likely to start a conversation, to suggest a *group* activity, and to avoid solitary tasks. His opposite number, the person low in sociability, is more likely to seek solitary tasks, to avoid group activity, and to remain passive in a new social situation. Both persons are in part structuring their social environment by their instrumental behavior. One is likely to find himself surrounded by other persons; the other is likely to be alone or with only one or two persons. One makes social contacts more interactive by the thrust of his social behavior; the other tends to convert a social contact into a nonsocial one by his lack of social initiative.

The *social* environment can be structured readily, but the *nonsocial* environment also can be affected. A highly active person can make sure that he is constantly busy merely by scheduling a huge list of tasks to perform. He may complain, half in jest, that he has a killing schedule, implying that the environment is forcing him to be active. But the truth in most instances is that he prefers it this way and programs his life so as to keep him busy. In effect, he selects his own environment.

REINFORCEMENT

Each of us offers feedback to others in social interaction. If we reinforce the responses others make to us, these responses should occur with greater frequency. In the absence of reinforcement, the responses of others should wane. Again consider sociability. If you meet a sociable person, he usually responds warmly. He smiles, becomes involved, and in general shows that the interaction is pleasant for him. Thus rewarded, you are more likely to seek him out again. But when you meet an unsociable person, he is likely to be unresponsive or even uncomfortable. He may not smile or if he does, it is a weak attempt at a smile; he may fidget and sweat; and he may let the conversation die. Given this response to your initial approach, you will be less likely to seek him out again. So each person in part determines the future of his social environment. The sociable person encourages further social contacts; the unsociable person turns them off.

In brief, there is a sense in which a person can make his own environment. He can do this as a *background stimulus object*, setting the tone for social interaction; as an *initiator*, stimulating others or programming his environment; or as a *reinforcer*, rewarding or not rewarding the efforts of others. But remember that this is a two-way street. The environment is acting on him in a precisely reciprocal way. The environment also sets the tone for social interaction, stimulates him, and differentially reinforces his behavior.

No one doubts that the environment can modify temperament, but there are limits. The effect of any particular environment depends in part on temperament. In the long run, even intense environmental pressure cannot *radically* alter a temperamental disposition. In our view, a low-active child cannot be made into a "perpetual motion machine." And a high-active child cannot be made to keep still and play quietly over long periods of time. Each child would react against the external pressure and return to his inborn level of activity. He might *temporarily* elevate or depress his pace of responding but would not keep it up. Sooner or later, he would drift back toward his natural level. In other words, temperament can alter the impact of the environment.

In rare instances, a person might deviate for a long time from his natural tendency. For example, a sociable person might take a job as a forest ranger. For months at a time he would live an isolated existence, almost devoid of contact with others. Or an unsociable person might be forced to take a job as the social director of a resort, where he would be thrown into constant association with others. Although rare, such things do occur. We suggest that they are rare because most persons are not foolish enough to defy their own inborn dispositions. But when such cases do occur, there must be an intense *strain* on the person. He would eventually become worn out from fighting his own strong disposition and from having to exist in a fashion that is alien to him. The kind of strain probably depends on both the temperament and which extreme the person is at (for example, high versus low sociability). More of this later.

To summarize, our model starts with inborn dispositions. The subsequent course of these dispositions is determined by a complex interaction with the environment, but the environment, in turn, is also affected by the dispositions. The social environment may be *shaped* by temperament initially or through feedback. Temperament may determine which environments are *selected*. There are limits to the *impact* of the environment, and temperament-environment mismatches can lead to strain.

THE DOMAIN OF TEMPERAMENT

What precisely is temperament? There is no simple answer. We begin with a definition by Allport:

> Temperament refers to the characteristic phenomena of an individual's nature, including his susceptibility to emotional stimulation, his customary strength and speed of response, the quality of his prevailing mood, and all the peculiarities of fluctuation and intensity of mood, these being phenomena regarded as dependent on constitutional make-up, and therefore largely hereditary in origin. [1961, p. 34]

Allport properly includes a hereditary component, which is necessary to distinguish temperament from other personality dispositions. Other aspects of his definition must be made explicit, specifically, the issues of style and generality of behavior.

Style versus Content

Any given behavior may be analyzed in terms of *content* and *style*. Content refers to *what* the response is: affection, aggression, problem solving, etc. Style refers to *how* the response is made: fast or slow, mild or intense, sparse and unelaborated or adorned and elaborated, etc. Temperament generally deals more with the stylistic aspects of behavior, although there are exceptions.

To illustrate the contrast between content and style, we shall examine the role of teacher in a college classroom. The *content* of the role is somewhat fixed and permits little variation from one teacher to the next. A teacher lectures, leads the class, maintains order, and evaluates the students' performance. The *manner* (style) in which these requirements are carried out varies considerably from one teacher to the next. At one extreme, a teacher might perform his role with considerable vigor, speak rapidly, interact closely and informally with the students, display spontaneity, shock them with surprise demonstrations, and maintain a carefree mood while lecturing. At the other extreme, a teacher might stay behind the podium, speak softly and in measured tones, maintain his distance from the students, sustain a serious tone while lecturing, and stick close to a formal syllabus.

These two aspects of roles—content and style—are the focus of two disparate approaches to personality. The *social-cultural* approach emphasizes man's place in society and the content of his behavior in social contexts. Role prescriptions and expectations are paramount here, and little attention is paid to the manner in which the role is played. The *individual differences* approach, in contrast, emphasizes the personal contribution of the individual playing the role: what does he bring to the role that is different from the next person? This is not to equate a focus on individual differences with an emphasis on style, but to indicate that some of the most important individual differences are stylistic. The teacher's role illustrates the importance of style in individual differences. Students clearly differentiate among teachers as *persons* not by the subject they teach but by the manner in which they teach. Teachers are evaluated not by the subject matter or the type of class but by how well they communicate and sustain interest, both of which derive much more from style than from content.

Parenthetically, the role of teacher has clearer expectations and is more formal and public than most of the roles that we play in everyday life. In the classroom the teacher can retreat behind the attributes of the role and to some extent conceal his personal characteristics. In the more informal and private roles of friend, wife, mother, or neighbor such concealment is more difficult. Role expectations are less detailed and rigid, and the person must imbue the role with more of his own personality. These considerations suggest that informal contexts are best for observing personality, and this is especially true of the temperamental aspects of personality.

Generalized versus Specific

Temperament is concerned with *broad* personality dispositions rather than highly specific acts or traits. One reason is that temperaments are inherited tendencies. Why should inherited behavioral tendencies be broad rather than narrow? The answer may be found by examining our evolutionary heritage. Lower animals tend to have many innate tendencies, and most of these are highly specific. During the evolutionary sequence that eventually led to man, there were two trends. First, there were fewer tendencies built in, and more behavior patterns were determined by learning. Second, the remaining innate tendencies were somewhat diffuse and generalized. So, in seeking inborn personality dispositions, we expect to find broad tendencies rather than narrow ones.

A broad tendency at birth may be expected to differentiate as the child matures. As the tendency differentiates, the relationship among its various components should weaken. So, if a given temperament differentiates during development, we would expect its components to correlate less and less as the years pass. But the correlation between each component and the overall temperament should remain high.

These points are well illustrated by intelligence. It is a *broad* inherited disposition. It *differentiates* during development into various components of intelligence. These components correlate less with one another in successive age groups. Nevertheless, there are substantial correlations between each component and total IQ.

In summary, temperament is concerned more with style than with content, more with expressive behavior than with instrumental (coping) behavior, and more with what a person brings to a role or situation than what either of these demand of him. Finally, temperaments are broad dispositions that are expected to differentiate during development, much like intelligence.

FOUR TEMPERAMENTS

Our theory suggests four temperaments: activity, emotionality, sociability, and impulsivity. We offer them in slightly rearranged order as the acronym EASI to make remembering them easier (pun intended). Level of *activity* refers to total energy output. The active person is typically busy and in a hurry. He likes to keep moving and may seem tireless. His speech and actions are vigorous.

Emotionality is equivalent to intensity of reaction. The emotional person is easily aroused, and he tends to have an excess of affect. It may appear as a strong temper, a tendency toward fearfulness, violent mood swings, or all these together. The autonomic nervous system is usually involved in such arousal, but we also include the *expressive* aspects of emotional arousal.

Sociability consists mainly of affiliativeness: a strong desire to be with others. For the sociable person, interaction with others is far more rewarding than most nonsocial reinforcers. We also assume that sociable persons are more *responsive* to others.

Impulsivity involves the tendency to respond quickly rather than inhibiting the response. We assume two main components: (1) resisting versus giving in to urges, impulses, or motivational states; and (2) responding immediately and impetuously to a stimulus versus lying back and planning before making a move.

These four temperaments are summarized in Table 1.1. How do the temperaments relate to one another? The discerning reader may have noticed some overlap. For example, sociability and activity may partially merge. A sociable person is expected to initiate contact with others. Such behavior may require an output of energy—more so than the relative passivity of an unsociable person. And a highly active person may well be energetic both socially and nonsocially. In either event, we expect a modest correlation between activity and sociability.

There may be two other built-in relationships. Activity level may be considered as an "engine" that supplies motive power. So can emotionality: the emotional person reacts intensely and powerfully. To continue the automobile metaphor, impulsivity may be viewed as the "brakes" (or lack of brakes). With a given set of brakes, a more powerful car stops more slowly than a less powerful car. In terms of temperament, an active person might appear more impulsive than an inactive person. For example, if two persons were required to sit quietly, the more active one would surely squirm and fidget. Such behavior would appear impulsive.

Similarly, an emotional person reacts intensely and therefore has a greater problem in controlling his emotions. If he vents his anger, shows his fear, or expresses his moods, he will be seen as impulsive. So we expect a modest correlation between impulsivity and both activity and emotionality.

We do not regard such overlap as a serious problem. Actually it is inevitable, given the way we define the four temperaments. Activity and emo-

TABLE 1.1 FOUR TEMPERAMENTS

Temperament	Extremes of the dimension	Aspect of behavior
Activity	Active–lethargic	How much
Emotionality	Emotional–impassive	Intensity
Sociability	Gregarious–detached	How close to others (proximity seeking)
Impulsivity	Impulsive–deliberate	Quickness vs. inhibition of response

tionality both involve a kind of "*push*," each of a different kind. Impulsivity involves inhibitory *control*, which may be used to oppose any motivational push. And sociability is a *directional* tendency, which cuts across the push to activity. It might be possible to devise a set of temperaments that would not overlap one another, but we could not find such a set that would meet the criteria for temperaments.

CRITERIA FOR TEMPERAMENTS

We suggest five criteria to be used in deciding which personality dispositions should be called temperaments. The crucial one is *inheritance,* which is central to the remaining four. An inherited component leads forward to developmental expectations of *stability during childhood* and *retention into maturity.* And it may be traced backward to *adaptive value* and *presence in our animal forebears.*

Genetic Component

The most important criterion of temperament is *inheritance,* for this is what distinguishes temperament from other personality dispositions. Many aspects of personality derive from socialization practices and the experiences of the developing child, but a theory of temperament cannot be concerned with them. Rather it must establish that important dimensions of personality are at least in part determined by the genes. Nor is it sufficient to point out that animals can be bred for certain characteristics (dogs, for example, can be bred for gentleness or ferocity), because more of animals' behavior may be genetically determined than man's behavior. A theory of temperament must demonstrate a genetic component in *man's* personality dispositions.

Stability During Development

An inherited tendency can be expected to be manifest throughout development. Presumably, it is something that inheres in the child as he matures, so it should be stable throughout development. We expect fluctuations during childhood and must allow for errors of measurement. And the tasks that confront the child may change appreciably as he matures. For example, the child moves from social interaction exclusively with the immediate family (especially parents) to a wider world of adults and peers, and this means that sociability becomes manifest in different ways. These considerations suggest that the criterion of stability during childhood should not be applied too stringently. We cannot expect a smooth curve of development in any trait, including such genetically determined anatomical traits as height and body build. But the criterion must be applied, and there are two reasons for doing so. First, it follows that if a disposition is inherited, it will be relatively stable during childhood. Second, if there is no stability, it must be assumed that it is wiped out or covered over by purely environmental variables and therefore is of little importance in determining adult personality.

Presence in Adults

If a personality disposition is inherited and shows at least moderate stability during childhood, it should be present in adults. This is a criterion for any ostensible personality dimension, whether or not there is a genetic component. This criterion is, in a sense, a one-way street. If the disposition is found in adults, this is merely *consistent* with its being a temperament; but it might have originated in childhood experience and have no genetic basis. If the disposition cannot be found in adults, either it is not really a temperament or it is so weak a disposition that it disappears by adulthood. In either case, a temperament theory would be seriously weakened.

Adaptiveness

Why are certain traits inherited? Darwin's theory of evolution provides the answer: they are adaptive. Traits that help the organism to thrive, procreate, and set the next generation on its way must come to predominate in the long run. Thus if a trait is shown to be inherited, this is presumptive evidence that it is adaptive. There are only two exceptions: (1) the trait might have been adaptive previously but no longer serves a purpose; and (2) the trait is in itself not adaptive and is present only because it is somehow *associated* with a trait that is adaptive. In brief, one criterion of a temperament is that it should be adaptive (or should previously have been adaptive).

Are the four temperaments of our theory adaptive? A reasonably high level of *activity* would help in coping with the physical environment, especially in seeking food and obtaining shelter. The potential for high levels of arousal—the essence of *emotionality*—is necessary as part of preparation to deal with threat, either by fighting or fleeing. Man thrives best in groups, which means that a tendency toward *sociability* would be adaptive. Finally, variations in *impulsivity* make sense in that some inhibitory control is basic to both higher mental processes and group living. Thus all four temperaments are adaptive.

But the criterion of adaptiveness can be met by a variety of personality dispositions. This makes it a weak criterion of temperament: necessary but not sufficient.

Presence in Animals

If a tendency has sufficient adaptive value to be passed on through the genes, it
is likely to be present not only in man but in animals close to man. Presumably, man—especially early man—shares with animals many of the problems of everyday life: obtaining food and shelter, sharing with others,
procreating, rearing the next generation, etc. It seems reasonable that in the
process of evolving, man retained some of the built-in tendencies that were
adaptive in his forebears.

Like adaptiveness, presence in animals is a rational criterion and therefore
not a crucial one. Nevertheless, it makes good sense, and it strengthens the
case for temperament if a disposition present in man also occurs in animals.
Our four temperaments, activity, emotionality, sociability, and impulsivity,
may be seen in a variety of mammals and especially in primates.

WHAT FOLLOWS

The Rest of the Theory

So far we have considered the four elemental temperaments and criteria for
evaluating them. The remainder of our theory offers details about the temperaments and how they interact with the environment. Each temperament is
closely examined to reveal its components or aspects. For example, both vigor
and tempo involve the kind of energy output that we associate with activity
temperament. If we assume that both are components of activity, surely they
are highly correlated. Perhaps they are highly correlated early in life and subsequently differentiated during development. Such analysis not only suggests a
different perspective for viewing personality but offers a means of testing the
theory, for example, the prediction that vigor and tempo are highly correlated.

The issue of testability raises a more general issue about our theory. Part of
the theory is not entirely new in the sense that others before us have suggested
similar or related innate personality dispositions. So part of our exposition will
be devoted to showing why our particular set of temperaments is better. Some
of our assumptions can be checked *directly* against facts that have already been
collected. Some of our hypotheses can be checked *indirectly* against facts that
were obtained by others for entirely different purposes. Some of our hypotheses

have led to our own research, and we shall be concerned with the outcome of these tests of the theory. Finally, some of the theory concerns speculations that have not been tested and may be hard to test directly. Some of these speculations concern the nature of the temperaments and others deal with implications for personality and abnormal psychology.

We believe that our theory is basically correct, but as scientists we know that at least some of its details will prove to be mistaken. Our task, then, is to be rigorous in stating hypotheses in testable form and to make sure that the theory *can* be proved wrong. And we shall speculate, on the assumption that the ideas may prove valuable as explanations or as leads to new research. Above all, we shall try to separate facts from hypotheses, and directly testable hypotheses from less testable speculations.

Our analysis of the temperaments extends to how they are measured. Most previous research has not tied measures to a theory of temperament, which leads to difficulties in assessing temperaments. For example, if we assess restlessness, is it a measure of impulsivity or activity? Our answer is *activity* (for details, see Chapter 3).

The temperament model involves an interaction between initial endowments and life experiences. Our theory suggests what happens to the temperaments during development. For example, the temperament of sociability may enter in different situations later in development than it does early in development. In addition, inputs from socializing agents probably modify the initial temperamental endowment.

Each temperament may be regarded as a fundamental building block of personality. But these elements do not occur singly in any person; each of us represents some combination of the four temperaments. Our theory uses combinations of two and three temperaments to account for such well-known personality patterns as extraversion, psychopathy, and hyperkinesis, as well as patterns that have received less attention. These attempts to explain particular "personalities" by combinations of temperaments is merely a first approximation. Hopefully, our speculations—which are testable—will encourage others to try combinations we have overlooked.

Plan of the Book

The temperaments are discussed singly in Chapters 3 to 6. Each chapter contains a description of at least one extreme of the temperament. These descriptions are not part of the theory but merely devices to provide concrete details about the behaviors relevant to the temperament. An analysis of each temperament is followed by a discussion of measures and then the developmental course of the temperament (except for activity). Gender differences have been established for three of the temperaments, and we discuss the origin of such differences in Chapter 7.

Temperaments do not occur in isolation, and in Chapter 8 we theorize about various combinations of two and three temperaments; also included are the concepts of introversion-extraversion and arousal. Parent-child interactions are treated in Chapter 9, which attempts to integrate research on inborn dispositions with research on child-rearing practices. Chapter 10 presents general conclusions, relates our theory to other theories of temperament, and speculates about both the physiological basis of temperaments and the direction of future research.

At this point the reader is roughly where we were several years ago with respect to temperament, possessing some abstract knowledge about temperaments but lacking empirical findings. We needed concrete evidence that our temperaments have an inherited basis and factorial unity. The appropriate research is described in Chapter 2.

CHAPTER

2

INHERITED BASIS
AND
FACTORIAL UNITY

This chapter has two aims: (1) to suggest that our postulated temperaments have an inherited basis, and (2) to show empirically that there are four separate temperaments. The first involves behavior genetics; the second, factor analysis. The issues are complex and technical, but the details are necessary to make an initial case for the temperaments. The reader uninterested in these quantitative issues may skip to Chapter 3. In succeeding chapters there is further evidence on the temperaments, and this chapter only lays the groundwork.

INHERITED BASIS

Each organism is born with a set of "blueprints" (genes), and both anatomical and behavioral traits are "constructed" with the available "materials" (environment). Without genes, there is no new organism; and the organism can exist only in an environment. Thus heredity and environment are so closely intertwined in any *individual* that they cannot be separated. Ultimately, the only way to separate their effects is to study *groups* of organisms. This can be done experimentally through breeding or manipulating environments, but such control must be limited to animals and cannot be extended to humans for obvious ethical reasons. The only recourse with humans is to observe groups of persons in whom we can estimate genetic and environmental similarity.

Human Behavior Genetics

Behavior genetics methods are like natural experiments in which groups are found who differ in genetic similarity or environmental similarity. The most popular method of determining human inheritance compares monozygotic and dizygotic twins. Monozygotic twins develop from the same fertilized ovum and so share the same set of inherited blueprints; for this reason, they are often called *identical twins*. Another way of describing them is to say that their *genotype* is identical. Because monozygotic twins are identical genetically, and observed (or phenotypic) differences between the twins can be ascribed to the environment.

Dizygotic twins develop from two separate fertilized ova. They are no more alike genetically than other brothers and sisters; on the average, they share 50% of their genes. Any observed (phenotypic) differences between fraternal twins are attributable to a combination of genetic and environmental causes.

The twin method assumes that environmental influences are essentially the same for the two types of twins. If the identical twins are observed to be more similar than the fraternal twins, this difference in their correlations is ascribed to the greater genetic similarity of the identical twins. This means that the trait is influenced by genetic factors. In theory, a trait entirely determined by genetic factors would yield an identical twin correlation of 1.0 and a fraternal twin correlation of .50.

Another method, *family studies*, traces the pedigree of traits over several generations. This method yields less conclusive results because it confounds genetic and environmental similarity. Parents who supply their children's genes also raise these children; siblings who share on the average 50% of their genes also share a common environment. A genetic hypothesis requires a positive correlation between parents and their children, or between siblings. So a family study can yield evidence consistent with a genetic hypothesis, but not proof.

A third behavior genetics method, *adoption studies*, untangles the familial confound between heredity and environment by studying children reared in foster homes. First, the children can be compared with their natural parents. Because these biological parents did not rear the children and therefore had no postnatal environmental influence, any similarities between the biological parents and their children must be attributed to heredity. Next, the children can be compared with their foster parents. Because these foster parents are entirely unrelated and therefore contributed no genes to the children, any similarities must be attributed to environmental influences.

The most convincing support for the inheritance of a trait comes from the *convergence* of evidence from twin, adoption, and pedigree studies. For a particular trait, if monozygotic twins are significantly more similar than dizygotic twins, if adopted children resemble their natural parents more than their adoptive parents, and if familial similarity on that trait conforms to genetic relatedness, the inheritance of that trait is beyond dispute. However, intelligence is the only personality trait for which data from all three methods has been amassed. For intelligence, all the data point to the same conclusion: there is a substantial inherited component in intelligence.

The inheritance of intelligence has been studied far more than other personality traits. The only evidence bearing on the inheritance of temperaments other than intelligence comes from a handful of twin studies. Optimally, adoption studies comparing adopted children with their natural and foster parents would be used in the study of personality. But such studies are hard to do. Data on the personality of natural parents of adopted children are seldom collected. Information about the adopting parents is elusive because of the conventional confidentiality of adoption agencies, and all adoption information is becoming increasingly difficult to obtain because of the decline of adoptions in the United States. In any event, there is little rationale for attempting to overcome these obstacles of adoption research until personality traits are screened for inheritance by the twin method.

OUR TWIN STUDY OF TEMPERAMENTS

The available twin studies of temperament are reviewed in the chapters on emotionality, activity, sociability, and impulsivity. On the whole, they tend to support the inheritance of the temperaments, but the studies vary considerably in the behaviors sampled and the way traits were defined. Accordingly, as a first step in the study of the four temperaments, we conducted a twin study that focused directly on the four traits that appeared to meet the logical criteria of temperaments.

EASI Temperament Survey

We constructed a 20-item questionnaire, five items for each temperament (see Table 2.1). The first item listed for each temperament is a general item, and the others are more specific. For example, the general emotionality item is

TABLE 2.1   THE EASI TEMPERAMENT SURVEY (I)

Emotionality

```
Child gets upset easily
Child tends to cry easily
Child is easily frightened
Child is easygoing or happy-go-lucky  (reverse)
Child has a quick temper
```

Activity

```
Child is always on the go
Child likes to be off and running as soon as he wakes up in the
morning
Child cannot sit still long
Child prefers quiet games such as block play or coloring to more
active games (reverse)
Child fidgets at meals and similar occasions
```

Sociability

```
Child likes to be with others
Child makes friends easily
Child tends to be shy  (reverse)
Child tends to be independent  (reverse)
Child prefers to play by himself rather than with others
(reverse)
```

Impulsivity

```
Child tends to be impulsive
Learning self-control is difficult for the child
Child gets bored easily
Child learns to resist temptation easily  (reverse)
Child goes from toy to toy quickly
```

"Child gets upset easily," and the more specific items have to do with crying, being frightened, good-naturedness, and quick temper. Each item was rated on a scale of 1 (a little) to 5 (a lot). Thus for each temperament, the possible range of scores was 5 to 25.

Sample

Mothers of 139 pairs of same-sexed twins completed the temperament survey by rating both of their twins. This sample overlaps that reported by Buss et al.

(1973) but is larger and more homogeneous in age. The average age of the twins was 55 months, and their age range was one to nine years. On the average, the mothers had completed two years of college. Their ethnicity was predominantly Anglo, and the average income for their families was $14,500. These characteristics of the sample reflect the general composition of the Mothers of Twins Club, from which this sample was drawn.

Zygosity Determination

Typically, blood is analyzed to determine whether twins are identical or fraternal. The basic logic is straightforward: because many genetic loci determine the makeup of blood, if the twins' blood differs in any way, the twins must be fraternal. If many features are examined and the twins differ on none, they must be identical twins. In recent years, an easier method of zygosity diagnosis has been developed. Physical attributes such as hair color and eye color are genetically determined and can thus be used in the same way as blood. Thus if twins differ in characteristics such as hair color or eye color they must be fraternal. Similarly, if a pair of twins does not differ on any of a large number of physical attributes, they can be assumed to be identical.

A questionnaire of physical similarity was developed by Nichols and Bilbro (1966), which yielded 93% accuracy of diagnosis as compared with blood analysis. Other questionnaires have offered similar results, with accuracy as high as 98% agreement with blood diagnosis (Cohen et al., 1973). Thus zygosity determination by questionnaire is highly accurate, and the infrequent errors in zygosity diagnosis tend to *reduce* the strength of any estimate of genetic influence. Misdiagnosing identical twins as fraternal will make the group labeled *fraternal twins* similar, thereby raising their correlation. Misdiagnosing fraternal twins as identical will make the group labeled *identical twins* less similar, thereby lowering their correlation. Thus both kinds of misdiagnosis decrease the difference between the correlations for identical and fraternal twins, yielding a lower estimate of genetic influence.

In our sample, zygosity was determined (without knowledge of the EASI Temperament Survey results) by a questionnaire modified from Nichols and Bilbro (1966). The original questionnaire was designed for ratings of adults, and we modified the items for parental ratings of children. We classified 81 pairs of twins as identical and 57 pairs as fraternal. Of the identical twins, 38 pairs were male and 43 were female; 33 fraternal twins were male and 24 were female. There was an unusual shortage of fraternal twin girls, but this shortage reflected the distribution of twins in the Mothers of Twins Clubs as estimated by the National Organization of Mothers of Twins Clubs. Any systematic bias caused by a shortage of fraternal twin girls would be reflected in consistent gender differences in heritability; there were no consistent gender differences, as will be seen below.

Correlations

The simplest way to determine similarity between twins is by intraclass correlation. We computed correlations for *each item* of the EASI Temperament Survey, mainly for the sake of completeness. The interested reader will find them in Appendix 1. The correlations for the four *scales* are presented in Table 2.2. The correlations are clearly higher for identical twins than for fraternal twins. The differences in correlations must be considered in light of standard errors, which are large in these small samples. The correlations differed by so much that the *F* ratios (identical vs. fraternal correlations) were all significant—with the exception of impulsivity in girls. The markedly greater similarity of identical twins suggests a genetic component for the EASI traits.

Another way of looking at these results is in terms of a statistic called *heritability*, which is the proportion of total variance accounted for by genetic factors. The correlations can be used to compute this statistic (Falconer, 1960). We prefer not to do so because the statistic implies far more precision than the data from small samples warrant (Loehlin & Nichols, in press).

TABLE 2.2 CORRELATIONS* AND STANDARD ERRORS FOR THE SCALES OF THE EASI TEMPERAMENT SURVEY (I)

| | Boys | | | | Girls | | | |
| | Identical (38 pairs) | | Fraternal (33 pairs) | | Identical (43 pairs) | | Fraternal (24 pairs) | |
	r	SE	r	SE	r	SE	r	SE
Emotionality	.68		.00		.60		.05	
		(.12)		(.18)		(.13)		(.21)
Activity	.73		.18		.50		.00	
		(.11)		(.18)		(.13)		(.21)
Sociability	.65		.20		.58		.06	
		(.13)		(.18)		(.13)		(.21)
Impulsivity	.84		.05		.71		.59	
		(.09)		(.18)		(.11)		(.17)

*Correlations listed are intraclass correlations that are equivalent to product-moment correlations computed by the double-entry method in which each pair of twins is entered twice with the order of the twins reversed.

Interpretation

The pattern of correlations in Table 2.2 argues strongly for a genetic component in at least three of the temperaments; the case for impulsivity is still in doubt. This does not mean that the EASI temperaments are entirely inherited. As we noted earlier, differences within pairs of identical twins must be environmental in origin, and the identical twin correlations are not 1.00. In addition, the differences between the identical and fraternal twin correlations in Table 2.2 were too large to be attributed solely to inheritance. When a trait is partly determined by genetic factors, the fraternal twin correlation should be roughly half the identical twin correlation regardless of the environmental input. Major departures from this expectation suggest environmental biases that differentially influence identical and fraternal twins, and this is the case for the correlations in Table 2.2. The problem is this: if there is a genetic component as indicated by the large difference between identical and fraternal twins, the genetic component should also be reflected in a lower but substantial fraternal twin correlation. Our fraternal twin correlations are too low. So there must be nongenetic influences making identical twins *more* alike or fraternal twins *less* alike, or both. These influences have been labeled *assimilation* and *contrast*, respectively (Loehlin & Nichols, in press).

Identical twins may have more *similar environments* than fraternal twins. In a large twin study of high school students, it was found that identical twins dressed more similarly, played together more, spent more time together as adolescents, and were treated more alike by their parents (Loehlin and Nichols, in press). These environmental factors are more similar for identical twins than fraternal twins, but do these factors make twins more similar in personality? Loehlin and Nichols found that identical twins who had more similar environments were *no more similar* in personality than identical twins who were treated less similarly. They concluded that "the greater similarity of our identical twins' experience in terms of dress, playing together, and so forth, cannot plausibly account for more than a very small fraction of their greater observed similarity." So the more similar environment of identical twins may not bias studies of personality in twins.

If the environments for the two types of twins do not cause differences in personality, why do the correlations in Table 2.2 depart from the expected pattern? Perhaps it was because we used *ratings* of young children. Most research to be examined in subsequent chapters used *self-report* data from adolescents. The self-report data tend to conform much more to the expected pattern of correlations for the two types of twins than do the rating data. But ratings, either by teachers or peers (Eysenck, 1956) or by an experimenter (Scarr, 1965, 1969) yield differences between the identical and fraternal twin correlations that are too large to be explained by a simple genetic model.

Raters may minimize differences within pairs of identical twins or maximize differences within pairs of fraternal twins, or both. These tendencies would inflate identical twin correlations or deflate fraternal twin correlations, or both. The outcome would be patterns of correlations that depart from the expected pattern.

Ultimately, these issues must be settled empirically. Ratings lead to one kind of error that gives us pause in concluding that our temperaments are inherited. Self-reports lead to other kinds of error (lying, social desirability, etc.) that may also cause doubt. But both self-report and rating studies have yielded data indicating heritability—a fact that will be documented in the next four chapters. Given such converging evidence, we feel relatively secure in concluding that our temperaments have an inherited component.

TEMPERAMENT FACTORS

The second major question of this chapter is: are the temperaments factorially sound? Answering this question involved three versions of the EASI Temperament Survey.

EASI-I

TWIN STUDY

The items of the 20-item temperament survey referred to in Table 2.1 and used in the twin study were intercorrelated, factor analyzed, and rotated to the Varimax solution for boys and girls (Buss et al., 1973). The items and their factor loadings are presented in Table 2.3. For both boys and girls, the majority of systematic variance was accounted for by four factors, essentially the four temperaments. At least three of the five items assigned to each a priori scale loaded highest on the appropriate factor. For each temperament factor, the general item loaded highest or second highest.

There were some discrepancies between a priori assignment and the outcome of the factor analysis. For both genders, the item "Child cannot sit still long" loaded on both the activity and impulsivity factors. And the factorial picture was somewhat clearer for boys than for girls. Thus for boys, the impulsivity items were factorially the purest, whereas for girls these items also loaded on the emotionality factor.

Table 2.4 lists the correlations among the a priori scales. For both genders, activity and impulsivity were related, and emotionality was marginally related to impulsivity. The relationship between activity and impulsivity was due to

TABLE 2.3   ITEMS AND FACTOR LOADINGS OF THE CHILD'S VERSION OF THE EASI-I

A priori Scale Assignment**	Boys (*N* = 140)				Girls (*N* = 116)			
	EMO	ACT	SOC	IMP	EMO	ACT	SOC	IMP
Emotionality								
Gets upset	.86				.67			
Cries easily	.76				.75			
Quick temper	.61				.48			
Easily frightened	.56				.55	.44		
Easygoing	-.57		.51					
Activity								
Always on the go		.73				.68		
Off and running		.80				.83		
Cannot sit still		.58		.55		.53		.54
Prefers quiet games								
Fidgets				.40		.31		.72
Sociability								
Likes to be with others			.77				.60	
Makes friends easily			.82				.81	
Tends to be shy			-.43				-.73	
Is independent								
Prefers to play by himself			-.62					
Impulsivity								
Impulsive		.68		.35				.79
Self-control		.79		.42				.45
Bored easily		.49		.70				
Learns to resist temptation				-.67				-.52
Goes from toy to toy		.63		.35				.66

* Only factor loadings greater than .30 are listed.
**Exact wording of the items listed in Table 2.1.

overlapping items (restlessness). When these items were revised in the EASI-II (discussed below) the correlation between activity and impulsivity dropped to a low value. With the exception of the correlation between activity and impulsivity, the temperaments are relatively independent.

Table 2.5 lists the means and standard deviations on the four temperaments. The size of the standard deviations indicates that the scales are sampling a

TABLE 2.4 INTERCORRELATIONS FOR THE *a priori* SCALES OF THE CHILDREN'S VERSION OF THE EASI-I

| | Boys (N = 144) | | | | Girls (N = 134) | | | |
	EMO	ACT	SOC	IMP	EMO	ACT	SOC	IMP
Emotionality		.13	-.19	.36		-.10	-.40	.32
Activity			.22	.59			.06	.49
Sociability				.05				.05

wide range of each temperament, from the low to the high end. The mean differences between boys and girls are small and random, a point we return to in subsequent chapters.

COLLEGE STUDY

The EASI-I was revised slightly to produce a self-report inventory for adults. The items were changed from the third person, "Child gets upset easily," to the first person, "I get upset easily." Also the wording of three of the items was changed to make them more appropriate for adults. This version was administered to a college sample of 162 men and 207 women. The factor analysis is presented in Table 2.6. The pattern of factor loadings is very similar to the children's version. The major exception is that for the college women of this sample, activity did not emerge as a distinct factor but was intertwined with sociability.

The intercorrelations of the a priori scales are listed in Table 2.7 and the means and standard deviations are listed in Table 2.8. None of these differs strikingly from the children's data. In summary, the factor analyses of the children's data and the adult data suggest that the four temperaments as

TABLE 2.5 MEANS AND STANDARD DEVIATIONS FOR THE CHILDREN'S VERSION OF THE EASI-I (mean = 55 mo; range = 2 - 9 yr)

| | Boys (N = 144) | | Girls (N = 134) | |
	Mean	Standard deviation	Mean	Standard deviation
Emotionality	13.6	(4.2)	13.6	(4.1)
Activity	18.1	(4.1)	16.5	(3.8)
Sociability	17.7	(3.1)	16.9	(3.1)
Impulsivity	14.8	(4.3)	14.3	(3.7)

TABLE 2.6   ITEMS AND FACTOR LOADINGS* FOR THE ADULT VERSION OF THE EASI-I

| | Factor loadings | | | | | | | |
| | Males (*N* = 162) | | | | Females (*N* = 207) | | | |
A priori Scale Assignment	EMO	ACT	SOC	IMP	EMO	ACT	SOC	IMP
Emotionality								
I get upset easily	.71				.67			
I tend to cry easily	.71				.70			
I have a quick temper	.34		.37	.34	.38			-.39
I am easily frightened	.65				.61			
I am easygoing or happy-go-lucky			.40				.55	
Activity								
I am always on the go		.68				.55	.55	
I like to be off and running as soon as I wake up in the morning		.54				.41	.40	
I cannot sit still long			.64		.53		.36	
For relaxation I prefer quiet, inactive pastimes to more active ones		-.38						-.32
I fidget at meals and similar occasions				.63	.40	.31		
Sociability								
I like to be with others			.65			-.51	.62	
I make friends easily	.47	.37					.78	
I tend to be shy			-.54				-.62	
I am independent of others			-.63			.71		
I usually prefer to do things alone			-.75			.72		
Impulsivity								
I tend to be impulsive		.43	.42					.68
I find self-control difficult	.49		.62					.60
I get bored easily			.62	.37				
I find it difficult to resist temptation			.52					.75
I tend to hop from interest to interest quickly			.63				.33	.33

*Only factor loadings greater than .30 are listed.

TABLE 2.7 INTERCORRELATIONS FOR THE *a priori* SCALES OF THE
EASI-I FOR SELF-REPORTS OF COLLEGE STUDENTS

	Men (N = 162)				Women (N = 207)			
	EMO	ACT	SOC	IMP	EMO	ACT	SOC	IMP
Emotionality		.00	-.16	.29		.01	-.01	.16
Activity			.29	.39			.12	.30
Sociability				.02				.03
Impulsivity								

TABLE 2.8 MEANS AND STANDARD DEVIATIONS FOR THE SCALES OF THE
EASI-I FOR COLLEGE ADULTS

	Men (N = 162)		Women (N = 207)	
	Mean	Standard deviation	Mean	Standard deviation
Emotionality	11.5	(3.1)	13.8	(3.8)
Activity	14.7	(3.5)	14.3	(3.3)
Sociability	16.4	(3.3)	16.9	(3.3)
Impulsivity	14.0	(3.3)	13.9	(3.4)

TABLE 2.9 TEST-RETEST RELIABILITIES FOR MOTHERS' RATINGS OF
THEIR CHILDREN AND THE MOTHERS' SELF-REPORTS ON THE EASI-I

	One-month, test-retest of mothers' ratings of their nursery-school children (N = 20)	One-month, test-retest of mothers' self-report (N = 20)
Emotionality	.91	.83
Activity	.82	.72
Sociability	.75	.83
Impulsivity	.82	.88

TABLE 2.10 ITEMS AND FACTOR LOADINGS* FOR THE ADULT VERSION OF THE EASI-II TEMPERAMENT SURVEY

A priori Scale Assignment**	Factor loadings							
	Males (N = 82)				Females (N = 89)			
	EMO	ACT	SOC	IMP	EMO	ACT	SOC	IMP
Emotionality								
Upset easily	.53			.35	.65			
Cry easily	.68				.75			
I tend to be irritable	.31			.64	(.25)		-.30	.47
Easily frightened	.70				.33		-.39	.37
I am somewhat emotional	.80				.80			
Activity								
Always on the go		.77				.41	.61	
Off and running		.49				.50		
I like to keep busy all of the time		.76				.72		
Prefer quiet pastimes				-.47	-.36	-.56		-.43
I am very energetic		.83				.59	.41	
Sociability								
Like to be with others			.64			-.52	.48	
Make friends easily			.60				.76	
Tend to be shy	.35						-.70	
Am independent of others			-.65		-.38		.35	.44
Usually prefer to do things alone			-.73				.64	
Impulsivity								
Impulsive			-.43	.45	.47			.41
Self-control				.62				.49
Bored easily				.49				.66
Resist temptation		.50		.55				.55
Hop from interest to interest	.50							.56

* Only factor loadings greater than .30 are listed.
**Exact wording of items same as Table 2.6 unless otherwise indicated.

TABLE 2.11   INTERCORRELATIONS FOR THE *a priori* SCALES OF THE
EASI–II FOR SELF–REPORTS OF COLLEGE STUDENTS

	Men (N = 82)				Women (N = 89)			
	EMO	ACT	SOC	IMP	EMO	ACT	SOC	IMP
Emotionality		−.01	−.07	.29		−.13	−.10	.37
Activity			.16	−.20			.34	.07
Sociability				−.04				−.03
Impulsivity								

measured by the EASI Temperament Survey are relatively independent factors.

In another study, the reliabilities of the children's rating version and the
adult self-report version of EASI-I were assessed. Mothers rated their nursery-
school children and themselves on the EASI-I and then rated their children
and themselves again about a month later. The test-retest reliabilities for the
rating measure and the adult self-report measure are listed in Table 2.9. The
average reliability for the children's ratings is .83; for the mothers' self-
reports, it is .82. These test-retest reliabilities compare favorably with the
average test-retest reliability of the scales of the Wechsler-Bellevue Intelligence
Test which, with a 1 to 26 weeks retest period, was .75 (Derner et al., 1950).
Thus the EASI Temperament Survey appears to possess adequate reliability.

EASI-II

We revised the EASI-I slightly to (1) eliminate the overlap of the two activity
items with the impulsivity scale, and (2) change two emotionality items that

TABLE 2.12   MEANS AND STANDARD DEVIATIONS FOR THE SCALES OF THE
EASI–II FOR COLLEGE ADULTS

	Men (N = 82)		Women (N = 89)	
	Mean	Standard deviation	Mean	Standard deviation
Emotionality	12.0	(3.4)	14.7	(3.3)
Activity	15.7	(3.1)	16.1	(3.4)
Sociability	15.6	(3.1)	17.3	(2.9)
Impulsivity	14.2	(2.8)	14.1	(3.1)

did not consistently load on the emotionality factor. We called this revised 20-item questionnaire EASI-II. The self-report version of EASI-II was administered to another college sample of 82 men and 89 women. The factor analyses, scale correlations, and means and standard deviations are presented in Tables 2.10, 2.11, and 2.12, respectively. In general, the revisions were successful. Activity and impulsivity were more discrete factors, correlated $-.20$ for the men and .07 for the women, neither of which is statistically significant.

The only significant relationship for both genders was between emotionality and impulsivity. This relationship between emotionality and impulsivity has shown up in all our research with the EASI. Given the nature of these two temperaments, they should be slightly correlated, as we noted in Chapter 1. Impulsivity may be regarded as "brakes" and emotionality as "engine." In our culture, emotions are required to be kept under control. An emotional person will be regarded as one who cannot control himself (impulsive). And an impulsive person will be regarded as one who is flightly, capricious, and easily upset (emotional). So there is a built-in, modest correlation between these two temperaments.

CONCLUSIONS

Our original twin study revealed much higher correlations for identical twins than for fraternal twins—and therefore a genetic component—for three of the four temperaments. The findings for impulsivity were mixed, and our conclusion is limited: a case has not been made for impulsivity as a temperament. More on this point in Chapter 6.

The identical versus fraternal twin difference in correlations—the hallmark of an inherited trait—was too large for the temperaments to be attributed solely to inheritance. This finding may be limited to (or at least more salient in) rating studies.

Raters tend to exaggerate the similarities of identical twins (assimilation) and the differences between fraternal twins (contrast). These problems require our attention as we attempt to interpret research findings on the personality of twins, but they should not obscure the major outcome of our twin study: the identical twins were rated as considerably more similar than the fraternal twins for emotionality, activity, sociability, and perhaps for impulsivity.

We also attempted to demonstrate factorial unity for each temperament, and the results were mixed. Most of the items assigned a priori to a given scale turned out to have appropriate factor loadings—both for twins rated by their mothers and college students rated by themselves. And the consistency of factor patterns for these two age groups—as well as for rating by others versus self-rating—is encouraging evidence for factorial stability. Nevertheless, there were some troublesome items that either failed to load on the a priori scales or loaded on more than one scale. These items were revised in the EASI-II and the outcome was better factorial unity.

In the next four chapters, each of the temperaments is analyzed. We suggest two components for each temperament. These components are included in an expanded (54-item) EASI Temperament Survey, EASI-III (see Appendix 2). But this is getting ahead of the story. We now turn to an analysis of each of the four temperaments.

CHAPTER

$$\boxed{3}$$

ACTIVITY

Activity level has already been defined in general terms as energy output: an active person moves around more, tends to be in motion, hurries more than others, and keeps busier than those around him. If he were an automobile, his powerful engine would idle faster, attain a higher rate of revolutions per minute, and run longer. Consider the case of a very active man in the middle years. The description emphasizes the *high points* of a person extreme in the temperament. The purpose is to furnish concrete examples, even at the risk of caricature (owing to the omission of details that would complete the personality description).

His vitality and profligate energy are reflected in most aspects of his behavior. He raps on doors loudly and pushes hard on doorbells and elevator buttons, often punching them several times. His progress on stairways is rapid: when going up, he takes two stairs at a time; when going down, his rhythmic gait sometimes becomes a gallop. His walk is brisk, and he must remember to slow down when merely strolling.

When speaking before a group, he paces incessantly; when seated, his arms, legs, head, and body tend to be in motion. He uses his arms and his hands to emphasize the content of speech, and his gestures are generally expansive and emphatic. His expressions are motile; for example, he signals assent or agreement by vigorous head nods. His exuberance carries over to speech: he speaks rapidly, loudly, and volubly. When thinking through an issue—

whether with others or alone—he tends to pace about the room like a caged animal. When forced to sit quietly, as in a waiting room or auditorium, his activity spills over into random restlessness and squirming. Knowing this, he brings materials that enable him to read or write. Thus the problem is not one of waiting per se (inhibitory control) but of remaining relatively passive and motionless (activity level).

His preferences in sports reflect his need for pulsating activity and a driving tempo. He likes tennis, handball, and squash best; these are followed by football, basketball, and volleyball; lower on the list are baseball, skating, swimming, and canoeing. Note that the best-liked sports involve not only a huge energy output but also bursts of vigorous exertion. Note also the sheer range of energy-depleting activities.

In general, he likes to keep busy and usually has several projects going simultaneously. When confined to relative inactivity—by illness or lack of opportunity—he chafes at the enforced idleness. Vacations are times to be doing, whether engaging in sports or sightseeing, as opposed to rest and quiet relaxation.

This description reveals how activity can pervade many aspects and areas of behavior. The various manifestations of high activity in one person help us to understand the temperament in the mundane terms of everyday life, but we are no further along in the analysis of the temperament in the more abstract terms of science. At issue here are distinctions between *vigor* and *tempo*, between *movements* and *acts*, and between *content* and *style*.

Vigor and Tempo

The very active person expends energy in vigorous activity (knocking harder on a door and playing games such as tennis and handball which require a huge energy output). He also maintains a quicker tempo (walks fast, talks rapidly, and takes stairs two at at a time). A single response may incorporate both aspects of activity: speaking louder (vigor) and more rapidly (tempo).

What is the relationship between vigor and tempo? We assume that they are alternative means of expending energy, and it is the expenditure of energy that defines activity level. Presumably, what is inherited is a "larger engine," a tendency to be more energetic (or the opposite, a "smaller engine" and a tendency to be less energetic). Other things being equal, high vigor should go with rapid tempo: the person who dissipates energy in high-amplitude activities like a spendthrift squandering money, also sets a pace analogous to that of a sprinter.

But other things may not be equal. A given social setting may strongly reward quickness rather than amplitude. Big-city life is proverbially fast-paced: rush to work, rush to be first in line, rush to get home, and in general *hurry*. In this milieu a very active person might expend his energy in rapid activity, not in vigorous activity; he might talk faster but not necessarily louder. In an environment with a more leisurely pace, his energy might go into slower but higher-amplitude activities. Of course, these illustrations from everyday life are merely examples, but not evidence. Until now, most measures of activity level have sampled tempo, not amplitude. Later in the chapter we suggest measures of vigor. Only when vigor and tempo are measured independently will we discover their relationship.

Movements and Acts

Activity is equivalent to movement: the person who moves more is called more active. But movements may be *random* or *patterned*. Random movements are essentially "spillovers" or discharges of energy without any special direction, for example, the squirming and fidgeting of restlessness. Patterned movements are *acts* or *responses*, and these of course are the basic units of behavior. Stated in the simplest terms, acts are coherent movements that have some function. The function may be instrumental, as in walking, talking, reading, manipulating, and so on. Instrumental behavior, by definition, moves the organism closer to a goal (or away from aversive stimuli). Not all acts are instrumental; some are *expressive* in that they express a temporary state of the organism, but they are ordinarily not functional in any instrumental sense.

What is the relevance of these distinctions for activity? It bears repeating that activity refers to movements and therefore to *all* behavior—whether functional or not, whether instrumental or expressive. We expect the very active person to engage in more instrumental behavior merely because he is doing something more of the time. But even when he is not *doing* in the sense of goal-directed responses, he is likely to engage in the aimless behavior that falls under the heading of restlessness.

The underlying assumption here is that the very active person is strongly motivated to be energetic. When there is no call for focused, instrumental behavior the push to be active will spill over into diffuse, noninstrumental behavior. This is analogous to the *displacement* behavior observed by ethologists (Tinbergen, 1952).

We are not implying that a very active person is necessarily inefficient in the sense of floundering and being clumsy. Early in the acquisition of skilled acts, the learner usually makes excessive movements. The novice cyclist waggles the handlebars too much, and the novice skater skitters like a drunkard. With practice, such acts become smoother and more fluid; the difference is that the excessive nonessential motions drop out. What happens to a highly active person when—as a function of greater skill—he expends less energy in performing the motor behavior? We predict that he will seek other outlets for burning up his energy and will thereby keep his activity level more or less constant. An example may be found in the case described above: the man usually has several projects underway simultaneously and chafes when inactivity is forced upon him. To state our position another way, activity temperament may be regarded as a drive or motivation the satiation of which requires energy-depleting behaviors.

Content and Style

Instrumental acts are grouped together by common consequences. Thus a door may be opened by shoving it with a hand, kicking it with a foot, nudging it with an elbow, or even bumping it with one's backside. All these responses have the same consequence—opening the door—and this instrumentality is called the *content* of the response. The goal (opening the door) is served by any of the responses, which is another way of saying that the responses have a common content. Nor for the goal itself does it matter whether the door is opened gently or violently.

But the force used on the door and the various ways of opening it do represent an important aspect of behavior: *style*. Whereas content is the *what* of the response, style is the *how*. And it is in the stylistic aspect of behavior that temperament makes a major contribution. The very active person is likely to open the door with more force and to move through it quickly. Similarly, if a distance is to be traversed on foot, the active person will usually stride purposefully rather than stroll slowly.

In many kinds of behavior, there is no reward for being vigorous or quick; the payoff remains the same whether the response is high or low amplitude, quick or slow. Yet one person will act with vigor and speed, and another with diminished amplitude and slower tempo. We ascribe these individual differences to activity temperament. In brief, the twin aspects of activity—vigor and tempo—are best seen in *how* a response is delivered (style).

MEASURES OF ACTIVITY

Measures Now in Use

Activity has been measured in infants who have difficulty in controlling movements and who cannot walk, in children who burn off enormous amounts of energy in play, and in adults who conserve energy by using automobiles, elevators, electric saws, and other implements, of an advanced technology. This diversity of subjects calls for a variety of measures, and researchers have responded with appropriate ingenuity. There are four kinds of measures: mechanical, open field, observational, and self-report (see Tables 3.1 to 3.4).

MECHANICAL MEASURES

These devices leave behind a record of the subject's total activity—a feature that offers two strong advantages. First, the measurement is completely objective and thus free of the subjective errors and distortions that accompany observers' ratings. Second, the record is *quantitative*, a large step forward in assessing behavior. Nevertheless, mechanical devices do have disadvantages. The *actometer* is sensitive to both rapid movements (tempo) and violent movements (vigor), and the total score reflects an unknown combination of tempo and vigor. A more serious defect is its sensitivity to certain kinds of motions and to movements as fine as tremors (Johnson, 1971). This fault arises because the actometers used to date are merely modified self-winding wristwatches. Surely, it would not be too difficult to manufacture an actometer designed not to wind up a watch but specifically to record movement.

The *fidgetometer* measures just what its name implies: diffuse, spillover activity. It virtually excludes instrumental movements of the hands or body, and it necessarily omits locomotion. Thus it might serve to assess activity in infants, but only if the investigator is aware that such activity in infants may be unrelated to the activity of older children (which includes walking, running, and other instrumental acts).

The *experimental measures* listed in Table 3.1 differ in that they are tasks in which the subject is instructed to do something as compared to the other measures, which are more naturalistic. Like mechanical devices, experimental measures are completely objective and leave behind a quantitative record. They all involve coordinated movements and therefore run the risk of confounding activity with skill. So far they have been used only with older children and adults, but simpler tasks should prove feasible with young children, for example, simple tapping, clapping hands, and jumping up and down.

OPEN FIELD

The *open field* measures focus directly on locomotion, but only at the cost of excluding all other activity; vigor is also neglected. There is an additional problem when open field measures are used with young children: they will not move about freely unless they are very secure, which means considerable familiarity with the situation. Most young children initially cling to a parent and

TABLE 3.1 MEASURES OF ACTIVITY: MECHANICAL INDICATORS OF MOVEMENT

Age	Description	Reference
Actometer		
From early childhood to adulthood	Adapted self-winding calendar wristwatch attached to the dominant arm and leg. It records movement on the hands and calendar of the watch; 1 to 3 wk test-retest reliability: .67	Schulman & Reisman, 1959
From early childhood to adulthood	1 to 2 wk test-retest reliability for boys: .31 for arms, .22 for legs; for girls: .76 for arms, .44 for legs	Maccoby et al., 1965
From early childhood to adulthood	Single day test-retest reliability: .52; actometer correlated only .12 with teachers' ratings of activity	Loo & Wenar, 1971
From early childhood to adulthood	The actometer inappropriately weights certain types of movement	Johnson, 1971
Fidgetometer		
Infancy only	Stabilimetric crib resting on an off-center fulcrum; records the number of times it pivots	Lipsitt & DeLucia, 1960; Escalona & Leitch, 1958
From early childhood to adulthood	Stabilimetric chair or cushion measuring wriggling; no test-retest reliability reported	Sprague & Toppe, 1966
From early childhood to adulthood	Ballistograph, a chair suspended by cables; 2 successive days test-retest reliability: .95; correlation with judges stopwatch timing of movement: .89	Foshee, 1958
From early childhood to adulthood	1-mo test-retest reliability: .56	Wolfensberger et al., 1962
Experimental measures		
From late childhood to adulthood	Measuring speed of turning cranks, sorting cards, tapping, writing, counting, clapping, etc.	Harrison, 1941; Frischeisen-Kohler, 1933

TABLE 3.2 MEASURES OF ACTIVITY: OPEN FIELD

Age	Description	Reference
From early childhood to adulthood	A gridwork of photoelectric cells; measures locomotion when a beam is broken; successive days test-retest reliability: .66 to .79	Ellis & Pryer, 1959
From early childhood to adulthood	Ultrasonic generator radiates signals; receiver monitors disturbances in the signals caused by moving objects and displays them on an oscillograph	Peacock & Williams, 1961
From early childhood to adulthood	No correlation between open-field locomotion and ballistograph scores	Foshee, Polk, & Cromwell, 1963
From early childhood to adulthood	Comparison of ultrasonic, photoelectric, and observational ratings in the open field; the ultrasonic approach is found lacking in reliability	Johnson, 1972
From early childhood to adulthood	Telemetric device placed on the subject transmits a signal that is monitored by a central receiving station; no test-retest reliability reported	Herron & Ramaden, 1967

explore a novel environment cautiously. So activity may well be confounded with emotionality when this measure is used with young children.

OBSERVATIONS

If activity simply is observed, it must be *evaluated* by the observer, even when the activity is recorded on film. Any evaluation of rating of activity involves *subjectivity*, the prime disadvantage of observational measures. The solution is to have two or more trained observers making the ratings. Agreement among raters—as measured by correlation—is reasonable proof of objectivity of measurement. One study (Goodenough, 1930) reported a correlation of .86 between two raters; this is good evidence for objectivity. Such agreement is facilitated by closely specifying the behaviors to be observed and how they are to be rated numerically.

TABLE 3.3 MEASURES OF ACTIVITY: OBSERVATIONAL RATINGS

Age	Description	Reference
From infancy to adulthood	Time-sampled filmed observations in which observers count specific movements during 5-second clips (correlated .87 with EMG)	Sainsbury, 1954
Infancy only	Film analyzer measures frame-to-frame displacement of the image at seven parts of the body	Kessen et al., 1961
From infancy to adulthood	Gross Body Movements Scale; time-sampling checklist of the presence of movement in different parts of the body; interrater reliability: .86	Carrier et al., 1961, in Werry & Sprague, 1970
From infancy to adulthood	Single rating of gross activity	Nelson, 1931; Escalona & Heider, 1959
From infancy to adulthood	Single rating of filmed observations	Korner, 1971
From infancy to adulthood	Single rating of taped interviews with parents of the children	Thomas et al., 1963
From infancy to adulthood	Rating of activity and rapidity	Schaefer & Bayley, 1963
Infancy only	The activity and body motion scales of The Infant Behavior Record of the Bayley Scales of Infant Development	Bayley, 1969
From early childhood to adulthood	Rating of tempo and energy level	Walker, 1962
From early childhood to adulthood	Rating of gross and specific activity, vigor, and tempo	Murphy, 1962
From early childhood to adulthood	Two observers rating a composite of global, hand, arm, and leg activity; interrater reliability: .86	Goodenough, 1930
Late childhood only	10-item Child Rating Scale of activity; one-week test-retest reliability: .86; correlation with ballistograph: .20	McConnell et al., 1964
Late childhood only	Werry-Weiss-Peters Activity Scale which involves ratings of activity in seven situations such as watching television, and at school; no reliability or validity data	Werry & Sprague, 1970

TABLE 3.4 MEASURES OF ACTIVITY: SELF-REPORT QUESTIONNAIRES

Age	Description	Reference
Early and late childhood	Number of games a child likes to play	Scarr, 1966
Late childhood and adolescence	Missouri Children's Behavior Checklist activity scale	Sines et al., 1969
Late childhood and adolescence	Missouri Children's Picture Series activity scale; consists of 238 pictures of children that the subject is asked to sort according to those that look like fun and those that do not; no test-retest reliability	Owen & Sines, 1970
Adolescence to adulthood	The energy scale of the Stern's Activities Index	Stern, Stein, & Bloom, 1956
Adolescence to adulthood	General Activity Scale of the Guilford-Zimmerman Temperament Survey	Guilford & Zimmerman, 1956
Adolescence to adulthood	Active and vigorous scales of the Thurstone Temperament Schedule	Thurstone, 1951
Adolescence to adulthood	EASI-I - general activity	Buss, Plomin, & Willerman, 1973
Adolescence to adulthood	EASI-III - tempo and vigor scales	Plomin, 1974

SELF-REPORTS

The basic problem with a self-report is its perspective. The subject may know himself better than anyone else, but he cannot see himself as others do, and his reports may be distorted by his needs, desires, and goals. Such distortions are less likely to occur for activity, perhaps because the extremes of activity are neither desirable nor undesirable. When persons are asked to compare their level of activity with that of others, they do not hesitate to declare that they are high, middle, or low. Nevertheless, self-reports are subject to unknown biases, and they should be checked against the assessments of neutral observers and other measures of activity. Self-reports can be obtained only from older children and adults, so other methods must be used with infants and young children.

Tempo and Vigor

Energy may be dissipated either by fast-paced responses or by high-amplitude responses. High-amplitude activity cannot be sustained, but low-amplitude activity can endure for hours. Consider running wind sprints versus jogging (see Figure 3.1). Wind sprints so exhaust the runner that he must rest before resuming them; the jogger needs no rest, and he maintains a steady pace. Let us assume that the total energy expenditure for the four minutes is equal in both activities. The jogger expends his energy in low-amplitude responses that endure, whereas the sprinter expends his energy in periodic high-amplitude responses. Which one is more active? The answer depends solely on total energy output. The two might be equally active but expend energy in different ways.

Thus it is possible that vigor and tempo are *negatively correlated*: the active person who engages in periodic vigorous activities does not engaged in enduring low-amplitude activities, and vice versa. However, perhaps vigor and tempo are *positively correlated*: the vigorous person also engages in many

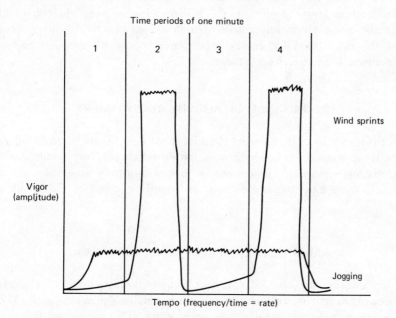

Figure 3.1. Tempo, vigor, and time sampling of behavior.

continuous activities. Finally, perhaps vigor and tempo are *uncorrelated*. If this were true, we would need to posit two different activity temperaments. For the present, we adhere to the simpler assumption that there is a single activity temperament which is manifested in either vigor and tempo, or both. The available evidence bearing on this assumption is supportive. Vigor and tempo seem to be related in newborns (Campbell, 1968; Bell, 1960), young children (Schaefer & Bayley, 1963), and adults (Thurstone, 1951). The Schaefer and Bayley study is particularly interesting because it found extremely high correlations for ratings of vigor and tempo during the first year of life (.94 for boys and .84 for girls) that dropped during the second and third years (.77, .67). However, the correlations in the third year were still quite high.

The final bit of evidence comes from the EASI-III (see Appendix 2). We constructed separate tempo and vigor subscales, each with five items. These were administered to several different populations, with N ranging from 129 to 267. The self-reports of college students of their vigor and tempo yielded correlations of .48 (women) and .50 (men). The self-reports of older persons— parents of twins—yielded correlations in the sixties. The correlations were also in the sixties when the spouses rated one another. And when parents rated their twin children, the correlations between tempo and vigor ranged from .62 to .77. Summarizing, the EASI-III yielded tempo-vigor correlations that varied from moderate to substantial. These data lead us to conclude that both vigor and tempo are merely different manifestations of activity temperament. How the two outlets for energy expenditure become differentiated during development is a question for future research.

INHERITANCE OF ACTIVITY TEMPERAMENT

What is the evidence that activity is an inherited disposition? Virtually all the research on humans has involved twins, but there have also been family studies (parents and children). The evidence is divided into twin studies that did or did not report intraclass correlations, and family studies (see Tables 3.5 to 3.7).

Studies That Reported Intraclass Correlations

All six investigations yielded data that support the hypothesis of a genetic component in activity. In each instance, the correlation for monozygotic (MZ) twins was significantly greater than for dizygotic (DZ) twins, and the girls' data replicated the boys' where both genders were included except for Schoenfeldt's study.

There is variability from one study to the next in the *size* of the correlations. The correlations in Willerman's study are high for both MZ and DZ twins. In the studies by Plomin and by Owen and Sines, the DZ correlations were negative. The measuring instrument used by Owen and Sines was a projective measure of unknown validity, which might account for their unusual results, but the Plomin study is more difficult to reconcile, particularly with the Buss et al. study which also used parental ratings of young twins. However, both the MZ and DZ twin correlations were lower in the Plomin study than in the Buss et al. study, so that the overall difference between the MZ and DZ twins, the basis for an estimate of heritability, is about the same in both studies.

Studies with No Correlations

In the twin studies that failed to report correlations (Table 3.6) the sample sizes ranged from a low of three pairs to a high of 53 pairs of twins. Most of the research yielded evidence that supports a genetic hypothesis for activity, and only two studies reported negative findings. Some of Freedman's (1965) data were negative, perhaps because of the small number of twins and the fact that they were infants. Vandenberg's (1967) negative findings might be due to his use of the Stern Activities Index; the activity scale of this index is of dubious value.

The three family studies (Table 3.7) yielded clearly positive findings, demonstrating similarities between parents and children in activity level. These findings are just as consistent with a completely environmental hypothesis of activity as with a genetic hypothesis. Nevertheless, a genetic hypothesis *requires* parent-child similarity, and therefore the data are at least consistent with a genetic hypothesis.

When all research in Tables 3.5 to 3.7 is considered, it strongly supports the hypothesis that activity temperament has a genetic component. Most of the findings were positive, and the results of the studies with larger samples, better controls, and more reliable instruments were especially confirmatory. What do these results suggest concerning further research in this area? Three kinds of studies should prove valuable. First, we need research that better specifies the correlations between monozygotic and between dizygotic twins for activity level. This would pin down more precisely the contributions of genes and environment to activity level. Larger samples and multimeasure studies are particularly needed. Second, we need other genetic studies, particularly adoption studies, to provide converging evidence that activity is inherited. Third,

TABLE 3.5   GENETIC STUDIES OF ACTIVITY LEVEL: STUDIES WITH INTRACLASS CORRELATIONS REPORTED

Measure	Number of MZ Pairs	Number of DZ Pairs	Age	Findings				Reference
				Males		Females		
				r_{MZ}	r_{DZ}	r_{MZ}	r_{DZ}	
Werry-Weiss-Peters Activity Scale	54	39	Early to late childhood	.92	.55*	.34	.62*	Willerman, 1973
EASI-I Temperament Survey—Activity Scale	78	50	Early to late childhood	.87	.17*	.71	.14*	Buss, Plomin, & Willerman, 1973
EASI-III Temperament Survey	60	51	2 – 6 yr					Plomin, 1974
Vigor				.48	-.11*	.67	-.18*	
Tempo				.25	-.39*	.49	-.44*	
Interview	24	28	Late childhood			.62	.37*	Scarr, 1966
Activity scale of the Missouri Children's Picture Series	18	24	Late childhood to adolescence	.24	-.29*	.58	-.52*	Owen & Sines, 1970

| Self-report and factored scale called "activity level" consisting of items about working and hobbies | 337 | 156 | 14 - 18 yr | .44 | .36 | .49 | .33* | Schoenfeldt, 1963 |

*Significant at .05

TABLE 3.6 GENETIC STUDIES OF ACTIVITY LEVEL: STUDIES WITH NO INTRACLASS CORRELATIONS REPORTED

Measure	Number of MZ Pairs	Number of DZ Pairs	Age	Findings	Reference
1958 version of the Bayley Infant Behavior Record--activity	9	10	Infancy	Significant activity: fine coordination Not significant activity: level of energy activity: gross coordination	Freedman, 1965
Objective tapping measure	53	49	Late childhood to adulthood	Not tested for significance, but MZs clearly more similar than DZs	Frischeisen-Kohler, 1933
For some twins in adolescence *and* in adulthood	35	33	Adolescence to adulthood	Not tested for significance, but MZs clearly more similar than DZs	Gottschaldt (in Vandenberg, 1967)
Ratings of interview data of activity	3	5	Infancy	Significant	Rutter, Korn, & Birch, 1963
Fidgetometer	3	6	Infancy	Significant	Van den Daele, 1971

Thurstone Temperament Survey—both the active and vigorous scales	45	35	Adolescence	Significant	Vandenberg, 1962
The energy scale of the Stern's Activities Index	50	38	Adolescence	Not significant	Vandenberg, 1967

TABLE 3.7 GENETIC STUDIES OF ACTIVITY LEVEL: FAMILY STUDIES

Measure	Sample size	Age	Findings	Reference
Werry-Weiss–Peters Activity Scale (completed retrospectively by parents about themselves)	43 children and their parents	Early childhood	Consistent with a genetic hypothesis, mother–child correlations for activity level were significant (correlations were .48 and .42, respectively)	Willerman & Plomin (in press)
Tapping measures	Not specified	Not specified	Data not analyzed by correlations; however, if both parents had a quick tempo, only 4% of their children had slow tempo, but if both parents had slow tempo, 71% of their children had slow tempo	Frischeisen-Kohler, 1933
"Energy" rating of child and self-report of mother	30 children and their mothers	Children were 1 yr old	Correlation of .40	Caldwell & Hersher, 1964

46

we need research that reveals the continuing interaction between genes and environment. Longitudinal studies of twins, adopted children, or even singletons would chart this interaction during development.

LONGITUDINAL STUDIES OF ACTIVITY TEMPERAMENT

There is a small body of research that traces the behavior of individual children as they develop, but in only a few of these studies was activity measured. For example, one of the best-known sources of longitudinal data is the Fels research project (see Kagan & Moss, 1962), but it failed to include measures of activity level. Thus there are fewer than a dozen longitudinal studies of activity; they are summarized in Table 3.8.

The first five investigations listed in the table all started with children less than one year old. All five reported essentially the same findings: little or no stability in activity, as revealed by low and generally nonsignificant correlations over time. Close examination of these studies suggests two explanations of the instability: the special problem of behavior during infancy and the comparability of behavior at different age levels.

Behavior During Infancy

The newborn human infant does little more than eat and sleep for the first few weeks, but waking time increases week by week, accompanied by greater alertness and awareness of surroundings. Motor activity also increases, but it lags behind sensory capabilities: the infant can see much more than he can *do*. The relative paucity of behavior raises a special problem for measurement of activity. There is simply not enough behavior to obtain a good assessment of activity level. Investigators have had recourse to observing squirming and restlessness *during sleep*, their implicit assumption being that movements during sleep are equivalent to movements during wakefulness. There is no evidence for this assumption, and given what is known about the various kinds and depths of sleep, it is unlikely that the diffuse, overflow movements of sleep are related to the many kinds of movements of wakefulness. The evidence bears out our expectation that there is no relationship between sleeping and waking activity (Schulman, Lipkin, Clarinda, & Mitchell, 1961; Cromwell, Wolf & Palk; both in Cromwell et al., 1963).

The problem of measuring activity in infancy is analogous to that of measuring intelligence in infancy. In both instances there is too little of the behavior under study, and the psychologist may be forced to measure anything remotely resembling that which he really wants to measure. In both instances,

TABLE 3.8 LONGITUDINAL STUDIES OF ACTIVITY LEVEL

Measure	Number	Age from beginning to end of study	Findings	Reference
Observational ratings	26	From 3 wk to 3 mo	Correlation of .25	Moss, 1967
For newborns: time-sampled, film-analyzed, displacement of hands and feet; for 8-mo olds: Bayley's (1959) Infant Behavior Profile	24	From first week of life to 8 mo	Correlation of .12	McGrade, 1968
Ratings from interviews with parents	80	From birth to 2 yr	Boys and girls combined 18 mo 27 mo 6 mo .24* -.15 18 mo .14 27 mo	Thomas et al., 1963

Open-field locomotion	130	From 8 to 27 mo	Correlation of .12 for boys and .08 for girls	Kagan, 1971
Ratings from interviews with parents	38	From birth to 3 yr	Boys and girls combined	Rutter et al., 1963

Boys and girls combined

	2	3
year 1	.41*	-.07
year 2		.10
year 3		

Ratings of activity (vigor) and rapidity (tempo)	54	From 1 to 3 yr	Activity	Schaefer & Bayley, 1963

Activity

	Boys		Girls	
	2 yr	3 yr	2 yr	3 yr
1 yr	.37	.41*	.64*	.54*
2 yr		.51*		.54*

Rapidity

	Boys		Girls	
1 yr	.48*	.35	.72*	.48*
2 yr		.62*		.57*

Ratings of rapidity		From 9-10 yr to 10½ yr	Boys .60* Girls .46	

49

TABLE 3.8 (CONTINUED) LONGITUDINAL STUDIES OF ACTIVITY LEVEL

Measure	Number	Age from beginning to end of study	Findings	Reference
1. Self-report on 16-item energy scale 2. Ratings by different teachers 3. Sociometric peer nominations	269 to 368	From 3rd grade to 4th; from 5th grade to 6th	(see below)	Walker, 1967
Ratings from Fels data	74	From birth to 10 yr	(see below)	Battle & Lacey, 1972
Ratings	136	Adolescence to adulthood	No correlations reported, but activity was stable over the 15 yr	Gottschaldt (in Vandenberg, 1967)

Findings (Walker, 1967):

	Boys		Girls	
	3–4	5–6	3–4	5–6
1.	.58*	.48*	.44*	.50*
2.	.54*	.47*	.37*	.61*
3.	.74*	.76*	.62*	.79*

Findings (Battle & Lacey, 1972):

	Boys			Girls		
	2	3	4	2	3	4
5–7 yr	.43*	.24	.23	.58*	.49*	.05
8–10 yr		.24	.27		.65*	.16
11–13 yr			.39*			.50*
14–16 yr						

*$p < .05$

50

activity and intelligence, measures taken during infancy do not correlate with measures taken during later childhood.

Different Behaviors at Different Ages

The reason for the lack of consistency (in both activity and intelligence) between infancy and later childhood is not hard to find: what is measured in infancy is not what is measured in later childhood. We know that this is true for intelligence. Infant intelligence tests are little more than schedules of sensory and motor achievements. Intelligence tests of childhood and adulthood contain virtually no sensory or motor items, but consist largely of cognitive items that cannot be used with sensory-motor infants.

We suggest that the same state of affairs exists for activity. Consider the research of Thomas et al. (1970), which traced children from two months to 10 years. At two months an infant was labeled *high* in activity on this basis: "Moves often in sleep. Wriggles when diaper is changed." He was judged *low* in activity on this basis: "Does not move when being dressed or during sleep." Now contrast the infancy activity measures with those at 10 years. High activity at 10 years: "Plays ball and engages in other sports. Cannot sit still long enough to do homework." Low activity: "Likes chess and reading. Eats very slowly." Let us leave aside the question of whether all these items measured activity and consider only their comparability. At two months the infant's activity is measured by diffuse squirming while being dressed or during sleep; at 10 years the child's activity is measured by highly specific preferences (chess, reading) and by his tempo of instrumental responding (eating). On the surface at least, the activities at the two ages are not at all comparable. Small wonder, then, that instability of activity is reported.

Another problem concerns infant crying and temper tantrums. One of the most vigorous things an infant does is to have a tantrum: he screams, waves his arms, and kicks his legs. The infant who has more frequent or more violent tantrums (or both) will receive a high activity score. But tantrums are surely better categorized under the heading of *emotionality* than *activity*. Researchers who include tantrums when measuring activity appear to be confounding activity with emotionality. This confound occurs only in infancy. As tantrums wane during childhood, the artificial relationship between emotionality and activity should disappear. The data support this expectation. Emotionality and activity correlate during the first one and a half years of life, not thereafter (Schaefer & Bayley, 1963). Also "bad mood" (emotionality) correlates with anxiety in the first year of life but not in older children (Rutter, Korn, & Birch, 1963). So both theory and data converge on a single conclusion: during infancy, tantrums and other emotional behavior should be excluded from the measurement of activity level.

If our analysis is correct, instability is a problem when the first measure is taken during the first year of life. When the first measure is taken later (12 months and older) activity should show at least moderate stability. The remainder of Table 3.8 bears out this expectation. There is the expected variation from one investigation to the next, but most of them are statistically significant. In brief, beyond the first year of life, activity shows at least a moderate degree of continuity, and this is consistent with its being a temperament.

PRESENCE IN ADULTHOOD

Activity temperament may be regarded as a foundation for certain later personality dispositions. Thus it is hard to see how a strong motive to achieve could develop in a low-active child. Similarly, any tendencies toward dominance or competitiveness would require at least an average level of activity. As a building block for later dispositions, activity temperament tends to become submerged as the adult personality develops. But activity is too basic a tendency to be concealed by the events of socialization and maturation, and we propose that it remains as one of the basic factors of the adult personality.

The evidence for this assertion comes mainly from factor analyses of self-report inventories. Our own EASI Temperament Survey has yielded a definite activity factor that is stable for both men and women across several samples of children and adults of both genders (see Chapter 2). And the latest revision, EASI-III, yields a very clean activity factor for both self-reports and ratings. Thurstone (1951) derived separate factors of vigor and activity (tempo) from his inventory, and the Guilford-Zimmerman Temperament Survey (1956) has a general activity factor.

Not all personality inventories yield an activity factor. Thus it has not emerged from either the Eysenck personality scale (Eysenck & Eysenck, 1963) or the Sixteen Personality Factor Questionnaire (Cattell, Saunders, & Stice, 1957). Of course, a factor cannot be found if appropriate items are not included, and many inventories contain few or no activity items. Thus Comrey (1961) originally did not include activity items in his factored personality system. Later he added appropriate items: "Analysis of the results by factor analytic methods showed that General Activity was well enough defined to warrant adding it to the Comrey factor system." (Duffy, Jamison, & Comrey, 1969, p. 295). More compelling evidence would be longitudinal data indicating that activity persists into adulthood. Only one investigation is relevant here, that of Gottschaldt (in Vandenberg, 1967), mentioned in Table 3.6.

Twins were tested first as adolescents and later as adults. Not only was there stability of activity for individuals, but the correlation for adult monozygotic twins remained higher than that for dizygotic twins. This research, taken together with the evidence for stability during childhood (see Table 3.8), argues strongly for considering activity as a temperament. Clearly, what is needed now is a longitudinal study that extends from infancy to adulthood, and it would be especially interesting to have a longitudinal study of twins.

CONCLUSIONS

We have established five criteria for temperaments, and it is appropriate to inquire how well activity meets them. In Chapter 1 we tried to show that activity is adaptive and has a long evolutionary history; thus it appears to meet the two logical criteria. This chapter deals with three empirical criteria. There is a definite inherited basis for activity level, as revealed mainly by twin studies. There is also at least moderate stability throughout childhood and persistence into adulthood. Thus in terms of both logical and empirical criteria, a good case can be made for activity as a temperament.

What next? More research is needed with twins and with children reared in foster homes to pin down the genetic component in activity. We also need to know what happens to activity level during the course of development, and only longitudinal research can yield this information. Before embarking on such research, we need to develop new and hopefully better measures of activity and discover how the present measures are related to one another.

In addition to these empirical issues, there are theoretical questions. Are there gender differences in activity? How does activity interact with the other temperaments? What is the impact of child-rearing practices on activity, and how does activity affect child-rearing practices? Our answers to these questions begin in Chapter 7.

Finally, we must add that activity occupies a special position among the temperaments. It is more "biological" in the sense that it involves expending energy, and the source of energy is internal, biochemical processes. It is also a diffuse tendency, permeating the entire range of behavior: every response varies in tempo and vigor. Of course, our interest is not in single responses but in the total energy dissipated in all responses. Thus activity is more diffuse and stylistic than the other temperaments. It does not necessarily involve personal interaction, and it is not as "dynamic" as emotionality or impulsivity. These attributes may account for its relative neglect by psychologists; as we noted earlier, many personality inventories do not tap activity level. We suggest that this neglect is unwarranted. Activity temperament is undoubtedly an important determiner of interests and vocations. Persons low in activity do not usually prefer marathon running or handball as a sport, or tap-dancing or steelworking as a vocation. And activity may be a factor in marital success. If a husband and wife are at opposite ends of the scale, there is bound to be some friction. The high-active spouse will believe the other one to be shiftless and lazy; the low-active spouse will look on the other as a manic nut. This is not to imply that marital partners must be equal in activity level, but only that a divergence is one source of marital conflict. In brief, we believe that activity temperament is an important basis of later personality dispositions, and psychologists would do well to study it more.

CHAPTER

EMOTIONALITY

Emotionality is best defined in terms of three words: *arousal, reactivity*, and *excitability*. The emotional person is aroused easily and reacts intensely. He is excitable in that he is easily stirred up and explosive in his reaction. His threshold for becoming disturbed is low, so he responds emotionally to situations that might not bother most persons. As a consequence, he has more explosive outbursts than the average person. And the magnitude of his reaction is disproportionate: where another might be mildly upset, he tends to be frenzied and agitated. Where another might wince, he screams. In brief, he is disposed to have stormy, emotional reactions.

Emotional behavior is well-known to all of us. It seems safe to say that every person has experienced the turbulent excitement of a strong emotional outburst. The private feelings appear to vary from one person to the next: stomach tied in knots, heart pounding, dry throat, inner turmoil and confusion, a feeling of queasiness, a sinking feeling in the chest, and a strong concern about what will happen next. We know about these covert, inner events because we have experienced them or had them reported by others.

The more public responses of emotion appear to be common to everyone. They consist of (1) surface manifestations of autonomic arousal, and (2) facial and skeletal-muscle responses. The autonomic signs may be mild in weak emotion and therefore difficult to discern. But in strong emotion they stand out clearly. Breathing becomes fast and shallow, the face becomes flushed (or, rarely, it becomes pale), arteries are seen throbbing in the throat or temple, hands clammy, and a sheen of sweat covers the face.

The facial expressions vary with the specific emotion, and anger can be distinguished from fear merely on the basis of photographs (Ekman, Sorenson, & Friesen, 1969). Nevertheless, one facial quality is shared by all strong emotions: tension. The muscles around the eyes, nose, and mouth become extremely tense, and the muscles of the throat constrict. Skeletal-muscle activity is an especially good index of emotion. Hands are typically clenched, and neck and shoulder muscles are rigid. There is often trembling, whether in panic or impotent rage. The common element in all these responses is *tension*. The muscles are contracting in preparation for, or as part of, a massive reaction to an emergency situation. The tension may spill over beyond tremors into random activity, restless pacing, aimless gesturing, or an edginess that gives rise to jerky, startled movements.

Such emotional episodes are transient. There is a sudden outburst, a gradual waning of excitation, and then arousal is back to resting levels. Virtually no one remains for long at a peak of emotional arousal. If emotional behavior is episodic and everyone has such episodes, what is the relevance of emotionality as a temperament? The individual differences reside in the *frequency* and *intensity* of the emotional behavior. The person high in the temperament presumably has a lower threshold for an emotional response and so has more of them. And presumably the amplitude of his response is greater, as manifested in the various indicators mentioned above.

As a result, the emotional person is like a powder keg that is ready to explode. A nervous irritability surrounds him like an aura. In groups he is likely to initiate turmoil and conflict. He is oversensitive to slights, threats, frustrations, and even sudden changes from the usual routine. He cannot stand stress and so cannot be counted on to endure and cope when consistency and stability are required. He cannot relax, has difficulty in concentrating, and may show muscular incoordination. In summary, the highly emotional person is likely to be maladapted to the stresses and strains of everyday life.

If high emotionality is maladaptive, does it not fail to meet one of the criteria of a temperament (adaptiveness)? The answer lies in the notion of *optimal* levels of excitability. Animals and men need to be arousable so that they can respond appropriately to emergency situations. To take an extreme case, when there is an immediate threat to life, a person must have mechanisms for coping with the danger. One such mechanism is the emergency preparation of the body for either flight or fight. It is precisely these autonomic and skeletal-muscle preparations that we label emotion. They are necessary forerunners of the massive effort that is about to begin; that is, they are adaptive. But if men or animals are excessively arousable, they spend too much of their time and energy preparing for phantom dangers, or they react too strongly with emergency mechanisms to an event that is only mildly threatening.

We did not raise this issue in our discussion of activity temperament, but similar considerations apply. A reasonable level of activity is obviously necessary in solving the everyday problems of living. But an excessively high level of activity would lead to overly fast and vigorous behavior, and no one would suggest that a manic person is coping with his environment. For most persons, the inherited range of activity level should be adaptive. For a few, the range will be too low or too high. Similarly, there are undoubtedly persons who are insufficiently emotional (or excessively emotional) and so respond inappropriately in emergencies. It is the large middle range of temperaments that is adaptive, not the extremes.

The Negative End

The discerning reader may have noticed our emphasis on unpleasant emotions (distress, fear, anger) to the exclusion of pleasant emotions (elation, friendship, love). We do not deny that there are positive *emotions*, but we suggest they are not part of *emotionality*. Remember that we are dealing with individual differences, specifically, with an inborn tendency to become emotional. We assume that persons differ in their innate tendency to become upset, distressed, and aroused in the face of threatening, annoying, or frustrating situations. Individual differences in the degree to which a person is elated, friendly, or loving are likely to be caused by the events of childhood, not by innate dispositions. If there is temperamental input into individual differences in *positive* emotions, it is likely to be activity (for elation) or sociability (for friendliness and warmth).

So we are deliberately restricting ourselves to the negative emotions, conceding that our theory cannot account for individual differences in all the emotions. In doing so, we follow everyday usage. A person labeled *emotional* is likely to show an excess of distress, fear, or rage. We do not ordinarily use the word *emotional* to describe happy-go-lucky, blithe spirits, or overly romantic persons; the term is reserved almost exclusively for those marked by the "darker" emotions. For example, if the term *emotional* were applied to a young child, it would elicit the picture of a cranky, fussy, intemperate child, who kicks, screams, and generally howls his discomfort to anyone within earshot. No one would invoke the word *emotional* as a label for a smiling, friendly child who is easily moved to laughter.

There is another reason for including only the negative emotions: they involve high levels of autonomic arousal. In the face of threat or noxious stimuli, the body prepares itself for massive action. Distress, fear, and anger are all marked by high levels of autonomic reactivity. Are there comparable levels of autonomic reactivity in the positive emotions? No, there is no need. There is no preparation for massive action in elation or love. These are quieter, benign feelings, and they are associated with minimal physiological reactivity.

Fear versus Anger

The two most common negative emotions are fear and anger. Many researchers believe that the two can be distinguished physiologically—specifically, that there are two different patterns of autonomic arousal, one for anger and one for fear. The experiments most cited in support of this contention are those of Ax (1953) and J. Schachter (1957). As both experiments used the same procedures and some of the same subjects, we shall discuss only the Ax experiment. Subjects were exposed to both threat of electric shock and harassment by an aide, and they reacted with behavioral signs of fear and anger, respectively. Of the 14 different physiological measures recorded for each subject, six of them significantly distinguished the fear state from the anger state. This finding has implications for the temperament of emotionality. If fear and anger have different autonomic patterns, perhaps we need two separate temperaments, one for each of these emotions. So it is important to examine the Ax study in more detail.

There are two matters relevant to the theoretical issue. The first concerns the way subjects were made angry or afraid. The subjects were angered by an "operator" who was an experimental accomplice:

> At the beginning of the anger stimulus, the operator entered the room stating that he must check the wiring because some calibration might be off. The experimenter objected but agreed to go into the other room and operate the polygraph. The operator shut off the music, criticized the nurse, and told the subject sarcastically that it would have helped if he had been on time. He checked the electrodes, roughly adjusted the subject, and criticized him for moving, noncooperation, and other behavior. After five minutes of abuse, the operator left. . . . [Ax, 1953, p. 435]

The subject was clearly provoked, but only by insults; he was not threatened with any bodily harm, and at no time was he in any danger. Contrast the anger provocation with the fear manipulation:

> The fear stimulus consisted of a gradually intermittent shock stimulus to the little finger which never reached an intensity sufficient to cause pain. When the subject reported the sensation, the experimenter expressed surprise, checked the wiring, pressed a key which caused sparks to jump near the subject, then exclaimed with

alarm that this was a dangerous high voltage short circuit. The experimenter created an atmosphere of alarm and confusion. After five minutes from the time the subject reported the shock, the experimenter removed the shock wire, assuring the subject that all danger was past. [p. 435]

This manipulation had the stamp of realism. The subjects were extremely frightened in what appeared to be a truly dangerous situation. One reported saying his prayers. Compare this with the anger manipulation: the subjects were annoyed by the nasty operator, but there was never any danger of harm. Surely, their anger was at a lower intensity than that of their fear.

The point of this detailed examination of procedure is that the fear and anger of the Ax study appear to be different in intensity: the subjects were much more scared than they were angry. Given this difference in intensity, the reported physiological differences might be due entirely to a difference in *level* of autonomic arousal rather than a difference between two separate emotions.

The second matter concerns data. Ax selected only the measures that differentiated significantly between fear and anger. For each of these measures, he computed the correlation for fear versus anger. In other words, he asked whether fear and anger are correlated positively, negatively, or not at all. The correlations ranged from .26 to .77, with a mean of .53. So, on the very physiological measures that distinguished fear from anger, the correlations between these two emotions were positive and fairly high. Suppose, for the sake of argument, that the fear and anger states in this experiment were not confounded with differences in intensity of arousal. Even if fear and anger were physiologically different, they are still correlated. The average correlation coefficient (.53) is little different from that obtained between vigor and tempo (the two components of activity temperament). Given the relationship between fear and anger, based on measures of autonomic reactivity, we feel justified in treating anger and fear as components of a single temperament, emotionality. There are behavioral data to support this position, and these will be discussed in the Measures section.

DEVELOPMENT

Emotionality is the only temperament that can be measured from the very beginning of life. Behavioral observations have been made on the second day of life (Freedman, 1971). And physiological recordings have been made on neonates, revealing clear individual differences in autonomic measures (Lipton, Steinschneider, & Richmond, 1961; Lipton & Steinschneider, 1964).

Our theory assumes that emotionality is defined by both behavioral and autonomic arousal. It follows that at birth these two aspects should be highly correlated. At present, there is no research bearing on this point, and it remains an untested assumption. We also assume that during childhood, these two aspects differentiate so that the correlation between them drops to a moderate level.

Our reasoning is based on the fact that autonomic reactivity is more covert than behavioral reactivity and is assumed to be less controllable. Some of the physiological reactions that occur in emotion can be seen, but most are internal and hidden from others. As such, they are less amenable to shaping and so are less susceptible to the forces that socialize children.

Behavioral reactivity is public and easily observed by others, and it is very much shaped during childhood. Children may be scolded for pouting or sulking, or they may be shamed for showing fear. On the other hand, children may be rewarded for struggling, screaming, or protesting vehemently: some parents will give in just to turn off the child's annoying vocalizations or mannerisms.

Thus autonomic and behavioral reactivity are subjected to differing degrees of control by others. Autonomic arousal is likely to be left untouched by any specific socialization practices or the rewards and punishments of everyday life. Behavioral arousal tends to be shaped by parents acting as socializing agents or merely as reinforcing agents in a dyadic interaction. In addition, behavioral arousal easily can be copied and so is influenced by imitation learning; autonomic arousal is ordinarily not imitated. Given all the additional learning that is imposed on behavioral arousal, it appears likely that its developmental course would diverge from that of autonomic arousal. It follows that the correlation between the two would drop during childhood.

Distress

The primordial negative emotion is *distress*, which may be considered undifferentiated emotionality. Distress can be observed easily in an infant from the day of birth. He crinkles his face as if to cry, but no tears are yet available; his face reddens, and his breath comes in gasps; he kicks his legs and waves his arms vigorously; and he may arch his back or try to move his head. The child is obviously uncomfortable, and his distress must usually be relieved by feeding him, picking him up, warming him, etc.

Milder stress was observed by Freedman (1971) in a unique study on ethnic differences in emotionality. The Chinese are known for their placidity, especially in comparison to the excitability of Americans. Presumably, this difference derives from cultural differences in the way children are socialized, but Freedman's research suggests that emotionality temperament may be a causal variable. The subjects were 24 American children and 24 children of Chinese parents, all born in a San Francisco hospital. They were observed on the second day of life (average, 33 hours old). The American children were found to be significantly more excitable and labile in affect than the Chinese children. Of special interest were their reactions to annoyance:

> In an item called *defensive movements*, the tester placed a cloth firmly over the supine baby's face for a few seconds. While the typical European-American infant immediately struggled to remove the cloth, the typical Chinese-American infant lay impassively, exhibiting few overt motor responses. [1971, p. 93]

These differences in emotionality cannot be attributed to sleepiness, for the Chinese infants were slightly (but not significantly) more alert than the American children.

These findings do not prove the case for emotionality as a temperament, but they are certainly consistent with the notion. The children showed clear differences in emotionality on the second day of life. These ethnic differences are surely inherited, for there is no way they could have been acquired so early in life. The only reasonable explanation must be that there are differences in gene pools between America and China. It is hard to believe that such group differences could exist in the absence of individual differences: if there were no inherited individual differences, how would different gene pools evolve? So the presence of ethnic differences at birth must be considered indirect evidence for emotionality as a temperament.

Fear and Anger

Fear has been reported to occur at roughly three months (Bridges, 1932). How do we know? The usual answer is that the infant cries, kicks, and tenses his body, but these are merely signs of distress. Bridges also mentions that the distress is a response to novelty, as when the infant is moved to a new place. But this is not a sufficient basis for inferring fear, for the distress response occurs in reaction to other stimuli. Fear must be defined in terms of *response* attributes, not antecedent stimuli. Later in life there are recognizable facial expressions, but during the first year of life the crucial defining property of the fear reaction is that *the infant attempts to avoid or escape from an aversive stimulus*. At approximately three months the infant has the requisite motor control to turn his head and body away or to recoil from a noxious stimulus. He also cries or screams, but this response is merely part of his general distress. What defines the reaction as a fear response is the infant's attempt at *flight*. Given his immaturity, the attempt is small and weak, but the infant does try to escape from the source of his discomfort, and this attempt is sufficient to differentiate the fear response from the more generalized distress reaction.

True anger does not occur until much later, probably not until one year. Bridges suggests that the first temper tantrum is not seen until 14 months but realizes that her sample was infant foundlings:

> If a child is not given his food or a coveted toy exactly when he wants it, he may respond by throwing himself suddenly on the bed or floor. He then screams, holds his breath, trembles, turns red, kicks or thrusts his feet out together. Tears flow and he will wave away anything that is not the desired object. . . . Anger is expressed more in protesting shouts, pushing and kicking, but less in tearful screaming. [1932, p. 332]

Note that the child does not shrink with fear but thrashes with anger. The fearful child cowers and recoils from aversive stimuli; the angry child attacks or pushes away noxious stimuli or negativistically shakes his head. The difference in direction of response becomes clear when the child is presented with an aversive object. If the child retreats and attempts to put distance between himself and the object, we infer that the object was threatening and the child responded with fear. But if the child smashes the object with his hand, pushes it, or throws it away, then we infer that the object annoyed the child and he responded with anger. These alternative responses are the precursors of the more effective flight versus fight reactions that develop later in childhood.

Recognizing Emotional Reactions

Mothers and some psychologists would object to our developmental timetable. They assert that the infant's emotions differentiate early and can be readily discriminated by an acute observer. We suggest that anyone who believes that he can discern *early* differences in emotions is probably falling into one of three kinds of errors.

First, fear or anger may be equated with distress. If the observer—usually the mother or other nonprofessional person—is asked how this particular reaction (fear or anger) differs from distress, the answer is usually an appeal to intuition.

Second, the observer may use antecedent conditions to label the child's emotional reaction. Thus the appearance of a stranger or a novel object is typically used to infer fear; the removal of a stimulus may be used to infer anger. But the eliciting stimuli are a poor basis for such inference. A stranger often induces fear, but some strangers may induce anger, especially after the first year of life. The appearance of a new baby may lead to jealous tantrums in its older sibling. Similarly, the removal of a stimulus may induce anger, but if the stimulus is a security blanket or toy, the response might better be labeled fear. Unfortunately, antecedent conditions comprise the major basis of discriminating emotions in young children. After investigating observers' ability to distinguish emotions, Sherman (1928) concluded:

> . . . the emotional responses of the newborn infant to the types of stimuli employed in the previously mentioned experiment are undifferentiated, and the success of the individual observer in recognizing and differentiating the emotional character of these responses is due to a knowledge of the causative stimulation conditions. [p. 388]

Third, observers tend to assume that infants have the same range of emotional reactions as older children and adults. As some persons impute human characteristics to animals, so they impute human adult features to infants. Thus if the situation would frighten an adult, the infant's distress is taken as fear. If the situation would anger an older child, the infant's distress is interpreted as rage.

These various errors can be avoided if observers clearly state the basis of their inferences: the *behavior* of the infant. Fear is marked by attempts to avoid or escape, anger by attempts to destroy or remove the aversive stimulus.

The Primacy of Fear

Fear differentiates from distress much earlier than anger, and it is a more pervasive reaction. The frequency of fear responses is many times that of anger responses during early childhood. One reason is speculative but logical in an evolutionary context: it is adaptive to avoid or escape from threats. The animal that crouches, freezes, burrows, runs, flies, or swims away is more likely to survive and leave offspring behind. Successive generations of animals tend to evolve a strong built-in tendency to react to threat with fear and escape responses. This tendency is built into virtually all animals, including man.

It would be maladaptive to react emotionally to *all* stimuli, and the young organism needs a basis for distinguishing harmful from beneficial stimuli. Schneirla (1959) suggested that the basis is stimulus *intensity*: high-intensity stimuli elicit fear and withdrawal; low-intensity stimuli elicit approach behavior (see Table 4.1).

The dichotomy drawn by Schneirla is essentially the same as that accepted by most researchers: fear versus curiosity. The young organism needs security before it explores the environment. In the absence of threat, it seeks novelty. But intense stimuli elicit fear and send the organism rushing for security. This

TABLE 4.1   APPROACH–WITHDRAWAL IN THE VERY YOUNG   (Modified from Schneirla, 1959)

Reaction	High-intensity stimuli	Low-intensity stimuli
Behavioral component	Vigorous mass action, shrinking, crying, tension	Pacified, local action, turning-toward, smiling
Autonomic component	"Interruptive" effects, sympathetic predominant	"Vegetative" effects, parasympathetic predominant

is as true for the human infant who clutches his mother as it is for the primate infant that clutches its mother. Fear occurs earlier than anger and is more basic.

Thus one reason for the primacy of fear is an adaptive end: survival of the individual. A second reason involves *instrumentality*. Little skill or coordination is needed to crouch, freeze, recoil, or scream for help; the response is little more than a reflex. But attacking or pushing away a noxious stimulus requires at least some motor coordination. Thus the behavioral concomitant of fear (escape) requires little instrumentality, and this minimal amount is present early in infancy (by three months in humans). But the behavioral concomitant of anger (attack or repulsion) requires some instrumentality, and the human infant evidently needs a year to develop the requisite skill and coordination.

A Developmental Model

During early childhood the primordial negative emotion, distress, differentiates into fear and anger. Later in childhood there are other differentiations, as cognitions play an increasingly important role in emotions. How do emotions differentiate? To answer this question we have borrowed Thompson's (1968) learning approach to development. We have modified it and extended it to form a developmental model of negative emotions (see Table 4.2).

Immediately after birth the neonate cannot really discriminate among stimuli in any way that is significant. His only reaction to discomfort, annoyance, or threat is the generalized reaction we call distress. At this stage the only learning he is capable of is habituation: getting accustomed to sudden or intense stimuli that are really benign or at least not noxious.

The first differentiation (in Thompson's terms) is in stimulus input. When the infant is a few months old, he can distinguish among various stimuli, especially social and emotional stimuli. He is now sufficiently developed to make escape or avoidance responses, so that we can separate his fear responses from the more generalized distress state. And previously neutral stimuli, through association with noxious stimuli, can evoke a strong negative reaction. This is of course classical conditioning. From then on, a variety of fears will be conditioned, as fear becomes the predominant negative emotional reaction.

By one year output becomes differentiated (again in Thompson's terms). Now the child can make responses that may remove or destroy a noxious stimulus. These responses allow us to identify his anger. Such responses are strengthened by their consequences, and this process is of course instrumental conditioning.

Some time during the second year of life the child starts to acquire language. Subsequently, he begins to use words and images to represent stimuli, and he gradually becomes a cognitive organism. By the fifth year of life he is actively using cognitions, and thereafter most of his learning will be of the cognitive variety. At this point he is capable of labeling his internal states and relating them to the stimuli that elicit these states. At first such labeling is infrequent and confused, but gradually the child becomes more skilled in both labeling

TABLE 4.2   DEVELOPMENTAL MODEL OF NEGATIVE EMOTIONS

Age	Dominant type of learning	Differentiation Stimulus input	Response output	Emotion
Neonate	Habituation	Low	Low	Distress
3 mo +	Classical conditioning	High	Low	Fear; specific fears and avoidance
12 mo +	Instrumental conditioning	High	High	Anger; varieties of aggression
Fourth year +	Cognitive learning			Attribution; finer discrimination of antecedent conditions and internal events (physiological and cognitive)

and attribution. Eventually, he develops more adult modes of attribution, which involve complex interactions of autonomic arousal, behavioral reactivity, and cognitions. This is not the place to discuss the mysteries of the intertwining of emotion and cognition (see Schachter & Singer, 1962; Valins, 1966; Bem, 1970; and Laird, 1974). All we can do is to indicate that the major differentiations in emotion after early childhood are based largely on cognition, and this takes us well beyond any input from temperament. Note that we are referring to *distinctions* among emotions, not the intensity with which they occur. Emotional intensity continues to be determined mainly by the person's inborn disposition.

MEASURES OF EMOTIONALITY

The physiological preparations for massive action involve *internal* systems of the body. Autonomic arousal must therefore be assessed by "plugging in" to the appropriate organ systems and measuring pulse, blood pressure, respiration, and so on. Emotionality is also *behavioral* reactivity, and this can be observed directly. Lastly, humans are knowledgeable organisms and can report their own states of being. In brief, there are three kinds of measures of emotionality: physiological, observational, and self-report. They are listed in Table 4.3, along with references that may be consulted for details of procedure.

Physiological Measures

The most common measures of autonomic arousal are heart rate, blood pressure, respiration, and galvanic skin response. The correlations among these various measures are low (Ax, 1953). For example, in some situations heart rate and galvanic skin response both increase, but in others heart rate goes down while galvanic skin response goes up. This has been called *situational stereotypy* (Lacey, 1959).

There are also individual differences in the pattern of autonomic arousal. Some persons react mainly with an increase in heart rate, others with an increase in galvanic skin responses, and so on. For each person the pattern may be slightly different and this patterning appears inherited to some extent (Alexander & Osborne, 1973). The presence of these individual differences complicates the task of assessing autonomic level of arousal. It means that the best measures of arousal will differ among persons and so a simple averaging of means will not suffice. Researchers must therefore check out their subjects to discover which are the best physiological indicators of emotion for each subject

TABLE 4.3   MEASURES OF EMOTIONALITY

	Reference
Physiological measures *of the autonomic nervous system*	
Heart rate, blood pressure, galvanic skin response, respiration	Lazarus, 1966 Lipton & Steinschneider, 1964 Sternbach, 1966
Observational measures	
General emotionality--excitement	Bell, 1960
Distress	Moss, 1967
Fear	Jersild & Holmes, 1935; Scarr & Salapatek, 1970
Anger	Buss, 1961
Facial expressions	Goodenough, 1931 Watson, 1972
Self-report measures	
Distress	Taylor, 1951
Fear	Cattell, 1957
Anger	Buss & Durkee, 1957 (see Appendix 2 for the EASI-III general emotionality, fear, and anger items)

and then use only those measures. In brief, the problem of individual differences in patterning poses no serious problem for our theory of emotionality.

But the problem of situational stereotypy does pose a problem. If each situation provokes a different pattern of autonomic reactivity, how can we maintain that there is a given level of autonomic arousal? One answer is that there are fewer patterns of excitation than was believed earlier, and there is good reason to retain the notion of general activation. In the words of a leading psychophysiologist:

Despite the existence of patterning . . . many different situations produce rather similar activating effects. Increased muscle tension, sympathetic nervous system activity, and EEG desynchronization can be produced by most emotions (perhaps not depression), by mental activity, physical exercise, changes in sensations—in short, by almost any *change* in conditions. In this sense activation seems to be a set of responses in the individual alerting him for whatever may come next, in the nature of a generalized preparatory act. Such a process probably has some survival value, since it increases the probability of speedy and vigorous responses if the situation should call for them. [Sternbach, 1966, pp. 72–73]

These remarks sum up our position. The presence of different patterns for various situations is a complicating factor, but it does not deny the usefulness of the notion of general activation. It all depends on one's goals. Psychophysiologists are trying to make sense out of a bewildering array of data. Consider the conclusion of a recent review:

The search for the physiological substrates of emotion has produced much research and theory. Inevitably, some of this has been sophisticated, useful and suggestive, and some has been naive, poorly conceived, and on occasion even obstructive. Unfortunately, however, the better work is inconclusive. [Strongman, 1973, p. 64]

Our goal does not involve the analysis of details about physiological processes. We are merely trying to make sense out of the organism's preparation for stressful situations. Given this goal, the notion of generalized activation appears to suffice. Nevertheless, the problems of psychophysiology do not disappear when researchers try to investigate emotionality, which suggests that autonomic measures may not be the best ones.

Finally, we suggest that all these problems might be resolved with appropriate data, and in this instance the appropriate data must come from genetic studies. If, in spite of all the complexity of autonomic responsivity, a case can be made for the inheritance of physiological arousal, our theory will be strengthened. The relevant data are discussed in the next section.

Behavioral Measures

Emotional behavior is easier to assess in children, who are relatively open and direct in expressing distress, fear, and anger. In our culture, children are taught to inhibit their fear and rage. The fearful child tends to be labeled *immature*, the angry child *spoiled* and *negativistic*. During development, there is increasing suppression and self-control of the more overt skeletal and facial expressions of emotion. As a consequence, behavioral measures are usually limited to children, especially young children.

Perhaps the best illustration of the waning of emotional ourbursts is the developmental course of the temper tantrum. It first appears during the second year of life, and it peaks during the two to four year range. The young child screams (or alternatively, holds his breath), kicks, tenses his body, and sometimes throws himself on the floor and bangs his head. Some of the movements look like parts of aggressive acts (pounding and flailing), and some have instrumentally aggressive components (screaming is aversive to parents). The pattern varies from one child to the next, and it varies with contingencies of reinforcement (whether or not the child gets his way as a result of the tantrum). But during the course of childhood, tantrums gradually disappear because of pressure from peers, eventual nonreinforcement by parents, and increasing self-control by the child.

The EASI-III (see Appendix 2) includes general emotionality, fear, and anger scales and has been used for ratings of children and adults. Data (Plomin, 1974) that we have collected using the EASI-III for children (average of three and a half years) and their parents can be used to examine the relationship among the components of emotionality. Fear and anger were positively and significantly correlated for the parents' ratings of their children and for the parents' ratings of their spouses. Although the correlations were not high, ranging from .20 to .30, fear and anger correlated more highly with the general emotionality scale. For the ratings of boys, fear correlated .66 and anger correlated .54 with general emotionality; for the ratings of girls, the correlations were .36 and .57. For the mothers' ratings of their husbands, the correlations were .28 and .62; for the fathers' ratings of their wives, the correlations were .54 and .62. These data suggest that fear and anger are related to each other and especially to general emotionality in both children and adults. It also seems that fear has differentiated from general emotionality for the men but not for the women, although the correlation between fear and general emotionality is higher for boys than for girls. This suggests a developmental trend in gender differences that is addressed in Chapter 7.

Self-Report Measures

As with any measure, the self-report represents a trade-off between disadvantages and advantages. Self-reports are limited to older children and adults, who have the requisite verbal comprehension and understanding of their own behavior. A more serious limitation is the subjectivity of questionnaires. Subjects lie, distort, or are unaware of their own feelings, expressions, or acts. There are methods for coping with lying, distortion, and ubiquitous response sets (see Wiggins, 1973), and the self-report can be a valuable tool in assessing emotionality.

The major advantage of the self-report, whether a questionnaire or an interview, lies in the reporting of material that is otherwise not available. When properly used, the interview can reveal information that is otherwise neglected. Hamilton (1959) interviewed anxiety neurotics and rated their symptoms. A factor analysis yielded two clusters of symptoms. The first consisted of various kinds of autonomic overactivity plus a variety of bodily complaints (digestive, genito-urinary, and so on). The second factor consisted of muscular tension, fears, and apprehension, and insomnia. Thus fear can show itself in one of two ways, somatic or behavioral. The duality was confirmed in another interview study, this time with a mixed group of psychiatric patients (Buss, 1962). A factor analysis yielded two factors: one involved both observed and reported autonomic signs (flushing, sweating, rapid breathing, heart racing, and "butterflies in the stomach"); and one involved restlessness, muscular tension, and worry.

The split appears to be between autonomic reactivity and a combination of motor (restlessness, tension) and ideational (worry) behavior. These findings neatly dovetail with Eysenck's (1961) hypothesis of inherited versus acquired components in fear. The inherited component is autonomic overreactivity, and the acquired component consists of the conditioned fear responses of restlessness and overconcern.

Are there analogous factors for anger? None has been revealed by research, but the following speculation appears reasonable. The autonomic components are the same in anger as in fear. The "spillover" of tension would be reflected in such violent motor activity as pounding on the table, shouting, slamming doors, or stamping on the floor. The ideational component would consist of hatred or at least strong dislike.

INHERITANCE OF EMOTIONALITY

Previous researchers have tended not to use the concept of emotionality, and only a few have studied it in twins. But there has been considerable research on variables related to emotionality, especially scales on personality inventories. The findings are discussed in four sections: general emotionality (Table 4.4), Cattell's and related scales (Table 4.5), neuroticism (Table 4.6), and autonomic activity (Table 4.7).

General Emotionality

The subjects in these studies were children, who have been less socialized than adults and who should therefore reveal the clearest evidence for inherited emotionality. Freedman (1965) found that monozygotic twins are more similar than dizygotic twins for fearfulness and reactivity but not for tension. His sample size was small, but the study is important because it provides evidence of inherited emotionality very early in life.

The next two entries in the table require special comment. Brown et al. (1967) and Vandenberg et al. (1968) reported negative findings; Wilson et al. (1971) reported positive findings. All three studies were part of the Louisville twin study, and they used the same subjects. The only difference was that Wilson et al. (1971) had a much larger sample size, so their data may be regarded as more reliable. In all three studies, mothers were interviewed and indicated for each item of behavior whether their twins were similar or dissimilar. This unorthodox method did yield evidence of heritability in the larger study (Wilson et al., 1971), but it appears to have two defects. First, it places an additional interpretive burden on the mother, who must not only evaluate how much of the trait each twin has but also must compare them. Second, it yields no quantitative data about the trait, only the relative similarity of the twins.

The last two studies of general emotionality, our own (Buss et al., 1973; Plomin, 1974) yielded mixed results. The first study, using the emotionality scale of the EASI-I, yielded strong evidence for the inheritance of emotionality for both boys and girls. The second study, using the three emotionality scales of the EASI-III, yielded strong evidence for the inheritance of general emotionality and fear in girls and of anger in boys. These data suggest that gender differences in emotionality must be considered (see Chapter 7).

Cattell's and Related Scales

As we mentioned above, most researchers have not investigated emotionality per se. Their measures have been an unknown mixture of emotionality temperament and other personality dispositions (the reader can verify this by examining the items on their scales). In this context, it is not surprising that the results of twin studies have been mixed (see Table 4.5). Significant differences between monozygotic and dizygotic twins have been found in roughly half the studies. In short, we suspect that the measures used in these studies tapped not only emotionality but other dispositions, and therefore we should not be surprised that the twin data are mixed and difficult to interpret.

Neuroticism

The same conclusion applies to studies of neuroticism and neurotic symptoms (Table 4.6). It is a reasonable assumption that an inherited tendency to be emotional would predispose a person to be neurotic, but it is equally reasonable to assume that no one becomes neurotic unless there is strong envi-

TABLE 4.4   TWIN STUDIES OF EMOTIONALITY: GENERAL EMOTIONALITY

Measure	Number of MZ Pairs	Number of DZ Pairs	Age	Findings	Reference
1959 version of the Bayley Infant Behavior Record	9	10	0 – 1 yr		Freedman, 1965
Fearfulness				Significant*	
Reactivity				Significant*	
Tension				Not significant	
Interview data from the Louisville twin study	35	39	0 – 6 yr		Brown, Stafford, & Vandenberg, 1967; Vandenberg, Stafford, & Brown, 1968
Temper				Not significant	
Tantrums				Not significant	
Crying				Not significant	
Interview data from the Louisville twin study "Temperament" (combination of temper frequency, temper intensity,	95	73	0 – 6 yr		Wilson, Brown, & Matheny, 1971

				Boys		Girls		
				r_{MZ}	r_{DZ}	r_{MZ}	r_{DZ}	
irritability, crying, and demanding attention) Reactivity				Significant*		Significant*		
EASI-I Temperament Survey Emotionality	78	50	55-mo average	.63	.00*	.73	.20*	Buss, Plomin, & Willerman, 1973
EASI-III Temperament Survey General emotionality	60	51	42-mo average	.59	.45	.29	-.35	Plomin, 1974
Fear				.81	.60	.59	.06	
Anger				.80	-.09	.26	-.21	

*$p < .05$

73

TABLE 4.5 TWIN STUDIES OF EMOTIONALITY: CATTELL'S AND OTHER SCALES RELATED TO EMOTIONALITY

Measure	Number of MZ Pairs	Number of DZ Pairs	Age	Findings	Reference
Cattell's Junior Personality Questionnaire	104	64	10 – 15 yr		Cattell, Blewett, & Beloff, 1955
C. Emotional stability				Significant*	
Q4. Nervous tension				Significant*	
Cattell's Junior Personality Questionnaire	45	37	14 – 18 yr		Vandenberg, 1962
C. Emotional stability				Significant*	
Q4. Nervous tension				Significant*	
Thurstone Temperament Survey Stability	45	37	14 – 18 yr	Not significant	Vandenberg, 1962

	MZ	DZ	Age	Boys r_{MZ}	Boys r_{DZ}	Girls r_{MZ}	Girls r_{DZ}	
Cattell's Junior High School Personality Questionnaire	34	34	14 – 18 yr					Gottesman, 1963
C. Emotional stability				.33	.76	.05	.12	
O. Placidity				.20	-.04	.50	.51	
Q4. Nervous tension				.12	.73	.35	.16	

	MZ	DZ	Age	r_{MZ} (Sexes combined)	r_{DZ}	
Cattell's 16 Personality Factor Scale (some twins separated)	40	45	Adolescent-adult			Canter (in Mittler, 1971)
C. Emotional stability				.37	.15	
O. Placidity				.38	.06*	
Q4. Nervous tension				.20	.10	
Second-order anxiety factor				.43	.08	
Gough Adjective Checklist rated by mothers	24	28	6 – 10 yr			Scarr, 1966
Counseling readiness (anxiety)				.56	.03*	
Stern's Activities Index Emotionality	50	38	14 – 18 yr	Significant for males but not for females		Vandenberg, 1967

*$p < .05$

TABLE 4.6 TWIN STUDIES OF EMOTIONALITY: NEUROTICISM

Measure	Number of MZ Pairs	Number of DZ Pairs	Age	Findings r_{MZ}	Findings r_{DZ}	Reference
"Neuroticism" factor (includes such measures as intelligence, tapping speed, flicker fusion)	25	25	13 – 15 yr	.85	.21*	Eysenck & Prell, 1951
Brown Personality Inventory (a test of neurotic symptoms)				.37	.27	Eysenck & Prell, 1951
Bernreuter Personality Inventory Neuroticism	40	44	12 – 19 yr	.63	.32*	Carter, 1933
Objective Analytic Test Battery Neuroticism	104	30	10 – 15 yr	Significant*		Cattell, Stice, & Kristy, 1957
Comrey Personality and Attitude Factors Neuroticism	111	90	14 – 18 yr	Not significant		Vandenberg, 1967
Early version of the Maudsley Personality Inventory Neuroticism	43	25	8 – 59 yr	.38	.11	Shields, 1962

Eysenck's Personality Inventory Neuroticism	25	29	Adolescent–adult	.53	.70	Canter (in Mittler, 1971)
Cattell's 16 Factor Personality Scale Second order factor of neuroticism				.36	.06	
Their own questionnaire Neuroticism	157	189	Adults	.28	.21	Bruun, Markkanen, & Partanen (in Mittler, 1971)
Woodworth–Matthews Personality Inventory (a test of neurotic symptoms)	50	50	Late childhood	.56	.37	Newman et al., 1937
Psychoneurotic complaints	88	31	13 – 69 yr	.53	.11*	Wilde, 1964
Psychosomatic complaints				.67	.34*	

*p<.05

TABLE 4.7 TWIN STUDIES OF EMOTIONALITY: AUTONOMIC ACTIVITY

Measure	Number of MZ Pairs	Number of DZ Pairs	Age	Findings r_{MZ}	r_{DZ}	Reference
Autonomic activity (pulse rate and blood pressure)	26	26	12 – 15 yr	.93	.72*	Eysenck, 1956
Autonomic reactivity (heart rate, GSR, and breathing rate) to a flash of lights, a bell, and a falling hammer	13 – 34	8 – 26	Adult	Breathing rate significant* for the flash and hammer stimuli		Vandenberg et al., 1965
Autonomic activity (heart rate and GSR)	21	None	Adult	No correlations reported, but high concordance for MZ twins		Block, 1967

*$p < .05$

78

ronmental facilitation. Thus our equation for the occurrence of neurotic symptoms is: emotionality + traumatic conditions = neurosis.

Remember, too, that there is evidence (cited earlier) for two factors. The first factor—a variety of somatic-autonomic complaints—is roughly equivalent to emotionality. The second factor—worry, restlessness, and motor tension—is probably conditioned. Eysenck's neurotic symptoms consist of a mixture of the two factors. Thus some of the items tap what we consider the inherited component (emotionality), and others tap the conditioned component of neurotic symptoms. This may explain why the majority of studies in Table 4.6 are negative. We contend that a pure measure of emotionality would yield strong evidence of heritability in twins, and the data in Table 4.6 provide support for our position. Neurotic symptoms may derive in part from high emotionality, but the environmental component is probably more important.

Autonomic Measures

There are few studies of autonomic measures in twins. Two of them (Eysenck, 1956; Block, 1967) showed that autonomic activity has an inherited component, but all the measures were taken *at rest*, not in response to stimuli. Autonomic *activity* may be related to autonomic *reactivity*, but the two are clearly different. It is not surprising that the resting level of the autonomic nervous system has a genetic component. Tonic activity is a basic physiological aspect of functioning, just as is basal metabolic rate. As such, it relates more to the everyday vegetative functioning of the body than it does to emotional reactions to threat.

One study (Vandenberg et al., 1965) provides preliminary data on autonomic *reactivity*. They used stimuli that were not as threatening as the original Ax (1953) manipulation of fear: a flash of light, an electrical doorbell, and a hammer that dropped in front of the subject. The measures of autonomic reactivity were heart rate, galvanic skin resistance, and breathing rate. On all three measures monozygotic twins reacted more similarly than dizygotic twins. This was the only study we could find on autonomic *reactivity* in twins, and the sample size was small. Clearly, we need more research on reactivity in twins.

LONGITUDINAL STUDIES OF EMOTIONALITY

Emotionality can be assessed at the very beginning of life. Crying is easily measured in terms of its frequency and intensity and there are consistent individual differences in the first few days of life (Bell, 1960; Birns, 1965; Bridger

& Birns, 1968; Lipton, Steinschneider, & Richmond, 1961; and Korner, 1971). Behavioral indicants of distress have also been used to measure emotionality early in life (Shirley, 1933). Direct physiological measurement of autonomic reactivity has shown consistent individual differences in the reaction of neonates to aversive stimuli such as blasts of air (Lipton & Steinschneider, 1964).

Table 4.8 lists the longitudinal studies of emotionality. The studies of infants in the first year of life show some stability for crying and fussing. However, Moss (1967) did not find a significant correlation between frequency of crying at three weeks and at three months. Only Shirley (1933) found consistently high correlations during the first year of life for crying and fussing. Her data may explain why emotionality does not appear to be stable during the first year. She observed and rated irritability (a combination of crying, screaming, and fussing) during both physical and anthropometric examinations. Irritability during the anthropometric examinations was considerably more stable: the correlation between 0- to 3-month ratings and 6- to 12-month ratings is .54. Shirley noted that:

> . . . the average irritability scores for the anthropometric examinations are shown to be almost twice as great, age for age, as those for the physical examination. . . . The reason for the greater irritability at the anthropometric examinations is perhaps that they entailed somewhat more handling and restraint of the baby. [pp. 28–39]

The babies were more aroused during the anthropometric examinations and thus greater ranges of reactivity could be assessed. This suggests that the greater stability of irritability in reaction to the anthropometric examinations may have occurred because reactivity was assessed better.

In only one other study (McGrade, 1968) was the emotionality of infants rated as a reaction to stimulation. The stimulation, however, was much milder—removal of a nipple and rubbing the infant's forehead—and stability was not as great. The other studies of crying and fussing measured emotionality only as it occurred spontaneously. This may lead to a problem because emotionality is a reaction to a stimulus. When stimulation—such as the handling and restraint in Shirley's study—is not supplied by the experimenter, error is introduced: there may or may not be an aversive stimulus for distress (for example, a wet diaper) or for fear (for example, a looming or strange object such as the observer). We predict that if stimulation were equally available to the observed infants, a highly emotional child would react more frequently and more intensely. We suggest that future studies supply standard aversive stimuli, such as air blasts, loud noises, bright lights, and restraint of the body.

The other studies during the first year show weak to moderate stability of emotional reactivity. Research on older children also demonstrates moderate stability for a number of variables related to emotionality: irritability, thresholds and intensity of reactivity, temper, conflict behavior, and fearfulness. A large-scale study by Walker (1967) is noteworthy. He found considerable one-year stability for third- and fourth-grade elementary children for emotional stability and fearfulness, as measured by self-report, teacher ratings, and sociometric peer nominations. Only one study (Tuddenham, 1959) attempted to assess stability into adulthood. The measure was an interview rating of "tenseness," and it did not show significant stability over the 15 years of the study.

This research has implications for our developmental model. In the first year, only excitement and distress are measured. There are no studies that specifically measure fear in early childhood, but anger is assessed in two studies of young children. Jersild and Markey (1935) reported that preschool children behave quite consistently in terms of conflict behavior. Wilson, Brown, and Matheny (1971) found that although temper frequency was stable from early in life, temper intensity was stable only after eight months and irritability was stable only after three years of age. As noted earlier, anger may be confused with distress early in life, but these few findings generally agree with our developmental scheme of emotionality. Clearly, we need longitudinal research on the differentiation of emotionality and the stability of its components throughout life.

PRESENCE IN ADULTHOOD

There are both theoretical and empirical grounds for believing that emotionality differentiates into fear and anger. So, in determining the presence of emotionality in adulthood, we should seek evidence for anger, fear, and undifferentiated emotionality. All the evidence comes from self-report questionnaires. There are only a few for anger, the clearest being the irritability scale of the Buss-Durkee inventory (1957). But no factor has emerged from the various personality inventories because items pertaining to temper are rarely included. The exception is EASI-III, which shows a clear anger factor.

The presence of fear in adulthood is much better documented. There are a number of anxiety questionnaires, and a fear factor has emerged from various personality inventories. One example should suffice. Guilford (1959) reported a *nervousness* factor could be extracted from several inventories, containing items such as: unable to relax, easily startled, cannot sleep, sweats easily, nervous habits (picking teeth), and tense.

Guilford (1959) also reported a general emotionality factor (emotionally excitable, gets upset easily), as well as a factor of *hypersensitivity* (feelings easily

TABLE 4.8 LONGITUDINAL STUDIES OF EMOTIONALITY

Measure	Number	Age from beginning to end of study	Findings	Reference
Observational ratings Fussing Crying Irritability (crying and fussing)	26	3 wk to 3 mo	Correlation of .42* .28 .37*	Moss, 1967
Newborns: time-sampled, film-analyzed displacement of hands and feet; 8-mo olds: Bayley (1959) Infant Behavior Profile	24	First week to 8 mo	Newborn reaction to stimulation of forehead and 8-mo tension and fear: not significant Newborn reaction to removal of nipple and 8-mo tension: .40* Fear: not significant	McGrade, 1968
Frequency of crying during testing situations	61	First month to 12 mo		Bayley, 1932

	5 mo	8 mo	11 mo
2 mo	.38*	.22	.15
5 mo		.26	.18
8 mo			.66
11 mo			

21	Birth to 52 wk	Ratings of irritability (combination of crying, fussing, and screaming)	Shirley, 1933

Irritability during physical exams

	2 mo	4 mo	8 mo
0 mo	.65*	.51*	.12
2 mo			.11
4 mo			.20
8 mo			

Irritability during anthropometric exams

	4 mo	8 mo
2 mo	.44*	.54*
4 mo		.52*
8 mo		

54	1 to 3 yr	Ratings of irritability (excitable-calm)	Schaefer & Bayley, 1963

	Boys			Girls		
	14	21	32	14	21	32
11 mo	.82*	.31	.31	.82*	.45*	.45*
14 mo		.32*	.56*		.62*	.46*
21 mo			.60*			.71*
32 mo						

80	Birth to 2 yr	Ratings from interview with parents	Thomas et al., 1963

Intensity of reaction

	9	14	20	24
3 mo	.45*	.41*	.38*	.30*
9 mo		.45*	.36*	.40*
14 mo			.49*	.40*
20 mo				.28*
24 mo				

83

TABLE 4.8 (CONTINUED) LONGITUDINAL STUDIES OF EMOTIONALITY

Measure	Number	Age from beginning to end of study	Findings	Reference
Observational ratings of conflict behavior during free play	24	3 – 4 yr to 4 – 5 yr	Threshold of responsiveness |	9	14	20	24 | |---|---|---|---|---| | 3 mo | .50* | .38* | .30* | .00 | | 9 mo | | .67* | .29* | .16 | | 14 mo | | | .37* | .20 | | 20 mo | | | | .29* | | 24 mo | | | | | Correlation of .79* for 1-yr retest of the total number of conflicts	Jersild & Markey, 1935
Ratings from interviews with parents	336	Birth to 6 yr	Crying appeared stable** Temper frequency stable** Temper intensity stable after 3 mo of age ** Irritability stable only after 3 yr of age	Wilson, Brown, & Matheny, 1971

Ratings from interview of the Berkeley Guidance Study   85   5 to 16 yr   Bronson, 1966

	Boys			Girls		
	9	12	15	9	12	15
Emotional stability						
6 yr	.65*	.37*	.25	.53*	.11*	.04
9 yr		.52*	.28		.36*	.35*
12 yr			.48*			.35*
15 yr						
Explosiveness						
6 yr	.58*	.44*	.34*	.50*	.30*	.17
9 yr		.59*	.53*		.64*	.07
12 yr			.63*			.35*
Reactivity						
6 yr	.61*	.30*	.22	.41*	.10	.21
9 yr		.54*	.56*		.61*	.37*
12 yr			.54*			.54*
Anxious-relaxed						
6 yr	.38*	.29*	.34*	.49*	.28	.07
9 yr		.54*	.42*		.46*	.22
12 yr			.53*			.38*
Fearfulness						
6 yr	.05	.32*	.21	.23	.34*	.55*
9 yr		.32*	.38*		.43*	.39*
12 yr			.40*			.26
Tantrums						
6 yr	.51*	.33*	.11	.33*	.24	-.10
9 yr		.47*	.16		.55*	.23
12 yr			.42*			.29

TABLE 4.8 (CONTINUED) LONGITUDINAL STUDIES OF EMOTIONALITY

Measure	Number	Age from beginning to end of study	Findings	Reference
Self-report Ratings by teachers Sociometric peer nominations	269 to 368	3rd grade to 4th; 5th grade to 6th	*(see Fearfulness table below)*	Kagan & Moss, 1962
Ratings of interview data of the Fels Longitudinal Study	89	Birth to 14 yr	Reaction to frustration *(see matrix below)*	Kagan & Moss, 1962
Interview ratings of relaxed-tense	72	Adolescence to adulthood	Correlations for Males: .18 Females: .21	Tuddenham, 1959

Fearfulness

	Boys		Girls	
	3rd–4th	5th–6th	3rd–4th	5th–6th
Self-report	.49*	.67*	.70*	.69*
Ratings by teachers	.45*	.40*	.57*	.36*
Sociometric peer nominations	.66*	.73*	.47*	.40*

Reaction to frustration

	Boys			Girls		
	5	8	12	5	8	12
1 yr	.67*	.50*	.00	.58*	.66*	.44*
5 yr		.75*	.24		.79*	.51*
8 yr			.60*			.76*
12 yr						

* $p < .05$
**No intercorrelational matrix was reported--only adjacent months were tested for significance of relationship.

hurt, worries about humiliating experience). A previous inventory (Guilford & Zimmerman, 1956) yielded a bipolar factor of emotional stability: evenness of mood, optimism, composure versus fluctuation of moods, feelings of guilt and worry. These general emotionality factors indicate that the temperament persists through development.

CONCLUSIONS

How does emotionality stack up against the five criteria of temperament? Clearly, it is adaptive to become alarmed quickly and escape before harm strikes or become enraged quickly and deal aggressively with threats to well-being. Concerning the other logical criterion, presence in animals close to man, the emotions of fear and anger may be seen in all mammals.

The three empirical criteria have also been met. Twin studies suggest an inherited component in general emotionality, and there is at least moderate stability throughout childhood. The evidence for presence in adulthood is weaker but sufficient in light of the paucity of information and the differentiation of emotionality into fear and anger. Thus in terms of logical and empirical criteria, we believe that a fair case has been made for emotionality as a temperament.

Much research needs to be done. A precise determination of heritability can be made only with large enough samples of twins to reduce the standard error to manageable proportions. This would require a twin sample of more than a thousand pairs, a number large enough to deter most investigators. The longitudinal research on emotionality is spotty, and we need sequential measures of arousability in the laboratory. This involves the repeated testing of children in a psychophysiological laboratory—a severe challenge to most researchers' resources, but clearly a necessary one.

We have included both fear and anger under emotionality. Many psychologists would not pair anger with fear, preferring to equate emotionality with fear. Diamond (1957), for example, makes his emotionality temperament synonymous with fear, and he includes anger under the separate heading of a temperament of aggressiveness. We believe that there are compelling reasons for linking anger and fear (see the first part of the chapter). Which position one accepts depends on how aggression and escape are construed, and how one relates animal aggression to human aggression. These issues would take us too far from temperament, but we shall add a few words in the final chapter.

Finally, what about mood? Persons high on emotionality would be expected to be somewhat changeable in mood, and perhaps even on the "down side." Mood is obviously related to emotionality, and we shall give this question fuller treatment in Chapter 8.

CHAPTER

5

SOCIABILITY

Sociability is the only temperament that has a directional component: seeking other persons, preferring their presence, and responding to them. The highly sociable person tends to work and play in groups. He would rather be part of the team than a loner, a member of a committee than a solitary worker. If his profession is writing, he finds it difficult to remain alone at his desk for hours at a time. A lonely job, such as a forest ranger or night watchman, is anathema to him. He is better off as a worker in a busy office or as a salesman in sustained contact with customers. If a scientist, he will probably be in the more interactive social sciences than in the more isolated physical sciences.

If our assumptions are correct, sociologists will prove to be more sociable than astronomers. Highly sociable persons are more likely to become teachers than researchers; if both, they tend to prefer the interaction of teaching to the relative isolation of research. And they gravitate toward work involving performance rather than design, invention, or composition. The sociable person is more likely to be a pilot than an airplane designer, a salesman than the inventor of the product being sold, or a violinist than a composer of music. This is not to imply that sociability is necessarily opposed to creativity—only that sociable persons, by definition, avoid solitary pursuits. To the extent that creative acts require solitude, the sociable person is handicapped. If the creative urge were strong enough, the sociable person would endure the discomfort of isolation and persevere in his work.

The sociable person tends to be a "joiner." He is likely to be a fraternity man or, if disdainful of fraternities, to be a member of a group that has similar functions. He belongs to several clubs and organizations, and he actively participates in them. He enjoys crowds and is more willing to tolerate the discomforts correlated with the presence of large numbers of people, as in ball parks and auditoriums, or of small groups in cramped quarters, as at parties.

Recreational activities are part of the same pattern. The preferred hobbies and games are those involving other persons. The sociable person tends to choose Scrabble over the similar but solitary crossword puzzle. He prefers playing the violin as part of a quartet rather than as a solo instrument. He elects to play golf as part of a twosome or a foursome rather than as a solitary golfer trying to beat par.

The interactive aspect of games has two different components. The first is *competition*: one struggles to beat an opponent whose aim is the same. What one player does determines the other's response in a continually changing pattern of action and reaction. This occurs in team sports such as baseball or football, in which offense and defense are determined formally by which team is at bat or possesses the ball. It also occurs in individual sports such as tennis or ping pong, in which offense and defense can shift with a single stroke. The same is true of the quieter but no less ferocious contests of table games such as chess: the more sociable person *competes* at chess; the less sociable person prefers to solve chess problems alone. In brief, the sociable person welcomes the give-and-take that marks competition with others.

The second component of interactive games, *cooperation*, occurs only in team sports. The singles player interacts only with his opponent; the team player interacts with both his opponents (competition) and his teammates (cooperation). Other things equal, we expect sociable persons to prefer team sports to individual sports because team sports are doubly social, through the give-and-take of competition and the camaraderie and group feeling of cooperation.

The sociable person tends to have a wide circle of friends and acquaintances. He gives more parties and attends more. He knows many persons and vocationally is likely to have "connections." None of this precludes a much smaller circle of close friends or an even smaller number of intimate relationships. Sociable and nonsociable persons may not differ in the affect-laden relationships of love, marriage, or family. Most normal human beings need an intimate relationship involving privacy, love, and often sex. Sociability enters into the more *public* relationships of friends, wider family, teammates, club members, and competitors. In these less intimate interactions, the sociable person shines and revels in the presence of others.

Sociability and Warmth

So far we have focused on the sociable person's *needs* and on his tendency to involve himself with others. What about his response to others? As might be expected, he is known as a warm, responsive person. Other things being equal, he smiles more than others, and he is more lavish in giving praise. As he would be rewarded by the presence of others, so he rewards them by attention, esteem, and even affection. Because of a natural orientation toward others, he can share feelings and sentiments. So he tends to be sympathetic, empathic, and even altruistic. In brief, as a highly social being, he responds to others with those attributes that mark specifically *human* reinforcements: attention, affection, esteem, sympathy, understanding, encouragement, and help.

In this formulation, need is separate from response. At first glance, the distinction might appear to be false because we infer the person's need from his response: if he *responds* by seeking to be with others, we infer that he has a *need* to be with them. But this applies only to the *directional* response of moving toward others. *Warmth*, on the other hand, refers to the person's behavior *after* he has made contact with others. Does he offer attention, help, or affection? Does he smile or indicate acceptance by closeness or gestures? *Need* refers to the polarity of presence-absence (moving toward versus moving away), whereas *warmth* refers to dimension of reactivity to others in a social context. We suggest that the person who wants to be with others (need) is also attentive, affectionate, and helpful in his interactions with others (response).

The thrust of these remarks is that sociability and warmth are opposite sides of the same coin. The sociable person has a strong need to be with others, but what is the nature of this need? It must be a set of attributes that are possessed by or can be supplied by other persons. We have already described what these uniquely human responses are: attention, affection, praise, understanding, and sympathy. When another person makes such responses, we call him *warm and responsive to others*. The warm person smiles often, laughs with others, is happy at their good fortune, praising of their worthy behavior, and understanding of their defects or failures. These are precisely the things that make social interaction so rewarding. We suggest that there is a kind of reciprocity in social exchange. The sociable person has a stronger need for attention, affection, etc., and he also has a stronger tendency to supply these things to others.

Two qualifications are immediately necessary. First, there is no precise equity between a person's social need and his response to others. We expect that *on the average* a sociable person's stronger need is matched by a stronger social responsivity. But it would be foolhardy to deny the presence of imbalance in both directions, for there are *takers* and *givers*. Takers sop up attention, affection, praise, and understanding, and offer little in return. Givers supply more than their share, and ask or demand little in return. Clearly, takers are more selfish and tend to be immature.

Second, although we have not made the point specifically, our discussion has concerned only adults. Children typically lack the experience and maturity needed to supply the understanding and help that adults can offer. Does this mean that children cannot display warmth? Of course they can, but the style is more affective and less cognitive. Children can share the joy of others' success, can offer attention, and above all can display a delightfully spontaneous affection (smiling, hugging, kissing, or jumping for joy). Children ordinarily do not and cannot fully reciprocate the affection, understanding, and help of an adult, but they are socially responsive in ways that allow us to label them as more or less warm.

In brief, we suggest two reciprocal dimensions. The first, called *sociability*, is a tendency to seek out and remain with others. Underlying this tendency is a set of correlated needs for attention, affection, sympathy, and solidarity. The second dimension, called *warmth*, involves social responsivity: responding to others with precisely the attributes that meet their social needs, such as attention and affection.

The two dimensions vary from the extremes of too much to too little (see Table 5.1). The adjectives in this table were scaled by clinical psychologists, using a rating scale of 1 to 9. The table contains the mean rankings, which vary from too much (*intrusive, overindulgent*) to too little (*solidarity, frigid*) of sociability and warmth, respectively.

The presence of two dimensions may be a source of confusion. Sociability

TABLE 5.1 DIMENSIONS OF SOCIABILITY AND WARMTH (Buss and Gerjuoy, 1957)

Sociability		Warmth	
Intrusive	2.0	Overindulgent	2.0
Gregarious	2.9	Doting	2.2
Convivial	3.3	Affectionate	3.5
Comradely	3.8	Tender	3.8
Companionable	4.0	Sympathetic	4.2
Accessible	4.8	Kindly	4.6
Reserved	5.3	Considerate	4.8
Reticent	5.6	Cool	5.8
Retiring	5.9	Detached	6.0
Shrinking	6.5	Unfeeling	6.5
Seclusive	7.2	Hardened	6.7
Solitary	7.5	Frigid	7.8
Isolated	7.8		

has traditionally referred to a *directional* tendency: to seek out and move toward other persons. To alter this definition would be to invite semantic confusion. Warmth, of course, refers to social responsiveness. What is novel in our approach is the insistence that the *temperament* of sociability includes *both* the directional component (traditionally called *sociability*) and the responsivity component (*warmth*). We assume that the sociable person not only seeks out others but is also warmly responsive to their presence. Stated another way, we believe that the two dimensions shown in Table 5.1 are highly correlated.

Positive and Negative

At its best, interaction between two persons offers some of the most cherished rewards: nurturance, affection, and attention. At its worst, social contacts can deliver some of the strongest punishments: rejection, hatred, and curtailment of freedom of action. The positives and negatives of social interaction may be regarded as complementary. For each positive aspect that would draw a person to others, there is a negative aspect that would drive him away (see Table 5.2). Thus a mother can soothe an upset child by picking him up and holding him, but this act restricts the child's movements and prevents independent actions by him. Play, games, or even conversation provide the stimulation that most of us seek and need; but play and games may lose their novelty and appeal, and conversations can be sufficiently dull to drive the participants to seek solitude. Most persons welcome attention and devise subtle means of obtaining it to supplement direct requests or demands for it. But the other person has another option that is extremely aversive: shunning or rejection. Most of us welcome affection from others, but what comes from the other person may not be liking but hatred. Similarly, others can be the source of praise and indications of success, but they can also deliver criticism and indications of failure. Finally, one's needs may require the feedback that can occur only in a social context (attention, affection, etc.), but the *cost* of meeting these needs may be acquiescence to the demands of others.

TABLE 5.2 POLARITIES OF SOCIAL INTERACTION

Positive	Negative
Soothing	Restriction
Stimulation	Boredom
Attention	Rejection
Affection	Hostility
Praise	Criticism
Needs	Demands

The thrust of this discussion is that social interaction is a mixed bag, not an unalloyed blessing. There are enough negative features associated with others to drive people away from one another. These negative aspects are probably just as aversive for sociable persons as for unsociable persons. Perhaps the person who needs attention has more to fear from rejection; when praise is sought, criticism stings more sharply. Thus the difference between sociable and unsociable persons may reside not in the negative features of social interaction, but in the positive features. These are so important to the sociable person that he tolerates the negative possibilities of boredom, rejection, etc. For the unsociable person, the positive features are simply not important enough to outweigh the negative features, and on balance social interactions are aversive.

Why do people seek others rather than remaining alone? We have suggested several social rewards—the "positives" of Table 5.2. The existence of these different social incentives raises an issue concerning sociability. First, if there are different incentives, does the highly sociable person have a strong need for *all* of them? There is no simple answer to this question. We assume that the person high in the temperament of sociability attempts to satisfy his needs *through persons*. If he seeks stimulation, he prefers it to come from other persons rather than from television, movies, drug taking, ·or any *solitary* activity. Thus for a nonsocial need, it is not the *amount* of the need that is crucial but the *way* in which it is met—socially rather than asocially.

Nevertheless, there are strictly *social* needs that cannot be met except through other persons: attention, affection, and praise. Are these needs stronger in sociable than in unsociable persons? If sociability is a unitary temperament, the answer must be *yes*. We are making the simplest assumption here, that the need for others is pervasive and generalized. This means that in sociable persons (1) strictly social needs (e.g., affection) are stronger, and (2) when there is a choice, other needs will be satisfied through persons rather than through objects or nonsocial events.

The second question concerns the persistence of social needs and incentives during development. For example, infants clearly need to be nurtured by a mother or substitute caretaker, but does this need endure into adulthood? The answer for all but a few immature adults is obviously *no*. This raises a further question: does sociability wane during childhood? Again the answer is *no*; the *need* for interaction continues unabated, but what people want and receive from one another changes. We suggest that there are developmental changes in the way that sociability is expressed.

DEVELOPMENT

We have organized the development of social interaction into three segments (see Table 5.3). The first, consisting of soothing and arousal, appears first in

TABLE 5.3 DEVELOPMENT OF SOCIABILITY

Aspect	Age Period
1. Soothing and arousal	Infancy through childhood
2. Affectionate relationships	
a. Nurturance received	Infancy through childhood
b. Peer interaction	Childhood through adulthood
c. Nurturance given	Adulthood
3. Affiliating	Adolescence through adulthood

early infancy and wanes thereafter. The second, consisting of the varieties of affectionate relationships, starts in infancy and continues in various forms through adulthood. The third, consisting of affiliating with groups of persons, starts as early as late childhood but typically in adolescence.

Soothing and Arousal

The newborn of all mammals tend to be easily frightened by the novel and unusual sights, sounds, and smells of an unfamiliar world. They root and cling to one another and to the mother for the contact and warmth that are synonymous with security. Primate infants prefer to cling to their mothers' hair, and they like to be held, touched, and stroked. Human infants have no maternal hair to cling to, but they also like being held, touched, stroked, and being kept warm by the mother's body heat. A disturbed or fearful infant can usually be calmed by being cradled by the mother, but soothing need not be accomplished *socially*; for some infants a cradle will suffice.

CUDDLERS AND NONCUDDLERS

There are pronounced individual differences during the first year of life in *how* an infant prefers to be soothed. Some infants like to be calmed part of the time by being held and part of the time merely by the noncontact presence of the mother. Some infants wish always to be held when disturbed, and some never. These two extreme groups have been identified as cuddlers and noncuddlers (Schaffer and Emerson, 1964):

> To illustrate the difference between the two groups, the following phrases may be quoted from the reports given by the mothers of the Non-Cuddlers regarding the infant's reaction to cuddling, i.e., that form of physical contact where the baby is picked up, held with both arms in an upright position on the adult's lap, pressed against her shoulder and usually given some skin-to-skin contact such as kissing or cheek stroking:

Gets restless when cuddled, turns face away and begins to struggle.

Will not allow it, fights to get away.

Has never liked this since able to struggle, squirms and whimpers.

Gets restless, pushes you away.

Wriggles and arches back, and only stops when you put down again.

Restless and whiny until allowed back in cot.

Will kick and thrash with his arms, and if you persist will begin to cry.

These phrases may be contrasted with the following from the mothers of the Cuddlers:

Cuddles you back.

Snuggles into you.

Holds quite still and puts on a soppy face.

Loves it.

Laps it up.

Would let me cuddle him for hours on end. [p. 3]

We believe that these opposing tendencies go beyond soothing and apply to social contacts generally. They are the earliest manifestations of the temperament of sociability. The cuddlers seek out others, especially the mother, because they prefer the presence of others. Schaffer and Emerson do not report on smiling or other social responses, but we suggest that cuddlers are more socially responsive. They would be reported by neutral observers as warmer, "easier," and more receptive and responsive children. Noncuddlers are probably colder, more difficult, and generally less responsive to persons. It follows that cuddlers should form a specific attachment to the mother *earlier* and that this attachment should be *stronger*. Both tendencies occurred but only the latter was at an acceptable level of statistical significance (Schaffer and Emerson, 1964, p. 6).

In brief, the tendencies to cuddle up to the mother, to prefer soft, fuzzy toys, and to accept restraint appear to reflect the earliest appearance of sociability temperament. A note of caution: other temperaments might have cut across the cuddle-noncuddler distinction. The noncuddlers were reported to develop motor skills earlier and to prefer rough-and-tumble play, so they might have been higher in *activity level*. They also reacted intensely to restrictions and so might be considered more *emotional*. These are merely speculations, but they cannot be ruled out. Clearly there is a pressing need for appropriate controls for the presence of other temperaments when social behavior is studied.

The need to be soothed is probably strongest during the first few weeks of life. Thereafter it slowly wanes, dropping lower and lower during childhood and virtually disappearing in adulthood. Mature adults need to be cradled and calmed only after such rare calamities as accidents, severe illness, or the death of a loved person.

AROUSAL

The opposing tendency—increasing arousal through exploration and manipulation—increases steadily from birth onward. And this is not solely a human developmental trend, for it characterizes primates generally:

> We cannot say with any certainty just when the growing primate begins to shift from its psychological preoccupation with the mother to the world at large. In most species, it probably starts at birth. It is certain, however, that a shift does occur, and it is obvious that the change is gradual and progressive. It represents the emergence of a basic orientation toward the world that differs radically from the mother-directed, arousal-reducing orientation that characterizes early infancy. Although the shift never wholly supplants this earlier orientation, it overshadows it increasingly as a factor in the day-to-day activities of the developing individual.
>
> The evidence for such a trend is abundant although on many points it can scarcely be considered systematic. Specific indications are, first, the increasing tendency to approach and interact with objects in the physical environment—the development of exploratory or investigatory activities; second, a progressive increase in the amount, vigor, and variety of motor play—the jumping, bouncing, climbing, and swinging, for which the primates are justly famous. . . . [Mason, 1968, p. 77]

HOMEOSTASIS

Thus there appear to be two opposing tendencies: the need for security and low arousal (obtained by soothing) and the need for stimuli and high arousal (obtained by exploration). There is a developmental trend for more stimulus seeking, but at any given time there is an optimal balance between the two. Mason (1965) suggests an optimal level of arousal, with deviations from this level inducing corrective tendencies. This homeostatic model requires evidence of such corrective tendencies, and Mason has the appropriate data.

He examined the preferences of infant chimpanzees for soothing versus arousal. Each infant was allowed to interact with two experimenters, seen singly, and each human had a distinctive costume (dark clothes and hood versus white clothes and hood). One experimenter always cradled and soothed the animal, allowing it to cling to him. The other always tickled and played roughly (but affectionately) with the animal. Gradually, each infant came to prefer the more intense stimulation and chose the appropriate experimenter— but only when in a state of *low* arousal. When arousal was *high*, the infants preferred to be soothed and calmed. Thus when an infant was placed in an un-familiar room, injected with amphetamine, or separated for some time from fellow animals (all arousal-inducing manipulations), the animal clung to the quiet, soothing experimenter.

There is related but indirect evidence in humans. When an infant is upset, it tends not to explore the environment. But when it is picked up and held and crying abates, visual exploration begins immediately (Korner & Grobstein, 1966). In summary, there appears to be an optimal level of arousal: excessive arousal sets up a need for soothing, and insufficient arousal sets up a need for stimulation. During the course of development, the optimal level of arousal ap-pears to increase. Children need to be soothed less and they prefer more stimulation.

How do these issues bear on sociability? We cannot equate the temperament of sociability with the need to be soothed. This would imply (1) a lower *balance point* of optimal arousal level, and there is no logical or empirical basis for this; (2) a tendency to become aroused more easily (arousability), but we have already suggested this as the defining property of another temperament (emotionality); and (3) a tendency toward immaturity—with so-ciable persons requiring more parental soothing and caretaking—and there is no logical or empirical basis for this, either.

Nor can we equate sociability with the need for stimulation (higher arousal). This would imply (1) that sociable children have a weaker need to be soothed, and there is not only no logical basis for this but evidence against it—cuddlers needed to be soothed as much as noncuddlers, but the former prefer-red being held; noncuddlers were soothed by proximity but resisted being held (Schaffer & Emerson, 1964)—and (2) that sociable persons become bored more easily and tend to seek excitement, and these two tendencies (boredom and sensation seeking) probably belong under the heading of *impulsivity*.

We conclude that there is no persuasive argument for equating sociability with a stronger need for either soothing or arousal. It is not the strength of a need that is crucial here, but how needs are satisfied. When the nonsociable child needs to be soothed, he prefers asocial means. He can be warmed by blankets, rocked in a rocker, or calmed by diminishing the level of visual, audi-tory, and tactile stimulation; none of these requires the intimate presence of a caretaker. But a sociable child prefers social soothing: to be touched, cradled, rocked in the caretaker's arms, and spoken to softly and reassuringly—all involving close, almost smothering contact with the caretaker.

When the nonsociable child craves excitement he prefers to be aroused by objects and events: television, phonograph, toys, and solitary games. He may tolerate others if they are part of the stimulation, but he can take them or leave them. When the sociable child craves excitement he seeks out others. He wants the reciprocal feedback that occurs only in social interaction. Thus the sociable infant delights in peekaboo and pat-a-cake, and the sociable child prefers competitive games to solitary play.

The point of this discussion is that, *with respect to soothing and arousal*, sociability is not a matter of greater or lesser *need*. Rather, it is a matter of *how* needs are satisfied. Whether the need is soothing or arousal, the sociable child wants it satisfied through other persons; the unsociable child either has no preference or prefers nonsocial means of being soothed or aroused. There is, of course, more to sociability than a preference for social soothing. The sociable child also seeks others for affection.

Affectionate Relationships

We are concerned here with interactions between two persons, the relationship being characterized by sufficient mutual liking to be maintained over time. The relationship need not be permanent (few are), but it should be more than transient; perhaps the best term is *enduring*.

Affectionate relationships may be divided into three developmental eras. With reference to the person being studied, they are nurturance received, peer interaction, and nurturance given. This sequence starts with the relatively helpless young child being dependent on an adult. It progresses to mutual give-and-take between more or less competent partners who are roughly equal in the relationship. And it ends with the adult taking a parental or supervisory role in aiding a less competent or relatively helpless person.

NURTURANCE RECEIVED

The barest minimum of nurturance is mere physical presence. At first glance the presence of another person might not appear to be nurturant, but in some contexts it clearly serves this function. Children and fearful adults sometimes become frightened when they are alone in unfamiliar surroundings. Similarly, an ill or injured person may find it aversive to be alone. In these situations, merely knowing that another is present tends to be reassuring; therefore accompanying another person may be nurturant.

Most children require more than a bare minimum of nurturance, and they seek the attention of any adult present. They want to be looked at, talked to, and perhaps even listened to—all involving the attention of the other person. Attention is fundamental to social interaction, for it is being the focus of another's attention that makes us feel special and unique. Each of us feels more human when he is looked at or listened to. What appears to be dehumanizing about modern society is that people are treated as a mass, and individuality is ignored. Attention enhances individuality.

But attention is affectively neutral, and most children crave at least some *affection*. They want to be smiled at and perhaps touched, stroked, held, hugged, and kissed. Children tend to enjoy being told that they are loved, that they are special and praiseworthy. They usually receive parental affection of both the physical and verbal varieties. Children also need and want *help*. Early in childhood they need to be carried, fed, cleaned, and dressed. Later, they need assistance in mastering tasks that are beyond their immature capabilities.

In brief, children want and seek three kinds of nurturance: *attention, affection*, and *instrumental help*. But there are striking individual differences in how much nurturance children need, differences that we attribute to variations in the temperament of sociability. The highly sociable child craves the presence of others and is more likely to cry when forced to be alone. He has a strong need for attention and learns early to obtain it from the adults around him: by smiling at others, by "performing" and being cute, and (if necessary) by making a nuisance of himself. The parent who tries to ignore a highly sociable child will lose out in the long run. The child will attempt to find others who are sufficiently attentive, or he will make enough mischief to guarantee parental attention. For a sociable child, even punishment is preferable to inattention. Such a child also needs much affection, as illustrated by the cuddlers observed by Schaffer and Emerson (1964). And the sociable child welcomes help from others. He likes attention, seeks and receives affection, and therefore he expects others to be helpful. All children gradually want to do things for themselves, but the sociable child is willing to be dependent longer.

We suggest that the sociable child's reactions match his wants and needs. He attends more to persons and responds affectionately. He smiles and laughs more and is willing to hug and kiss others. When very young, he is unable to offer help but his highly sociable reaction to others (attention and smiling) strongly rewards their nurturant responses. Thus a *positive* feedback cycle is established. The sociable child seeks nurturance; when he receives attention, affection, or help, he reinforces these responses by adults with his own social responses (smiling, etc.). Such reinforcement makes the adults more nurturant, and the cycle continues.

In our view, the cycle for the unsociable child is one of *negative* feedback. He needs and seeks little nurturance, and his responses to it—his general affective response—is cool. Wanting less nurturance, he is less rewarded by it. He generally smiles less and prefers not to be hugged and kissed (he is a noncuddler). Adults who offer attention and affection tend to be turned off by the child's cool reception, or they may feel slighted at the child's rejection of their attempts to be affectionate. As he matures, the unsociable child strongly prefers to do things for himself. More than most children, he rejects help and tends to become negativistic if he is not allowed to master tasks alone. In contrast to the sociable child who shapes adults with his warm responsivity, the unsociable child shapes adults with his coolness or rejection. Gradually, adults offer less attention, affection, and help, and the unsociable child receives a level of nurturance that is more or less consistent with the low need for it. Excessive attempts by parents to offer more nurturance or force greater sociability should sooner or later lead to rebellion by the child. As the sociable child may remain dependent and catered to, so the unsociable child may become negativistic and hostile.

Maturing children spend more and more time with age mates, and their predominant social interactions shift from receiving nurturance to the give-and-take of equals. Children gradually act less as passive recipients of attention and affection, and more as active participants of shared attention and affection. They learn to entertain others as well as being entertained, and they offer affection as well as receive it. As they would be helped to accomplish tasks, so they help others. They learn to merge their own selfish ends with those of a partner so that both may attain their goals. They start to share their possessions, giving as well as receiving goods. In brief, they move from a position of helpless and selfish receptivity to one of helpful and more unselfish sharing. This general tendency—a well-known part of socialization—provides a basis for the equitable relationships of adulthood. Our interest here centers on the different paths taken by children high and low in sociability.

We have already suggested that the highly sociable child *needs* more attention, affection, and help. He continues to seek these from peers just as he did from parents, but his style is different. As described above, his peer relationships will be marked by *equity*. He not only seeks but gives attention, affection, and help. Thus the needs persist, but the way they are satisfied changes to fit the context of peer interaction.

This means that the large change is in the child's *responsivity*. The sociable child *attends* more to others and observes them more. Such observation is one of the basic aspects of imitation learning (Bandura, 1969). It follows that the highly sociable child, by paying more attention to others, learns more by imitation. The unsociable child attends to others less, and so imitates less (Fouts & Click, unpublished).

The sociable child is more *affectionate* toward peers; his friendships tend to be warmer and closer. The combination of greater attention and more shared liking should produce more sympathy for others. The sociable child can better share his friend's affect because his friend is more important to him. Therefore sociable children should tend to become more empathic than unsociable children.

We see the sociable child as seeking and giving more instrumental *help*. It follows that he becomes more involved in *group* tasks and shows a greater willingness to share goods and credit for success. The unsociable child tends to reject help and wishes to pursue his goals independently. He prefers solitary activities and rightfully sees no need to share credit for his own accomplishments. He is less susceptible to group pressure for conformity and tends to go his own way. If achievement is demanded of him, he has less conflict about beating out others for the prize. The highly sociable child may be torn between a desire to win in competition and a need to cooperate with others. He will be a better "team player"; the unsociable child fits better as the individual star. In line with these tendencies, sociable children should prefer team sports (football), unsociable children individual sports (tennis). It is during childhood and adolescence that children discover the sports, games, and hobbies that match their temperament: sociable children gravitate toward group and competitive pursuits, and unsociable children toward solitary and noncompetitive pursuits.

The sociable child has an easier path to follow in childhood. He accepts the demands of socialization and group pressure for conformity because his strong social needs are satisfied by others. And his warm responsiveness to others tends to make him liked and accepted, thereby enhancing the positive side of social interaction.

The unsociable child finds childhood more difficult. Being more independent, he resists group pressures and finds them overly restrictive. His need for others is less and therefore he is less receptive to their presence or interference. His response to others is cooler, and therefore he is less liked and accepted. The positive side of social interaction, which is low to begin with, sinks lower in the face of social rejection and the relative absence of affection from others (which he turns off). He has little empathy for others and is less able to see the need for sharing and cooperation. These tendencies point up the aversive aspects of social relations and drive him away from others. Thus he is less social, less socialized, and less in harmony with the give-and-take of group living.

NURTURANCE GIVING

Humans start life as helpless infants who need the care of parents or substitute caretakers. The children progress to self-help and eventually most adults reach the position of caring for the next generation. Thus *giving* nurturance—the reciprocal of *receiving* nurturance—may be regarded as the last step in socialization. Most adults attain this status, if not through parenthood then through nursing, teaching, and a variety of pursuits that all involve helping others.

In light of our previous comments, there is little to add about high- and low-sociable persons. Sociable adults tend naturally to give nurturance in the appropriate context. They not only see the need because of their greater sympathy but are eager to share because of their social orientation. Moreover, they enjoy the reciprocity of the two-person interaction and are strongly rewarded by the affection that rebounds to them. Unsociable persons find these rewards less potent, they are less sympathetic, and they find the interaction more aversive. In brief, unsociable persons start life needing less nurturance and as adults wind up giving less.

Affiliating

So far we have discussed two-person interactions, which are usually characterized by reciprocal affection, attention, and perhaps even help. But many social activities occur in organized groups, whose memberships vary from a handful to millions of persons. We prefer to use the term *affiliating* in the sense of belonging to a group because the term *affiliation* has unfortunately been equated with gregariousness and sociability.

PRIMARY AND SECONDARY GROUPS

Groups have been divided into two kinds on the basis of number of persons and nature of the interaction. *Primary* groups consist of up to a few dozen persons who regularly see one another. Thus the group is small, the participation direct, and the contact face-to-face. The function of the group may be work, as in groups of cooks in a restaurant or construction workers on a building site. Or the group may be recreational, as in a local bridge club or baseball team. The identity of the group depends on how formally it is organized. Work groups are usually informal and unlabeled, whereas teams and clubs usually have a name (Titans, Aces) and a structure (captain, manager). Concerning sociability, the important point is that primary groups involve direct participation of the members, who often become involved in affectionate, nurturant, and attentional activities with each other. Thus primary group interaction is merely a short step away from two-person interaction.

Secondary group interaction is more distant and vicarious. Such groups include large numbers of persons, who are so spread out geographically as to preclude face-to-face contact. Examples are nationality (American), religion (Catholic), gender (woman), and profession (physician). Virtually all psychologists share a vocational identity and consider themselves as part of the same professional group whether or not they belong to the national association. But most do not see or work with each other and are generally ignorant of the individual existence of one another.

The importance of secondary groups resides in their size, power, and status. Children are taught of our national heritage and they learn pride in being an

American. They can discern the power of the country in military, economic, and scientific terms, and they may discover the value of an American passport when traveling abroad. Most Americans have been conditioned to value the appropriate symbol, Old Glory, and desecration of the flag can inspire murderous rage among many citizens.

On a more limited scale, many persons strongly identify with athletic teams. Thus the New York Mets, the Green Bay Packers, and the Boston Celtics all have rabid fans, who not only attend games and request autographs but write letters to the athletes and meet them at airports after outstanding victories. None of the fans participates in games, and there is no face-to-face interaction. Being a fan is like being a member of any secondary group: the identity may be strong but it is vicarious. The team itself is a primary group; the fans comprise a secondary group. Thus the interaction of members of secondary groups is indirect, cognitive, and distant, in contrast to the interaction of primary groups, which is direct, instrumental (or affective), and close.

SOCIABLE AND UNSOCIABLE

Primary groups, we have suggested, are but a step away from two-person interactions. And we have already stated that sociable persons have more frequent and more intense two-person interactions than do unsociable persons. It follows that sociable persons belong to more primary groups and participate in them more actively. Such groups help to satisfy their strong social needs and provide opportunities for meeting other needs (status, getting the job done, recreation) through others. Moreover, the highly sociable person's warm response to others in the group helps to yield reciprocal reinforcement from other members, thereby strengthening his bonds to the particular group and to membership in groups generally.

The unsociable person has none of these reasons for affiliating. Because social needs are low, there is little motivation to be around groups of people. He prefers to meet his nonsocial needs asocially, and thus he seeks status through individual accomplishment, tries to get the job done alone, and engages in relatively solitary recreations (hiking, fishing, or cross-country running). Moreover, his relative unresponsiveness in groups turns others off, and his few social responses to group members tend to go unrewarded, thereby weakening his bonds to the particular group and to membership in groups generally.

Thus sociability may play a large role in whether and how persons affiliate with *primary* groups, but sociability is of little or no consequence in relation to *secondary* groups. Such groups do not meet most of the social needs of the sociable person. There is little or no attention, no affection, at best a distant kind of help, and none of the give-and-take of face-to-face encounters. There is no way to show one's individual warmth or sympathy, or to receive these from another. So the fundamental reasons for being gregarious are either absent or seriously diminished.

Also diminished are the *negative* aspects of encounters with others. In secondary groups, there is virtually no individually directed hostility or rejection and little danger of social intrusiveness. One need not possess any particular social skills, and there is no reason for social anxiety. All the negative features that drive unsociable persons from others are negated or minimized in secondary groups. Unsociable persons have less reason to avoid such groups, and sociable persons have less reason to join such groups. So, other things being equal, the temperament of sociability should play no role in the tendency to join, participate, and identify with secondary groups.

BIRTH ORDER

It is widely believed that the order of birth is a major determinant of the desire to be with others, especially when one is afraid. Schachter (1959) first demonstrated that firstborn children prefer to be with others when threatened, and there is some corroborating evidence. Nevertheless, during the past decade, two developments have seriously weakened the factual basis of the birth order effect. First, inspection of the research has revealed serious problems of method (for example, lumping only children with firstborns of larger families). Second, negative findings have tended to cancel out the earlier positive ones. The reader should consult Schooler (1973) for a penetrating review of the literature. At present it is not clear whether birth order determines "affiliation," and so we do not discuss the issue as part of sociability.

MEASURES OF SOCIABILITY

Two theoretical issues bear directly on how sociability is measured. First, there are developmental trends in how sociability is manifested. In children, soothing, arousal, and receiving nurturance are the major aspects of sociability, but more egalitarian relationships characterize sociability in adolescents and adults. Thus the appropriate measure of sociability depends in part on the age of the subject.

Second, we have distinguished two aspects of sociability: need and responsivity to others. These can be and have been measured separately, and we have organized the various measures in accordance with this split. Unfortunately, no one has correlated a need measure with a responsivity measure, so our hypothesis is as yet untested.

Measures of sociability have been divided into those involving behavioral observation (see Table 5.4) and those involving self-report (see Table 5.5). The behavioral measures are subdivided into those tapping need and those tapping responsivity. In infants, an excellent measure is how close they stay to the mother, especially when they need soothing. This yields the cuddler–noncuddler distinction discussed earlier (Schaffer & Emerson, 1964). The soothing ministrations of the mother occur in what Hall (1966) calls the *intimate* zone of human distances. This zone is important in infancy; it distinguishes cuddlers from noncuddlers. Its importance for sociability wanes with age because most social interaction takes place in the two zones beyond the intimate zone, the *personal* and the *social* zones. The personal zone is ordinarily used by friends for conversation and other interaction; it extends from an arm's reach to a little over 4 feet. The social zone, from 4 to 12 feet, encompasses the space in which impersonal interactions occur, those among business acquaintances but not friends. The personal and social zones vary from one culture to the next (Hall, 1966), but within any given culture there are wide variations among individuals. We believe that one source of this variability is sociability: more sociable persons place themselves closer to friends (personal zone) and to strangers or acquaintances (social zone) than do less sociable persons. When spacing is investigated in the laboratory, care must be taken to avoid such confounds as fear of offending the other person (by either moving in too close or staying too far back). Nevertheless, with appropriate controls, spacing should be an excellent measure in the laboratory. It can also be used in the field

TABLE 5.4 EXAMPLES OF SOCIABILITY MEASURES: BEHAVIORAL MEASURES

	Description	Reference
Need (direction)	Closeness to mother	Schaffer & Emerson, 1964
	Personal space (preferred distance from others)	Hall, 1966
	Choosing to wait or work alone or with others	Schachter, 1959
	Participation in primary groups	Gough, 1965
Responsivity (warmth)	Warmth, smiling	Bayes, 1972
	Eye contact	Exline, 1963
	Pupil dilation	Hess, 1965
	Other facial expressions, and amount of talking with or about others	Mehrabian, 1970
	Intimacy of talk	Sermat & Smyth, 1973

TABLE 5.5 EXAMPLES OF SOCIABILITY MEASURES: SELF-REPORT MEASURES

Description	Reference
Sociability scale of the EASI-III Temperament Survey	See Chapter 2 and Appendix 2
Social Introversion scale of the Guilford-Zimmerman Temperament Survey	Guilford & Zimmerman, 1956
Sociability scale of the Thurstone Temperament Survey	Thurstone, 1951
Sociability and Self-sufficiency scales of the Bernreuter Personality Inventory	Bernreuter, 1935
Sociability scale of the California Psychological Inventory	Gough, 1957
Affiliation scale of the Adjective Check List	Gough & Heilbrun, 1965
Shyness and Dependence Factors of the Comrey Personality Factor System	Comrey, 1961
Affiliation scale of the Edwards Personal Preference Schedule	Edwards, 1954
Affiliation scale of the Personality Research Form	Jackson, 1967

Sixteen Personality Factor Questionnaire
  Factor A. Reserved (schizothymia) vs. outgoing (affect others)
  Factor H. Shy (threctia) vs. venturesome (parmia)
  Factor Q_2. Group dependent vs. self-sufficient
	Cattell, Saunders, & Stice, 1957

without any controls but with the advantages conferred by naturalistic observation.

Of the remaining two behavioral measures of need, Schachter's (1959) is certainly the better known. He threatened subjects with impending electric shock and let them choose whether to wait alone or with others. He found that fear induces gregariousness, but more recent research has shown that embarrassment can lead to social withdrawal depending on who the other members of the group are (Firestone, Kaplan, & Russell, 1973). In Gough's variation (Gough & Heilbrun, 1965), subjects were allowed to work alone or in groups. Both of these choice situations could be connected to manipulations of the need to be with others. Thus subjects might be isolated from others beforehand (Gerwirtz & Baer, 1958) or even shunned by other persons (Fenigstein, 1973) and then allowed a choice of whether to be alone or with others. Surely sociability would partially determine the outcome.

Behavioral measurement of need is difficult and indirect because the need must be *inferred* from the behavior. And the best measures involve an either/or choice, which does not yield a quantitative estimate of the need. It is much easier to assess responsivity, which can be measured directly and quantitatively. One study of warmth stands out because it is the only one that tried to specify the behavioral cues for warmth. Bayes (1972) videotaped interviews of college students and had judges rate them for global warmth and for eight behavioral cues for warmth. Two cues stood out from the others in terms of correlation with the global rating of warmth: smiling and positive comments about others. A factor analysis yielded two factors. The first consisted of the global warmth rating, smiling, and positive comments about others; the second included speech rate and head and body motion, both aspects of activity level. Thus when warmth is assessed, activity level enters into the evaluation. This means that activity level should be controlled when sociability is assessed to avoid a confound between them.

The other measures of responsivity listed in Table 5.4 require only brief comment. Eye contact (Exline, 1963) is now widely used in social psychological experiments, and we suggest that some of the variance in that research may be attributed to individual differences in sociability. Dilation of the pupil has been widely used as an index of interest; if the object of interest is another person, the measure is entirely appropriate for sociability. Mehrabian (1970) has considered a variety of facial expressions that indicate a positive or negative response to others. Finally, the content of the conversation in terms of degree of intimacy appears to be a reasonable measure of sociability (Sermat & Smyth, 1973).

Concerning self-report measures (Table 5.5), virtually every major personality inventory has a sociability scale. Most emphasize the need for dyadic or primary group interaction. Responsivity to others is rarely sampled, perhaps because it is hard to assess by self-report. We made a preliminary attempt to study both components in our questionnaire (Plomin, 1974). We included two sociability scales that proved to be factorially distinct. The first, *general sociability,* is primarily a measure of need because the items include preferring to do things with others and having many friends. The second scale, which we labeled *affection,* is related to warmth but is really a measure of need for affection. So we were frustrated in our attempt to measure warmth or responsiveness by self-report and rating questionnaire (although warmth can be measured by observation; see Table 5.4). The general sociability and affection scales correlated .34 for adults' self-report and .21 for children rated by their parents. So far, sociability has emerged as a more or less unitary factor in research with self-report instruments. For example, Guilford and Zimmerman inspected their Social Introversion scale and isolated what they thought were seven subscales. Factor analyses then revealed that six of the subscales all loaded high on a general factor. But it remains to be seen whether factors within sociability will emerge when need is separated from responsivity.

THE INHERITANCE OF SOCIABILITY

Is sociability inherited? The evidence bearing on this question is summarized in Tables 5.6 and 5.7. The research falls into two groups: (1) studies of children rated by observers or parents (Table 5.6) and (2) self-report studies of adolescents and adults (Table 5.7).

Rating Studies of Children

The evidence here suggests moderate to strong heritability for sociability. There are genetic differences in responsiveness to people during the first year of life (Freedman, 1965). Although the sample was small and no correlations were presented, the ratio of the differences within pairs was highly significant ($p < .005$). In fact, this ratio was larger than that of any other behavior measured by the Bayley Infant Behavior Record in Freedman's study.

The Wilson et al. (1971) study is difficult to interpret because of the way the data were collected: mothers were asked whether their twins were the same or different in smiling, seeking affection, accepting people, and demanding attention. This "same-different" dichotomy forced mothers to decide the point at which quantitative difference between twins became qualitative, so they not only observed behavior but were forced to interpret it. The resulting data could not be presented in correlational form, nor could heritability be estimated. Nonetheless, the monozygotic twins were consistently more concordant—mothers rated them as "same" more often—than dizygotic twins at all ages from six months to six years.

In a study of 128 pairs of twins ranging in age from two to 16 years, Buss et al. (1973) found the sociability scale of the EASI-I Temperament Survey to be clearly heritable for both boys and girls. This twin study was replicated using the EASI-III (Plomin, 1974). The sociability items of the EASI-III were the same as the EASI-I items, but a related scale measuring affection was included. Both studies showed the identical twins to be considerably more similar than the fraternal twins in sociability. The correlations in the second study were lower for both types of twins and even negative for the fraternals, but such fluctuations are usual in twin studies with small N. The important point is that both studies provided evidence of heritability.

Scarr (1966a) asked mothers to rate their 6- to 10-year-old twin girls on the Gough Adjective Checklist (Gough & Heilbrun, 1965). Three Adjective Checklist scales appear at first glance to be related to sociability: Succorance, Nurturance, and Affiliation. Closer examination of the adjectives in each scale reveals that only the Affiliation scale clearly involves sociability. This scale has 34 adjectives, most of which are related to sociability: *kind, pleasant, talkative, warm*, etc. The Succorance scale included adjectives like *self-pitying* and *whiny*; the Nurturance scale included *arrogant, nagging*, and *loyal*. There is no a priori reason for assuming that self-pity and arrogance are inherited, and Scarr's data confirm this expectation. The Affiliation scale was found to show significant heritability, the other two scales not. In addition to the mothers' ratings, an observer rated the twins on some of the Fels Behavior Scales, and the Friendliness scale was highly heritable.

Self-Report Studies of Adolescents and Adults

Research with adolescents and adults (Table 5.7) consistently shows moderate heritability, as measured by a wide variety of sociability scales. However, few of the studies report correlations, which makes it difficult to estimate the heritability of sociability. Nevertheless, the magnitude of the variance ratios and the two studies that report correlations suggest that the heritability estimate is lower in adults than in children.

CATTELL'S FACTORED SCALES

Studies using Cattell's factored scales have been grouped at the end of Table 5.7. Factor A has been called "reserved versus outgoing" and factor Q_2 is

TABLE 5.6 GENETIC STUDIES OF SOCIABILITY: RATING STUDIES OF CHILDREN

Measure	Number of MZ Pairs	Number of DZ Pairs	Age	Findings	Reference
Ratings on the 1958 version of the Bayley Infant Behavior Record—social orientation (responsiveness to persons rather than to objects)	9	10	0 – 1 yr	Significant difference* between MZ and DZ twins (no correlations reported)	Freedman, 1965
Mothers' ratings of twins' concordance in Smiling Seeking affection Accepting people Demanding attention	95	73	6 – 72 mo	MZs more concordant at all ages (correlations not possible from data)	Wilson et al., 1971
EASI–I Temperament Survey—Sociability	78	50	55-mo average	Boys: MZ .63 DZ .25* Girls: MZ .53 DZ .20*	Buss et al., 1973

			Boys		Girls		
			MZ	DZ	MZ	DZ	
EASI-III Temperament Survey	60	51	2 – 6 yr				Plomin, 1974
Sociability			.49	−.16	.46	−.03	
Affection			.36	.02	.49	−.03	

			All girls		
			MZ	DZ	
Gough Adjective Checklist as rated by the mothers	24	28	6 – 10 yr		Scarr, 1966
Need for affiliation			.83	.56*	
Need for nurturance			.55	.50	
Observer's rating on Fels Behavior Scales					
Friendliness			.86	.35*	

*p < .05

111

TABLE 5.7 GENETIC STUDIES OF SOCIABILITY: SELF-REPORT OF ADOLESCENTS AND ADULTS

Measure	Number of MZ Pairs	Number of DZ Pairs	Age	Findings	Reference
Thurstone Temperament Survey Sociable	45	37	14 – 18 yr	Significant difference* between MZ and DZ twins (no correlations reported)	Vandenberg, 1962
California Personality Inventory Sociability	498	319	14 – 18 yr	Boys: MZ .53, DZ .25*; Girls: MZ .54, DZ .33*	Nichols, 1966
California Personality Inventory Sociability	79	68	14 – 18 yr	Significant difference* between MZ and DZ twins for girls; boys approached significance (no correlations reported)	Gottesman, 1966
Project Talent-- Factored Scale of Sociability	337	156	14 – 18 yr	Boys: MZ .55, DZ .43; Girls: MZ .60, DZ .35*	Schoenfeldt, 1968
Sociability scale	157	189	adults	Significant difference* between MZ and DZ twins (no correlations reported)	Bruun et al., 1967 (in Vandenberg, 1967)

	MZ	DZ	Age	Results	Reference
Comrey Personality and Attitude Factors Shyness	111	90	14 – 18 yr	Significant difference* between MZ and DZ twins (no correlations reported)	Vandenberg, 1967
Dependence				Not significant	
Stern's Activity Index Nurturance	50	38	14 – 18 yr	Significant difference* between MZ and DZ twins (no correlations reported)	Vandenberg, 1967
Affiliation				Not significant	
The sociability items of the extraversion scale of the Eysenck Personality Inventory	25 15 (separated for more than 5 yr)	29 16	Adolescent to adult	MZ DZ .51 .25* (.91) (.25)	Canter, 1969
Cattell's Sixteen Personality Factor Test	25	29	Adolescent to adult		Canter, 1969
A. Reserved vs. outgoing				.49 .29	
Q_2. Group dependent vs. self-sufficient				.39 .01	

TABLE 5.7 (CONTINUED) GENETIC STUDIES OF SOCIABILITY: SELF-REPORT OF ADOLESCENTS AND ADULTS

Measure	Number of MZ Pairs	Number of DZ Pairs	Age	Findings				Reference
				Boys		Girls		
				MZ	DZ	MZ	DZ	
Cattell's Junior Personality Questionnaire	34	34	14 – 18 yr					Gottesman, 1963
A. Reserved vs. outgoing				-.10	.05	.26	.40	
Q₂. Group dependent vs. self-sufficient				.51	.42	.54	-.02*	
Cattell's Junior Personality Questionnaire	45	37	14 – 18 yr	Not significant (no correlations reported)				Vandenberg, 1962
A. Reserved vs. outgoing								
Cattell's Junior Personality Questionnaire	52	32	14 – 18 yr	Not significant (no correlations reported)				Cattell et al., 1955
A. Reserved vs. outgoing								

*p < .05

usually called "group dependent versus self-sufficient." In contrast to the other studies, there is little evidence of heritability for either factor. Similar results were found for Cattell scales of emotionality (see Chapter 4) and impulsivity (see Chapter 6). Of the hypotheses that might account for the discrepant results with Cattell's scales, two stand out. First, being "reserved" and "dependent" may be related only indirectly to sociability. Second, the reliability of Cattell's scales tends to be low (Cattell et al., 1955).

With the exception of Cattell's scales, sociability has amassed the strongest and most consistent genetic support of the four temperaments. This conclusion is echoed by Scarr (1969) in her review of twin studies. Clearly, individual differences in sociability are at least partially determined by initial endowment. This conclusion may fly in the face of an older tradition of studying social interaction, but it is entirely consistent with more recent trends concerning the direction of effects between a parent and child. Thus Rheingold (1969) has proposed " . . . that the human infant begins life as a social organism, that while still very young he behaves in a social fashion, and that he socializes others more than he is socialized" (p. 779).

LONGITUDINAL STUDIES OF SOCIABILITY

The appropriate research is summarized in Tables 5.8 and 5.9. The only study of infants during the first year of life (Moss, 1967) found some stability for smiling but none for the amount of time the child looks at the mother. But the correlation over time for smiling was nonsignificant, and so the overall findings were essentially negative (no stability). This is not surprising in light of our developmental model of sociability, which assumes that the manifestations of sociability change with age. Smiling goes through asocial, indiscriminately social, and discriminately social phases during the first six months of life (Schaffer & Emerson, 1964). Thus there is no basis for stability of smiling per se over time, unless the investigator specifies the particular context. Similarly, the child who is a cuddler at one year will probably not be a cuddler at seven years of age. The need for soothing gives way to the need for nurturance, and then to the need for more egalitarian social interaction. There is a direct implication for longitudinal research: there may be low stability for any particular manifestation of sociability *as a need*. Furthermore, *responsivity* should show more stability because its manifestations change little during the course of development.

According to the findings in Table 5.8, ratings of responsiveness to persons and of shyness during the second and third years of life showed considerable stability for girls and moderate stability for boys (Schaefer & Bayley, 1963). The reason for this gender difference is not clear, but it is only one of many

TABLE 5.8 LONGITUDINAL STUDIES OF SOCIABILITY: CHILDHOOD

Measure	Number	Age from beginning to end of study	Findings	Reference
Ratings of smiling and amount of time with eyes on mother	26	3 wk to 3 mo	Correlation of .32 for smiling; −.12 for eyes on mother	Moss, 1967
Rating of responsiveness to persons	48	1 yr to 3 yr	(see sub-table below)	Schaefer & Bayley, 1963
Ratings of shyness			(see sub-table below)	
Ratings of friendliness		2 to 8 yr	(see sub-table below)	
Ratings of "friendly"		9 to 12 yr	Correlation of .63*	

Rating of responsiveness to persons

	Boys		Girls	
	2 yr	3 yr	2 yr	3 yr
1 yr	.34	.25	.49*	.65*
2 yr		.28		.47*
3 yr				

Ratings of shyness

	Boys		Girls	
	2 yr	3 yr	2 yr	3 yr
1 yr	.32	.29	.62*	.41*
2 yr		.48*		.66*

Ratings of friendliness

	Boys			Girls		
	4 yr	6 yr	8 yr	4 yr	6 yr	8 yr
2 yr	.45*	.28	.19	.39	.22	−.12
4 yr		.54*	.56*		.45*	.34
6 yr			.49*			.48*
8 yr						

Measure	N	Age range	Findings	Reference
Ratings from interviews with parents	336	Birth to 6 yr	Smiling was stable from 12 mo*; Demanding attention was stable from 36 mo**; Seeking affection was stable from 3 mo**; Accepting people was stable from 6 mo**	Wilson, Brown, & Matheny, 1971
Ratings of interpersonal orientation	38	3 to 5 yr	(see correlations below)	Emmerich, 1964
Ratings from interview data of the Berkeley Guidance Study; Shy vs. socially easy	85	5 to 16 yr	(see correlations below)	Bronson, 1966
Sociability	269 to 368	3rd grade to 4th; 5th grade to 6th	(see correlations below)	Walker, 1967

Emmerich, 1964 — Ratings of interpersonal orientation

	Boys and girls	
	2 yr	3 yr
3–4 yr	.62*	.74*
4–4½ yr		.60*
4½–5 yr		.58

Bronson, 1966 — Ratings from interview data of the Berkeley Guidance Study

	Boys			Girls		
	9 yr	12 yr	15 yr	9 yr	12 yr	15 yr
6 yr	.60*	.32*	.61*	.52*	.44*	.44*
9 yr		.67*	.58*		.73*	.65*
12 yr			.52*			.70*
15 yr						

Walker, 1967 — Sociability

	Boys		Girls	
	3rd–4th	5th–6th	3rd–4th	5th–6th
Self-report	.35*	.59*	.54*	.43*
Teacher ratings	.39*	.41*	.43*	.59*
Peer nominations	.48*	.37*	.27*	.55*

* $p < .05$

** No intercorrelational matrix was reported—only adjacent months were tested for significance of relationship.

such differences in Table 5.8 that are hard to explain. Ratings of "friendliness" did not show stability from two years to eight years, but this measure considered "only those responses which bear specifically upon task performance" (Schaefer & Bayley, 1963, p. 30) and so may be confounded with ability.

Let us turn to the data for adults in Table 5.9. The Fels Longitudinal Study (Kagan & Moss, 1962) shows high stability for "withdrawal from social interaction" from 12 years to adulthood (approximately 24 years of age). The study also included measures that appear at first glance to be measures of sociability: dependency and independence. But dependency was defined as requests for instrumental aid as well as separation anxiety, and independence was defined as behavior in threatening and problem solving situations. Thus "dependency" and "independence" in this research include much more than sociability and are only peripherally related to it.

The remainder of studies in Table 5.9 need no detailed comment. Admittedly, there are variations in the amount of stability from one study to the next and between boys and girls. But the pattern of studies reveals adequate stability of sociability during the developmental sequence. In fact, sociability appears to be the most stable of the temperaments.

PRESENCE IN ADULTHOOD

Temperamental differences among children might become submerged or masked during socialization and, thus disguised, elude our search for adult personality traits. But the environment might also accentuate temperamental differences. A very sociable child emits positive social cues (warmth) and these in turn elicit positive social interactions. This positive feedback cycle enhances social interactions and tends to strengthen the child's social responses. A child low in sociability neither emits nor elicits the positive aspects of social interaction, and the relative absence of reinforcement further diminishes his initially weak social responses.

Two sources of evidence support the hypothesis that sociability continues into adulthood. First, longitudinal studies of sociability suggest that sociability is at least moderately stable in adulthood, even for 20 years (Kelly, 1955; Tuddenham, 1959; Kagan & Moss, 1962). Second, all major personality self-report questionnaires measure some aspect of sociability. This includes questionnaires developed by factor analysis. Furthermore, factor analyses of the many subscales of rationally constructed questionnaires find that sociability is a factor underlying several subscales (Sherman & Poe, 1970, for Edwards Personal Preference Schedule; Nichols & Schnell, 1963, for the California Psychological Inventory).

TABLE 5.9 LONGITUDINAL STUDIES OF SOCIABILITY: ADOLESCENCE AND ADULTHOOD

Measure	Number	Age from beginning to end of study	Findings		Reference
Ratings from interview data of the Fels Longitudinal Study Withdrawal from social interaction	71	12 yr to adulthood	Boys .65*	Girls .56*	Kagan & Moss, 1962
Sociability scale of the Bernreuter Personality Inventory	50	College men in their first 3 yr of college	Start to year 1: .77* Year 1 to year 2: .55* Year 2 to year 3: .66*		Farnsworth, 1938
Sociability scale of the Bernreuter Personality Inventory	368	Adults over a 20-yr period	Correlation of .46*		Kelly, 1955
Interview ratings of social vs. detached	72	Adolescence to adulthood (as much as 20 yr)	Men: correlation of .53* Women: correlation of .29*		Tuddenham, 1959

*$p < .05$

Taken together, this evidence strongly suggests that sociability continues to be a major source of individual differences in adulthood as well as childhood. This is not proof that sociability is a temperament, but it is consistent with the notion.

CONCLUSIONS

We have suggested five criteria for evaluating temperaments, two logical ones and three empirical ones. Sociability clearly has an adaptive payoff: the tendency to associate with others provides the "glue" that keeps groups and communities together as functioning units. It aids in defense, child rearing, and division of labor, all processes that can be accomplished better socially than by individuals. And animals close to man tend to be highly sociable, especially those closest to man (primates). Thus the logical criteria seem to be met.

Sociability also passes the empirical tests of temperament. The twin research reveals a definite genetic component, there is reasonable stability throughout development, and sociability is widely regarded as one of the basic dimensions of adult personality. The empirical case for it is the best of the four temperaments. In brief, we are on firm ground in regarding sociability as a temperament in terms of both logical and empirical criteria.

An important theoretical issue concerns the distinction between need and responsivity. We see them as two sides of the same coin, but in spite of numerous examples in everyday life (everyone knows persons who are both gregarious and warm, or both seclusive and cold), there is no research that establishes a high correlation between the two. Warmth is an important determiner of sociability over time. The warm person reinforces others with his presence, thereby eliciting positive feedback from others; this enhances gregariousness. The cool person fails to reinforce others (or is even negative), making the interaction less pleasant for them and therefore eventually for him; the outcome is a weaker tendency to associate with others. Again, there is not research bearing on this issue, and the answer will have to come from longitudinal research in naturalistic settings.

The developmental course of sociability is another important issue. The human infant is so helpless that its survival literally depends on the care of a parent. Sociability at this age is seen in relation to soothing, arousal, and receiving nurturance. As the child develops, he enters into more capable relationships with peers and even with older persons. The child who continues to need and demand soothing or nurturance when he is long past infancy must be labeled immature. Such immaturity is more likely to occur in highly sociable children, whose need for others is intense, than it is in relatively unsociable children, who can more easily get along without the presence of others. The testable hypothesis here is: excessively dependent children will prove to be higher on the temperament of sociability.

Finally, the issues of arousal and activity are linked to personality. Other persons are the source of considerable stimulation, and so one motive for associating with others is the need for arousal. This means that a sensation seeker tends to be more sociable than a nonsensation seeker. Sensation seeking is one aspect of impulsivity (see Chapter 6), so there may be a built-in relationship between impulsivity and sociability. There may be a similar built-in relationship between sociability and activity level. As we mentioned earlier, other things being equal, active persons do more of everything, including interacting socially. These relationships raise the general issue of how the temperaments interact, which is the topic of Chapter 8.

CHAPTER

$$\boxed{6}$$

IMPULSIVITY

Impulsivity is the most troublesome of the four temperaments. In the twin study reported in Chapter 2, an inherited component was found for boys but not for girls, and we concluded that a case had not yet been made for impulsivity as a temperament. There were also some problems with impulsivity as a relatively pure factor, again for girls only. So we are confronted with two questions: (1) precisely what is impulsivity in the sense of factorial unity, and (2) is there an inherited component?

To answer the first question, we shall start with descriptions of impulsivity as a personality trait. Its core meaning, in psychological usage, involves inhibitory control or lack of such control. As such, it varies from reckless, impetuous behavior to restrained, overcautious behavior. A full-bodied description of these extremes has been offered by Diamond:

> They may be called thoughtless, weak-willed, impetuous, suggestible, distractible, imprudent, absent-minded, fickle, criminal, or bad losers. This incomplete listing is enough to show that many kinds of control are needed, in different situations. Furthermore, excess of control can be as damaging as its deficit. One must be quick in emergency, spontaneous in conversation, and relaxed in play. The individual who suffers from excess of control may be described as indecisive, compulsive, stubborn, rigid, overinhibited, suffering from choice anxiety, or at the extreme, as catatonic—that is, suffering from an exaggeration of control so great as to present the appearance of organic paralysis. For one individual, to

choose between two motion picture programs, neither of which has anything very special to recommend it may be a difficult decision. For another, a decision in favor of one course of action is instantly forgotten the moment another is suggested, even before there has been a chance to weigh one against the other. Both are equally suffering from defects of control. [1957, pp. 395–396]

This account not only fleshes out the dimension of control but also reveals that the term *impulsivity* has other referents. Further details have been supplied by Murray:

Impulsion is the tendency to respond quickly and without reflection. It is a rather coarse variable which includes: (1) short reaction time to social press, (2) quick intuitive behavior, (3) emotional driveness, (4) lack of forethought, (5) readiness to begin work without a carefully constructed plan. The subject is usually somewhat restless, quick to move, quick to make up his mind, quick to voice his opinion. He often says the first thing that comes into his head, and does not always consider the future consequences of his conduct.

Deliberation is easier to observe than Impulsion. It is marked by: (1) long reaction time to social press, (2) inhibition of initial impulses, (3) hesitation, caution, and reflection before action, (4) a long period of planning and organizing before beginning a piece of work. The subject may have obsessional doubts: a "load" of considerations which he must "lift" before beginning. He usually experiences difficulty in an emergency. [1938, pp. 205–206]

These descriptions help to make the point that impulsivity consists of more than the dimension of control. We think that inhibitory control lies at the core of impulsivity, but other facets of impulsivity are included in these descriptions: decision time, persistence, and boredom or sensation seeking. We shall discuss each in turn.

The notion of impulses is merely one way of viewing the *tendency to act*, which usually falls under the heading of motivation. This is not the context in which to discuss motivation. We may merely note in passing that impulses refer to both need states (appetitive and aversive) and incentives (goals). If there were no opposing tendencies, the impulse would be expressed in behavior. But this situation surely is rare, and usually there is some basis for inhibiting a response. We can say with tongue in cheek that everything that is really enjoyable is either immoral or involves too many calories. But there is some truth in this remark, for most behavior is accomplished only at some cost to the responder: time, effort, money, or even punishment. All social groups require conformity, and all societies have both codes of morality and standards of maturity. In brief, there are often strong reasons for inhibiting a response.

It may be necessary to eliminate a response from one's repertoire and never engage in the behavior. For example, nuns are expected never to have coitus, and orthodox Jews must never eat pork. But such complete suppression of behavior is rare; it is more usual to inhibit behavior only for a given time. In some cultures a girl should remain a virgin only until marriage, Catholics are expected to do without meat only on Fridays or only during Lent, and orthodox Jews refrain from eating only on specified fast days. In short, the usual demand for inhibitory control is *delay*, not complete suppression.

In any event, delay is the essence of inhibition of response. As time passes, other stimuli elicit different responses, and other needs press for satiation. If the person can successfully delay the prohibited response, the tendency to make the response may weaken. Consider the injunction to count to 100 before acting in anger. The physiological arousal of anger cannot remain at an intense level, and as it wanes the tendency toward angry aggression wanes. The delay may be sufficient to weaken the impulse and thereby inhibit the response. Similarly, in a frightening situation if the escape response is delayed, the fear stimulus may diminish or the person may discover a coping response; in either case, waiting would be sufficient to inhibit the "cowardly" escape response. Thus the basic issue in inhibitory control is the ability to delay.

In terms of group living, the most important inhibitory control concerns *delay of gratification*. The infant cannot wait; if he is hungry, wet, or cold, he complains in the vocal terms that all parents understand. The infant is allowed his impulsiveness, but one of the major tasks of socialization is to teach him to wait before making consummatory responses. The world is not arranged for each of us to have our wants satisfied the moment they become salient. If one is cold, the heat must be turned on (the fire lit); if one is hungry, the food must be obtained or prepared. Unless the world is one's oyster, there is an inevitable delay between the wish and its gratification; children must learn to wait.

Children must also learn to *resist temptation*. It is tempting to appropriate another's toys or money, and it is hard to resist lying when it will avoid punishment. In these examples the child is confronted with an immediate payoff, acquisition of a reward or avoidance of a punishment. What society tries to teach him is the link between the prohibited (but tempting) response and its *eventual* punishment. This has been called *time-binding*: linking immediate behavior with its eventual consequences. What the child learns is to delay his immediate consummatory response because of the probability of a subsequent better consummatory response, a strong subsequent punishment, or both.

DECISION TIME

The delay of instrumental responses, although of less importance for a society, is still not a trivial issue. The issue here is *decision time*. The impulsive person craves spontaneous action and chafes when asked to plan and to put off deciding until alternative courses of action are considered. The deliberate person wants to explore all possibilities and foresee all consequences before committing himself; he feels pressured if asked to decide quickly and without close attention to details. Is it better to adopt one strategy rather than the other?

> A person who sought guidance from aphorisms would find it awkward to reconcile 'Haste makes waste!' and 'Look before you leap!' with 'He who hesitates is lost!' He might well conclude that these pieces of advice should be reserved for different occasions, for it is certainly true that precipitous speech or action can be ruinous in some circumstances whereas in others delay may be fatal and quick action imperative. Yet it is easy to observe that a great many people have a fixed preference for one style or the other regardless of circumstances. Haste makes waste except where he who hesitates is lost, but rare is the person who can always perfectly suit his speed to the occasion. [White, 1972, p. 176]

So neither strategy is always preferable. Americans tend to be a "can do" people who like to "get on with it." Our frontier heritage has given us folk heroes who are quick on the trigger and our war heroes are those who "Damn the torpedoes, full speed ahead!"

Persistence

Quickness of response is a basic defining property of impulsivity. Impulsive persons readily initiate new activities; deliberate persons are slower to take action. It is only a small extrapolation to assume that the person who initiates a response quickly terminates it quickly. If the reason for *turning on* quickly is to seek novelty, this is also a reason for *turning off* quickly: new stimuli and responses soon lose their novelty and alternatives are sought. Anyone who tends to seek novelty is, by definition, less persistent.

Even if the impulsive person does not become bored more quickly, he should still be less persistent. Suppose that two persons are working at a routine task and are tempted to leave it for something more exciting. The household accounts must be settled, but it is a beautiful day for sailing; or the car must be washed, but there is a football game to be watched. We know that the impulsive person has trouble in suppressing impulses, in waiting, and in tolerating aversiveness over time. If the task is dull, boring, or tiring, he will quit it sooner than a nonimpulsive person.

A low tolerance for aversiveness is one side of the coin; the other is low resistance to temptation. If the necessary task is annoying and the alternative is attractive, the impulsive person will be quicker to switch to the more attractive activity. Unable to delay gratification, he will abandon the dull, boring task for the exciting, rewarding activity. In brief, there are three reasons for the impulsive's lack of persistence:

1. His general quickness in responding—to turn off as well as to turn on (switching to a new response means giving up the old one).
2. His inability to tolerate aversive events over time, so that boring or tiring tasks are soon abandoned.
3. His low resistance to temptation, which renders him less able to fight off the lure of more interesting activities.

Boredom or Sensation Seeking

We have already suggested that impulsives seem to suffer more from boredom. It may be related to their quickness of response: turn on faster, turn off faster. This assumes faster habituation; that is, stimuli lose their novelty faster for impulsives.

It is possible, however, that impulsives habituate at the same rates as anyone else and that their level of boredom is not especially high. But they may be less able to tolerate the boredom. It has been suggested several times that impulsives have trouble in tolerating aversiveness. Perhaps they are no more bored than anyone else but have more trouble in abiding boredom.

In either case—faster habituation or intolerance of aversiveness—impulsives appear to have a problem with boredom. The usual solution is to seek novel stimuli and responses. Impulsives prefer to do things on the spur of the moment, relish the unpredictable, delight in spontaneity, and in general are more than willing to try something new and exciting. They love fads and adventure; they abhor the familiar and the routine. In their desire to avoid boredom, they are usually sensation seekers.

Comment

When we started thinking about temperaments and initiated research on them, we defined impulsivity in terms of inhibitory control. This slant is reflected in the EASI-I Impulsivity scale, which consists mainly of self-control items. But as we thought further and surveyed the literature, we were forced to admit that impulsivity might be considerably more complex than merely inhibitory control. This complexity prevents us from discussing the developmental course of impulsivity until we discover what impulsivity is in terms of how it is measured and how the various measures relate to one another.

MEASURES OF IMPULSIVITY

Our discussion of measures is inclusive because at this stage, all four aspects of impulsivity are relevant.

Experimental Measures

Impulsivity has been studied extensively in the laboratory. The various measures are listed in Table 6.1.

TABLE 6.1 EXAMPLES OF IMPULSIVITY MEASURES: EXPERIMENTAL

Measure	Aspect of Impulsivity	Reference
Delay in touching forbidden object	Delay of gratification	Aronfreed & Reber, 1965
		Grinder, 1962
Delay in receiving better reward		Mischel, 1961
Matching-to-sample decision speed	Decision time	Kagan, 1966
The Porteus Mazes		Foulds, 1951
		Porteus, 1950
Time to guess the next card in a game of chance; time to free associate to words		Eysenck & Prell, 1941
		Carter, 1933
Time subject stays with a dull task (writing "c" and "d" for 30 minutes)	Persistence	London et al., 1972
Persistence in the face of obstacles		Thornton, 1939
		Rethlingshafer, 1942
		Barker et al., 1941
		Hartshorne et al., 1929
Waiting with minimal stimulation	Boredom-sensation seeking	Jones et al., 1961
Preferred rate of stimulus presentation		Berlyne, 1960
Preferred predictability of stimulation		Jones et al., 1964

INHIBITORY CONTROL

The two basic paradigms involve resistance to temptation and deciding to wait for a greater reward. In the best known resistance to temptation procedure, a child is presented with two toys, one attractive and the other unattractive (Aronfreed & Reber, 1965). The child is told to pick up a toy and tell the experimenter all about it. He is also told that some of the toys are for older boys and he is not to choose them. There are nine training trials (the toys are changed for each trial), and the experimenter says, "No, that's for older boys," each time the child picks up the attractive toy. Then the experimenter leaves the room with a bogus excuse, allowing the child to be alone with an unattractive and an attractive toy. The measures are whether the child picks up the attractive toy and if so, how soon.

The ability to wait for a better reward has been studied by Mischel (1961), who gave these instructions:

> I would like to give each of you a piece of candy but I don't have enough of these (indicating the larger, more preferred reinforcement) with me today. So you can either get this one (indicating the smaller, less preferred reinforcement) right now, today, or, if you want to wait for this one (indicating) which I will bring back next Friday (one week delay interval). [p. 4]

The measure was simply whether the child decided to take the inferior reward immediately or to wait one week for the superior reward. Here the better reward was opposed by the aversiveness of delay, whereas in the Aronfreed paradigm the better reward was opposed by the tendency to obey rules.

Parenthetically, inhibitory control has also been studied by asking subjects to make very slow movements: drawing, walking, and turning a crank (Maccoby et al., 1965). We have omitted these measures from Table 6.1 because of the likelihood of a confound with activity level. The highly active person, by definition, has a faster tempo and therefore tends to perform *any* task faster. It is more difficult for him to slow down than it is for a person with low activity, whose tempo is bound to be slower. Thus the inhibition (slowing down) of movement would be a useful measure of impulsivity only if activity level were controlled.

DECISION TIME

The most popular means of assessing decision time was developed by Kagan (1966), who regards it as a cognitive style. Although several tasks have been used, the most frequent one is the matching-to-sample task that originated in work with primates (Harlow, 1949). The sample is a drawing of, say, a doll, and there are five other figures, all drawings of dolls similar to the sample; the subject must select the figure that is identical to the sample. There are no time limits or instructions for speed, and the measure is simply the amount of time taken to respond. There is a substantial negative correlation between time and errors; the subject who takes longer tends to make the finer discriminations necessary for success.

The major problem with the matching-to-sample task as a measure of impulsivity is a possible confound with intelligence. Brighter persons tend to be better problem solvers; if a task requires more time, they will spend more time. So if a person responds quickly, it might be because he is impulsive or not intelligent, or both; if a person responds slowly, it might be because he is deliberate (Kagan uses the term *reflective*) or intelligent, or both.

A similar problem exists when the Porteus mazes (Porteus, 1950) are used to measure impulsivity. Solving the paper-and-pencil mazes requires foresight, planning, and the ability to delay responding until a reasonable spatial strategy has been developed. Clearly, there is an intellectual component, and the task can be used only if intelligence is equated or controlled by a statistical procedure such as covariance.

The last two measures, time to guess the next card and free association time, have been used infrequently, but they have the advantage of being free of a confound with intelligence. These tasks are purer measures of impulsivity because no cognitive skill is required and therefore intelligence does not determine speed of response. It should be possible to construct similar tasks involving no cognitive skills; for example, in Mischel's delay of gratification paradigm, one might measure not only the subject's decision but also how long it took to make the decision. But regardless of the nature of the task, it should be kept free of both intelligence and any implicit demand for speed.

PERSISTENCE

The easiest way to measure persistence is to have someone do a really dull task, for example, copy letters for half an hour (London et al., 1972). The problem is that persistence is confounded with boredom. The solution is to present a task that is difficult but not boring. For example, subjects have been asked to make as many words as possible out of the letters B, R, T, A, O, and U (Thornton, 1939; Rethlingshafer, 1942). Another measure was persistence in reading a text that became increasingly difficult because of spacing and errors in punctuation and capitalization; this correlated well with persistence in making words out of letters. Finally, children can be presented with an insurmountable obstacle to determine how long they persist in attempting to overcome it (Barker et al., 1941).

These measures involve: (1) waiting with minimal stimulation or, (2) the preferred rate and predictability of stimulus presentation. Because few of these experimental measures have been used to study individual differences in impulsivity, there is a dearth of information concerning their interrelationship. And we do not know the relationship between experimental measures and self-report questionnaires of impulsivity.

Self-Report Questionnaires

The major self-report measures related to impulsivity are listed in Table 6.2. The items of the scales have been examined in an attempt to determine the particular component of impulsivity emphasized by each measure.

GUILFORD-ZIMMERMAN TEMPERAMENT SURVEY

The Rhathymia scale of the original Guilford scales (1940) included both sensation seeking and inhibitory control-decision time items. Examples of the former are "happy-go-lucky," "carefree," and "crave excitement"; examples of the latter include "act on the spur of the moment without thinking things over," "often say things and later regret them," and "plan work beforehand." In 1956, Guilford and Zimmerman factor analyzed the Guilford scales, using the following items from the Rhathymia scale: four "carefree" items, five "impulsiveness" (decision time) items, three "seriousness versus unconcern" items, and three "liking for action and excitement" items. The decision time items did not load on the same factor as the other items, which are primarily boredom-sensation seeking items.

THURSTONE TEMPERAMENT SCHEDULE

Thurstone (1951) factor analyzed Guilford's items, and this led to the development of the Thurstone Temperament Schedule (Thurstone, 1953). Guilford's Rhathymia scale—including both the decision time and boredom-sensation items—was replicated and labeled "Impulsive."

EYSENCK PERSONALITY INVENTORY

Eysenck also used the Guilford Rhathymia items as part of his scale of Extraversion (Eysenck & Eysenck, 1963b). Carrigan (1960) questioned the unidimensionality of Eysenck's Extraversion factor, and Eysenck and Eysenck (1963a) discovered two factors in extraversion, sociability and impulsivity (see Chapter 8).

TABLE 6.2   EXAMPLES OF IMPULSIVITY MEASURES: SELF-REPORT AND
RATING QUESTIONNAIRES

Measure	Aspect of Impulsivity*	Reference
Impulsivity scales of the EASI-III	Inhibitory control Decision time Persistence Sensation seeking	Appendix 2
Rhathymia scale of the Guilford-Zimmerman Temperament Schedule	Sensation seeking Decision time	Thurstone, 1953
Impulsivity items of the extraversion scale of the Eysenck Personality Inventory	Sensation seeking Decision time	Eysenck & Eysenck, 1963b
Cattell's 16 Personality Factor Test		Cattell, Saunders, & Stice, 1957
Factor F. Serious vs. happy-go-lucky	Sensation seeking	
Factor G. Expedient vs. conscientious	Persistence Inhibitory control	
Factor Q_3. Uncontrolled vs. controlled	Inhibitory control	
Barratt Impulsiveness Scale-II		Barratt, 1965
Speed of cognitive response	Decision time	
Lack of impulse control	Persistence	
Adventure seeking and risk taking	Sensation seeking	
Zuckerman's Sensation Seeking Scale	Sensation seeking	Zuckerman et al., 1964 Zuckerman, 1971

*Determined by inspection of items.

The highest loading impulsivity items were nearly identical to Guilford's decision time items:

Are you inclined to stop and think things over before acting?

Are you given to acting on impulses of the moment which later land you in difficulties?

Do you often act on the spur of the moment without stopping to think?

In addition, some of Guilford's sensation seeking items loaded on impulsivity:

Do you tend toward a rather reckless optimism?

Would you rate yourself as a happy-go-lucky individual?

Would you do almost anything for a dare?

Thus Eysenck's Extraversion scale contains a mixture of sociability and impulsivity items, and the impulsivity items include both decision time and boredom-sensation seeking items.

CATTELL'S 16 PERSONALITY FACTOR TEST

Cattell's factored scales are not easy to relate to impulsivity. Three impulsivity-related factors appear in Cattell's 16 Personality Factor Test (Cattell, Saunders, & Stice, 1957), and a summary of Cattell's early factor analytic studies of rating data described two of them (Cattell, 1946):

Factor F. Serious (surgency) versus happy-go-lucky (agitated, melancholic, desurgency) highest loading clusters:

1. Cheerful, enthusiastic, witty versus unhappy, frustrated.
2. Optimistic versus melancholic.
3. Sociable, hearty versus seclusive, shy.
4. Tough, solid, talkative versus introspective, sensitive.

Factor G. Expedient (positive character integration) versus conscientious (immature, dependent character):

1. Wise, mature, polished versus dependent, silly, incoherent.
2. Strong-willed, conscientious versus indolent, incoherent, impulsive.
3. Realistic, facing life versus demoralized, autistic.

Factor analyses based on questionnaire data replicated these factors and added an additional factor labeled Q_3, uncontrolled versus controlled (self-sentiment control).

The highest loading clusters defining these factors make it clear that Cattell's factors are complex and not easily interpretable. Factor F, however, seems to be closest to boredom-sensation seeking; Factor G has traces of persistence and inhibitory control-delay of gratification, and Factor Q3 is some combination of the two.

BARRATT'S IMPULSIVENESS SCALE

Barratt's (1965) factored subscales closely correspond to the components of impulsivity that we have described but miss inhibitory control items. Examples of the highest loading items on each factor are the following:

Decision time: I make up my mind quickly.

Persistence: I like work requiring patience and carefulness.

Boredom-Sensation seeking: I like being where there is something going on all the time.

Unfortunately, no work has been done using these factored scales of impulsivity, and Barratt's own work (1965) used a priori scales which bear little resemblance to the factors.

ZUCKERMAN'S SENSATION-SEEKING SCALE

Zuckerman et al. (1964) designed the Sensation-Seeking Scale (SSS) to measure "optimal stimulation level." Of the 34 items, 26 for males and 30 for females loaded above .3 on a general sensation-seeking factor. Farley (1967), however, found that only 16 items loaded on a general factor. The highest loading items were as follows:

I sometimes like to do things that are a little frightening.

I would like to take off on a trip with no preplanned or definite route or timetable.

I would like to learn to fly an airplane.

Zuckerman and Link (1968) verified the presence of several factors in the SSS. In 1971, Zuckerman added 63 new items and foun' a general factor and orthogonally rotated factors for sensation seeking in different areas such as sports and social life. Although no intercorrelations were reported, Zuckerman noted that the general factor was "highly related" to the other factors and that the other factors were also intercorrelated. Thus the highest loading items on Zuckerman's SSS appear to be a good measure of self-reported sensation seeking.

Relationships Among the Components of Impulsivity

Extant impulsivity scales contain various mixtures of the components of impulsivity. This makes it difficult to determine which components belong under impulsivity. Because this question is crucial to an understanding of impulsivity, we will examine the relationships among the scales.

Barratt's (1965) study yielded separate factors for decision time, persistence, and sensation seeking, but he did not report intercorrelations among them. His a priori scales from the same items include persistence, motor inhibition, and action-orientation; these may be analogous to persistence, inhibitory control, and boredom-sensation seeking. The a priori scales intercorrelate from .30 to .41, suggesting some commonality among them.

Barratt (1965) has also correlated his a priori impulsivity subscales with the Guilford-Zimmerman Rhathymia scale (a version which includes both the decision time and sensation-seeking items), Thurstone's Impulsive scale, and Cattell's factors F, G, and Q_3. The majority of the correlations are significant, and Cattell's factors G and Q_3 show the lowest correlations. The highest correlations (.46 to .62) were for the scales that primarily focus on sensation seeking: Barrett's action-oriented subscale, Cattell's Factor F, Guilford's Rhathymia scale, and Thurstone's Impulsiveness scale. These are also the highest loading items in a factor analysis of the tests in Barratt's study. The persistence and motor inhibition subscales of the Barratt scale were the only scales that did not emphasize sensation seeking. They correlated with the other scales, but only at marginally significant levels.

Zuckerman's Sensation-Seeking Scale has been related to extraversion. Farley and Farley (1970) found, as we would predict, that the SSS correlates more highly with the impulsivity items than with the sociability items of the extraversion scale of the Eysenck Personality Inventory. The SSS should correlate more highly with the boredom-sensation seeking items ("Would you do almost anything for a dare?") than the decision time items ("Are you inclined to stop and think things over before acting?") of the extraversion scale. Zuckerman and Link (1968) found an insignificant correlation between SSS and EPI extraversion, but they did not compute the correlation between the SSS and the impulsivity items to Eysenck's extraversion scale.

Two facts emerge from these studies. First, there is some relationship among the several components of impulsivity, at least among persistence, decision time, and sensation seeking. Second, sensation seeking has been overemphasized in impulsivity scales, and inhibitory control has been neglected.

A more direct test of the relationship among the components of impulsivity is needed. The EASI-III includes subscales of five items for each of the four components of impulsivity (see Appendix 2). These items were administered to 137 middle-class families of young twins (Plomin, 1974). Each parent rated himself and his spouse on the adult version of the EASI-III, and both parents rated both twins on a child version of a similar questionnaire. Factor analyses of all the EASI items revealed a clear persistence factor. However, the other impulsivity components did not emerge as clearly in the adult self-report and rating data. Despite this lack of factorial clarity, the a priori impulsivity scales were positively and significantly intercorrelated. The intercorrelations are presented in Table 6.3. The correlations for the children's EASI are the average correlations for the mothers' and fathers' ratings of both boys and girls, but all four of these intercorrelational matrices were similar. The correlations between sensation seeking and both persistence and decision time are the lowest. The highest correlations were obtained between inhibitory control and each of the other three components. Nearly the same pattern of results can be seen in the adult data in part B of Table 6.3. This provides tenuous support for our hypothesis that inhibitory control is at the core of impulsivity.

We also examined test-retest reliabilities. Inhibitory control had the lowest test-retest reliability (.56 over two to three months) for the mothers' ratings of their twins. Although the observed correlations between inhibitory control and the other components of impulsivity are almost the same in the child and adult data, correlations corrected for unreliability would yield much higher values for the child data. These findings suggest two conclusions. First, there appears

TABLE 6.3   INTERCORRELATIONS FOR THE IMPULSIVITY SCALES OF EASI-III

(a)   Average correlations* for the mothers' and fathers' ratings of boys and girls on the children's version of the EASI-III. N = 137 mothers rating 129 boys and 145 girls and 193 fathers rating 187 boys and 199 girls.

	Persistence	Decision time	Sensation seeking
Inhibitory control	.33	.24	.34
Persistence		.23	.14
Decision time			.18

(b)   Average correlations* for the mothers' and fathers' self-report and ratings of their spouses on the adult version of the EASI-III. N = 137 mothers and 137 fathers.

	Persistence	Decision time	Sensation seeking
Inhibitory control	.26	.29	.33
Persistence		.26	.13
Decision time			.34

---

*Correlations greater than .09, $p < .05$; correlations greater than .12, $p < .01$.

to be some relationship among the components of impulsivity. Second, the data are consistent with the hypothesis that inhibitory control is at the core of these components. Now we can theorize about the developmental course of impulsivity.

DEVELOPMENT

During childhood, inhibitory control increases with age. The newborn infant is virtually a reflexive organism who reacts immediately to internal needs and external stimuli. The socialized adult can exercise self-control in a variety of contexts, ranging from the suppression of internal needs such as hunger to the exercise of moral restraint when no one is watching. Society clearly benefits when individual members inhibit themselves because personal needs are more easily submerged to those of the group. And each person benefits in the sense of acquiring discipline and recognizing that he has the ability to control himself. But self-control is often achieved only at the cost of an important attribute: spontaneity. Too often the delightful unpredictability of the child is exchanged for the staid caution and predictability of the adult. Many adults regret the lack of opportunity to engage in unrestrained behavior that will not be punished. One answer in today's world is to resort to alcohol or other drugs and plead innocence because of "being under the influence."

SEQUENCE

Self-control is not demanded or initiated over all behaviors simultaneously. We can discern a sequential pattern of inhibitory control over age-graded behaviors during development. It starts with control over body functions. Toilet training is typically initiated during the second year of life, and most children have bowel and bladder control by age three years. The conditioning process is not especially difficult, and there is no basis for assuming that impulsivity temperament is an important determinant.

During the third year of life, most children start learning to delay gratification and to control affect. Both processes are slow, and complete control is rarely achieved before adulthood (and some adults never do). Children in our society—especially middle-class children—are taught to postpone reward. They learn to save money, sometimes merely to inculcate thrift and otherwise to buy an expensive object. They are taught to wait until others are seated at the dinner table, until it is their turn in a line, until they reach a given age, etc. Children tend to chafe at such delays, but most children learn to tolerate the annoyance (or even to avoid becoming irritated).

Children in our culture must also inhibit emotionality. Temper tantrums and excessive crying are simply not tolerated. Boys must learn to control fear and signs of weakness (e.g., crying), and girls must learn to control anger. Some adults never master self-control of affect, but adults are clearly less open, less explosive, and generally less expressive of affect than are children.

The last kind of self-control to be initiated during childhood concerns decision making. Only when children become clearly cognitive organisms—at roughly five years of age—can such training begin. Then children can be urged to "look before you leap" and to suppress the initial impulse to act. This occurs mainly in the context of intellectual activities (principally in school). Thinking through problems requires reasoning and judgment, neither of which thrives in an atmosphere of haste. Impetuosity has no place in real intellectual tasks such as mathematics and chess.

The temperamentally impulsive child finds it difficult to acquire self-control. He has trouble in delaying gratification and holding back responses involving a choice, and he has considerable difficulty in inhibiting fear and anger. Thus the impulsive child has a hard time during development. Socializing agents are continually pressuring him to postpone gratification, to suppress affect, including boredom, and to delay decisions—all of which run counter to his disposition to be impetuous. The deliberate child has an easier time of it. The demands for control fit neatly with his natural disposition to take his time and delay responding. His main problems arise in peer interactions, when playmates may demand the spontaneity and sense of adventure he does not possess.

SOCIALIZATION

Society works very hard to train children in self-control, which is one of the major goals of socialization. However, not all the components of impulsivity seem to undergo the same degree of socialization pressure. It is likely that inhibitory control is a focal issue in socialization because self-control seems so important in socialization. The other components are also important in socialization, but to less extent. For example, decision time is not an issue during early childhood, persistence does not seem to be as amenable to shaping because it involves long-term behavior, and sensation seeking seems to us to be worked on the least during socialization and perhaps even in adulthood. If there is differential socialization pressure on the components of impulsivity, it would explain the lack of strong interrelationships among the components.

In general, very strong socialization pressure is applied toward impulsivity, probably more than against the other temperamental dispositions. Socialization agents largely ignore *activity level*, attending to it only in those few contexts where it interferes with group goals ("stop fidgeting in class" or, conversely, "pull your share of the load"). Only the expressive aspects of *emo-*

tionality suffer interference from socializing agents, and there is considerable tolerance for "sensitive children." Concerning *sociability*, children are pressured to socialize, but their reaction to the pressure is important. They can discourage excessive pressure by being cool and socially unresponsive and so arrive at an amenable compromise between their own sociability temperament and the demands of others for interaction. Thus impulsivity is shaped and perhaps altered more than any other temperament. This has two possible implications. First, the environment may claim a larger share of the variance, leaving less for the genetic component. As a consequence, heritability estimates would be lower. Second, the impact of the environment would be stronger with increasing age. Thus heritability estimates should be diminished considerably in older children and adults; and longitudinal research should reveal only minimal stability throughout childhood.

These comments apply mainly to the middle class, which emphasizes the self-control aspects of socialization. Lower-class children must also learn to inhibit, but there is considerably less constraint concerning expression of affect and delay of gratification. There are fewer controls concerning sex and aggression, and postponement of fun in favor of working toward distant goals is often openly ridiculed. To the extent that these class differences occur, impulsivity temperament should be revealed more clearly in lower-class children and adults. They are less socialized for control, and therefore the environment should not claim a major share of the variance. We suggest that most research on impulsivity, which has used middle-class subjects almost exclusively, underplays the role of temperament. This is an empirical issue, which can be resolved by comparing middle-class with lower class children. The issue is not whether lower-class persons are more impulsive but whether inheritance plays a larger role in their impulsivity.

THE INHERITANCE OF IMPULSIVITY

Table 6.4 lists twin studies of inhibitory control. Three studies involved children who were rated by their parents. Buss et al. (1973) found high heritability for boys but no heritability for girls. Plomin (1974), using midrater estimates of the twins' EASI, found high heritability for both boys and girls, although the heritability was less for the girls. Scarr (1966) also found little evidence of a genetic factor in impulsivity for girls. The evidence of three studies of self-control in high school students is also mixed. Nichols (1966) discovered a significant genetic factor for self-control in a very large twin study, as measured by the California Psychological Inventory for both boys and girls. Gottesman (1966), using the same inventory but small samples, found a significant difference between monozygotic and dizygotic twins for girls only. And

Vandenberg et al. (1967) found no evidence of a genetic factor for either boys or girls as measured by the self-control scale of the Comrey Personality and Attitude Factor Scales.

Table 6.5 lists twin studies that used Cattell's studies. In the section on measures we noted the difficulty in interpreting the factored scales. The five studies using Cattell's factor Q_3 *uncontrolled versus controlled*, are unanimous: there is no genetic component. However, Cattell's scales also failed to yield heritability for emotionality and sociability when nearly all other studies showed heritability (see Chapters 4 and 5). So these negative findings do not necessarily deny that impulsivity is inherited.

Table 6.6 lists twin studies of decision time and other measures related to impulsivity. It is divided into three parts: experimental measures, self-reports, and a miscellaneous category.

The data provide a weak case for a genetic component for decision time. Of the four experimental twin studies of decision time, only Eysenck and Prell (1951) found significantly greater similarity in monozygotic twins. Thus, on the whole, there is little support for an inherited component of decision time, as measured experimentally. Two reasons may underlie these negative findings. The first concerns reliability. Scarr (1966b) and Eysenck and Prell (1951) used a single trial as their measure of decision time, and no test-retest reliabilities are available for their measures. Second, decision time in a single situation such as picking a toy to play with or guessing which card will come next in a game of chance, may be too focalized to allow a broad temperamental disposition to display itself. Both considerations suggest that decision time should be measured in several situations and also over several trials.

Two self-report studies of reflectiveness—which may be related to decision time—add to the pattern of mixed results (see Part 2 of Table 6.6). In one study, Vandenberg (1967) suggested that it is heritable in boys but not girls; in another (1962) he found no evidence for heritability. Plomin (1974), however, found significant heritability in a rating study of decision time in young twins. These studies also used general measures of impulsivity that combine inhibitory control, decision time, sensation seeking, and persistence items. Once again, Vandenberg found evidence for heritability in one study (1962) but not in the other (1967). Another study of general impulsivity (Schoenfeldt, 1968) also found no evidence for heritability.

In short, the genetic evidence for impulsivity is very weak. There is some evidence for an inherited component for inhibitory control (excluding studies using Cattell's factors), but it is not consistent across studies or across genders. Furthermore, there is little evidence suggesting an inherited component for decision time. The other components of impulsivity have seldom been studied, although Plomin (1974) found significant heritability for both boys and girls for persistence and sensation seeking. If impulsivity is indeed a temperament,

TABLE 6.4 TWIN STUDIES OF IMPULSIVITY: INHIBITORY CONTROL

Measure	Number of MZ Pairs	Number of DZ Pairs	Age	Findings Boys MZ	Boys DZ	Girls MZ	Girls DZ	Reference
EASI-I Temperament Survey Impulsivity	78	50	55-mo average	.90	.17*	.85	.78	Buss et al., 1973
EASI-III Inhibitory control	60	51	42-mo average	.65	−.07*	.49	.12*	Plomin, 1974
Rating by the mother on the Gough Adjective Checklist Self-control	24	28	97 mo	All girls MZ: .51 DZ: .31				Scarr, 1966
California Personality Inventory Self-control	79	68	High school	No correlations reported Girls: MZs more similar than DZs* Boys: MZs not significantly more similar than DZs				Gottesman, 1966

140

| California Personality Inventory
Self-control | 333 | 484 | High school | .56 | .27* | .57 | .36* | Nichols, 1966 |
| Comrey Personality and Attitude Factor Scales
Self-control | 111 | 90 | High school | No correlations reported MZs not significantly more similar than DZs | | | | Vandenberg et al., 1967 (in Vandenberg, 1967) |

*p<.05

TABLE 6.5   TWIN STUDIES OF IMPULSIVITY: CATTELL'S SCALES OF INHIBITORY CONTROL

Measure	Number of MZ Pairs	Number of DZ Pairs	Age	Findings	Reference
Cattell's Junior Personality Questionnaire Q_3. Uncontrolled vs. controlled	104	64	High school	No correlations reported MZs not significantly more similar than DZs	Cattell et al., 1955
Objective Analytic Test Battery Will power	104	30	High school	No correlations reported MZs not significantly more similar than DZs	Cattell et al., 1957
Cattell's High School Personality Questionnaire Q_2. Uncontrolled vs. controlled	34	34	High school	Boys MZ −.01 DZ −.22 Girls MZ .56 DZ .34	Gottesman, 1963
Cattell's Junior Personality Questionnaire Q_3. Uncontrolled vs. controlled	36	45	High school	No correlations reported MZs not significantly more similar than DZs	Vandenberg, 1962
Cattell's Sixteen Personality Factor Test Q_3. Uncontrolled vs. controlled	40	45	Adolescent-adult	MZ: .22 DZ: .23	Canter, 1969 (in Mittler, 1971)

TABLE 6.6 TWIN STUDIES OF IMPULSIVITY: DECISION TIME

Measure	Number of MZ Pairs	Number of DZ Pairs	Age	Findings				Reference
1. Experimental measures of decision time								
Decision time for selecting a toy	24	28	6 – 10 yr	MZ: .34	DZ: .04			Scarr, 1966 (b)
Time to free associate to words	38	34	9 – 17 yr	MZ: .39	DZ: .23			Carter, 1939
Downey Will Temperament Test Speed of decision	50	50	Elementary and high school	MZ: .50	DZ: .69			Newman et al., 1937
Decision time to guess a card in a game of chance	25	25	13 – 15 yr	MZ: .34	DZ: -.12*			Eysenck & Prell, 1951
2. Self-report of decision time								
EASI-III Decision time	60	51	42-mo average	Boys: MZ .57	DZ .01*	Girls: MZ .72	DZ -.32*	Plomin, 1974
Thurstone Temperament Schedule Reflective	36	45	14 – 18 yr	No correlations reported MZs not significantly more similar than DZs				Vandenberg, 1962

143

TABLE 6.6 (CONTINUED) TWIN STUDIES OF IMPULSIVITY: DECISION TIME

Measure	Number of MZ Pairs	Number of DZ Pairs	Age	Findings	Reference
Stern's Activities Index Reflectiveness	50	38	14 – 18 yr	No correlations reported Girls: no difference Boys: MZs more similar than DZs	Vandenberg, 1967
3. *Miscellaneous*					
Thurstone Temperament Survey Impulsivity	36	45	14 – 18 yr	No correlations reported MZs more similar than DZs	Vandenberg, 1962
Stern's Activities Index Impulsivity	50	38	14 – 18 yr	No correlations reported MZs not significantly more similar than DZs	Vandenberg, 1967
Project Talent Questionnaire Impulsion	337	156	14 – 18 yr	Boys: MZ .24, DZ .21; Girls: MZ .32, DZ .11	Schoenfeldt, 1968

*$p < .05$

perhaps it has not been measured adequately, or it may be submerged during the socialization process. Of course, impulsivity may not be a temperament, and it would not be revealed as such even if all the measurement problems were resolved. But this issue requires a discussion of all the criteria of temperament and is therefore left for the end of the chapter.

LONGITUDINAL STUDIES OF IMPULSIVITY

The longitudinal research reviewed in this book was by and large not directed specifically toward temperaments. This proved to be no problem for the other three temperaments because measures appropriate to them were included along with many other personality variables. But, for reasons unknown to us, measures of inhibitory control were *not* usually included. As a result there are virtually no longitudinal studies of impulsivity.

Kagan (1971) measured decision time at 27 months on the Embedded Figures Test and at 48 months on the Matching Familiar Figures Test. The youth of the subjects, the use of two different tests, and the small sample (18 girls and 12 boys), all worked against obtaining a large correlation. Nevertheless, the correlation for girls was substantial, .57, but for boys it was only .13. Any conclusions from these data must be highly tentative. The findings are not inconsistent with stability throughout development, but they do not provide strong support for stability.

PRESENCE IN ADULTHOOD

There is some indication that impulsivity continues to underlie adult individual differences. The major personality inventories, especially the empirically constructed ones, have scales that are related to impulsivity (see Table 6.2). However, in the Measures section we pointed out that most of the scales emphasize sensation seeking and decision time and neglect inhibitory control. We suggest that this is an important oversight because delay of gratification and resistance to temptation are at the core of the confrontation between impulsivity and socialization. Thus, although impulsivity is a factor on several adult personality scales, not all its components are represented.

CONCLUSIONS

Is impulsivity a temperament? There are three empirical criteria: presence in adults, stability during childhood, and heritability. The trait is clearly present

in adults, and there is no evidence bearing on stability because of lack of research. But these two criteria are not as basic as inheritance. The heritability
data are mixed. Roughly half the studies have yielded positive evidence and the
other half, negative evidence. In several instances, a larger sample would have
yielded a significant difference in correlations between monozygotic and
dizygotic twins, thereby tipping the weight of evidence in a positive direction.
But such a change would not radically alter the way we interpret the data:
they are mixed. So, in answer to the question posed in the first sentence, *a case
has not yet been made for impulsivity as a temperament.* This is of course a
compromise between two extreme positions, and so it is necessary to examine
both extremes.

Suppose we were to conclude that impulsivity really is a temperament. This
would nicely account for the positive evidence and leave the negative evidence
unexplained. Why do roughly half the studies fail to show heritability? There
are two possible reasons. First, it is not clear precisely what impulsivity is. It
is measured differently from one study to the next. Perhaps the studies with
negative findings were not assessing "true" impulsivity and so failed to find a
genetic component. If this were so, we should seek to discover precisely what
we all mean by impulsivity and return to twin research only after that point is
well established.

A second possibility concerns the impact of the environment. Activity is little
influenced by socialization, and only the expressive aspects of emotionality are
shaped by socialization agents. There is considerable pressure for children to
socialize, but this is countered by the child's own responsivity (or lack of
responsivity), and the outcome is at best a compromise between the child's
original endowment and the demands of those around him. Of all the temperaments, impulsivity is most affected by the environment. As we noted earlier,
one of the major tasks of socialization is to produce self-control in adult
members of society, and the child cannot counter the pressure in any effective
way; at most he can rebel and perhaps get into serious trouble.

If the environment has a strong impact on impulsivity, several implications
follow. First, there should be clear developmental trends in the amount of impulsivity shown by children; we already know that inhibitory control increases
with age. Second, heritability estimates (as derived from twin research) should
drop off sharply with age, but there are no data on this point. Third, individual differences in impulsivity should show up more clearly in children of the
lower class (who receive less training in inhibition) than in the children of the
middle class, but again there is no evidence.

Now consider the other extreme position, that impulsivity is not a
temperament. How do we account for the positive findings? Again we start
with the fact that impulsivity is measured differently from one study to the
next. In some of the research it might be assessed in a way that includes other

inherited dispositions. For example, it might be confounded with emotionality. Subjects would vary in their control over emotions, not because of differences in impulsivity but because of differences in emotionality: subjects who scored high in impulsivity would really be high in emotionality, a temperament already known to have a genetic component. The same kind of confound might exist for activity. Children who are fidgety and restless might be assessed as impulsive because of a high activity level rather than a lack of control. We already know that activity level has an inherited component, so positive findings in at least some twin studies would be no surprise. In brief, the positive findings in twin research might be caused by a confound between impulsivity and a personality disposition known to have a genetic component.

As theorists, we prefer to believe that impulsivity might be a temperament, but as scientists we see little basis for choosing either of the extreme positions. Neither one offers a satisfactory explanation of the findings, but the two positions have different implications. If impulsivity is a temperament, we should continue to seek evidence that would establish a genetic component. We already know that there is likely to be an environmental influence, so taking this position would not shut off any direction of research. On the other hand, if impulsivity is not a temperament, we should stop looking for an inherited component: all the variance resides in the environment. There are two objections to this. First, it would place a heavy burden on environmental variables and, as we describe in Chapter 9, the evidence for environmental variables is weak. Second, it would foreclose research on the inheritance of impulsivity, and we believe that it is much too early to do so. History records many examples of a muddled area being clarified by subsequent research. There is of course the danger of extending the life of a hypothesis far beyond its possible worth, but we suggest that it is much too early to worry about that possibility. Let us at least keep open the question of whether impulsivity is a temperament and so repeat our evaluation of the evidence to date: the case is not yet proved.

CHAPTER

7

GENDER
DIFFERENCES

Are there gender differences in temperament? There must be some basis for
believing that there are or we would not devote an entire chapter to the topic.
But there is not necessarily a gender difference in every temperament. In fact,
we could find none for impulsivity.

If gender differences can be documented, the next question is, what determines them? Reduced to the simplest terms, there are only two answers.
Gender differences may be built-in and therefore biological, or they may derive
from gender role training and therefore be anthropological/psychological.
How can we decide between these alternatives? Each approach must have implications that are different from those of the other. For example, if there is a
biological basis for men being temperamentally different from women, the difference should be universal. But if socialization practices produce the gender
difference, it should appear in some cultures but not in others.

A nontemperament example may make this point clear. In America, most
men can throw a baseball with at least moderate speed and accuracy, and the
throwing motion is coordinated. Most women are clumsy and uncoordinated
in the way they throw a baseball. A possible cause of this gender difference is
anatomical differences between men and women in the shoulder joint. Not so:
their shoulder joints are essentially the same. The crucial fact lies not in

148

anatomy but in a cultural difference; European men throw a baseball essentially the way American women do. They have virtually no experience in throwing baseballs, largely because they concentrate so much on soccer. Before any American criticizes European men for throwing like women, he should remember that perhaps American men kick a soccer ball the way women do. The point of this example is that we can evaluate the two approaches to the gender difference by testing their implications. If the underlying cause is biological, the shoulder joints of men should be different from those of women. The absence of a difference weakens the biological hypothesis. If the underlying cause is psychological/anthropological, there should be differences from one society to the next. The presence of such differences strengthens the psychological/anthropological hypothesis.

ACTIVITY

Theoretical Issues

It is widely believed that males are more active than females, and there is some evidence to sustain this belief. Let us assume for the moment that there is a gender difference. If the difference were innate, it might show up at two points during life. It might exist from birth onward, and we would discern it as soon as activity could be measured reliably. The earliest age at which activity shows the required stability is one year. Thus if there is a gender difference from birth onward, it should be clearly manifest by at least 12 months of age.

Second, the gender difference might be related to the hormonal changes that occur in early puberty. The secondary sex characteristics (hair, breasts, hips, height, and so on) that so clearly differentiate men from women are inherited, but they do not appear until male or female hormones increase beyond their childhood levels. Any difference in activity level might similarly be triggered by hormonal changes and would first appear during adolescence.

On the other hand, any gender difference in activity might be caused entirely by cultural differences in gender roles. This hypothesis has two implications. First, each culture would have its own pattern of gender differences, depending on how boys and girls are trained. Thus in one society boys might be more active and in another, girls more active; in a third, there might be no differences in activity level.

Second, the age at which a gender difference first appears would be directly linked to the onset of gender role training as it relates to activity. Consider the example of certain Jews in Europe during the past few centuries. The men were expected to become Talmudic scholars, spending their days studying and praying. The women were expected to care for the family and even earn a living. In this group, a gender difference in activity would not emerge until adulthood, and it would be the women who were more active.

In present-day America any culture-related gender differences in activity would occur when boys and girls learn games and sports appropriate to their gender. If boys' games are more active than girls' games, then a gender difference in activity should emerge in early childhood. Moreover, it should disappear when adult men and women stop games that require very high levels of energy, say, during middle age.

Of course, it might be argued that boys' games are more active because boys are the more active gender; that is, innate differences *cause* gender differences in games. If this were true, then boys' games would be more active in *all* cultures. This hypothesis would also require that boys be more active than girls as soon as activity can be measured—at one year of age. Thus the origin of a gender difference would be best resolved by discovering *when* the difference first appears.

When Gender Differences Appear

Age is a crucial variable in gender differences in activity, and the turning point appears to be four years. Below four years, no gender differences in activity emerge from virtually all the studies; above four years, a number of studies report that males are more active. The details are shown in Table 7.1.

Consider first the activity level of children four years and younger; the studies are almost unanimous in reporting no gender differences. The sole exception was the investigation of Goldberg and Lewis (1969) of 13-month old children:

> Boys were independent, showed more exploratory behavior, played with toys requiring gross motor activity, were more vigorous, and tended to run and bang in their play. [p. 30]

Why are these findings directly opposed to all the other findings with preschool children? Perhaps it was *where* the children were observed. The children and their mothers came to a playroom that contained a variety of toys. The context was novel for the child, and the only security was the presence of the mother. It is well-known that a novel situation threatens *all* primate young, who cling to the mother for security. Only when they are very secure do the young investigate their environment and initiate high-energy activities. In this investigation, the girls tended to stay closer to their mothers, explored less, and initiated fewer activities. Thus their lower activity was probably caused by greater insecurity, a stronger attachment to the mother, or both. This explanation could easily be tested. Each young child should be observed in his own home, in a familiar room. If our explanation is correct and if all the other studies on young children are valid, there should be no differences in activity between boys and girls when they behave in a familiar environment.

Now consider the results with children older than four years. Here the findings are mixed; some studies report a gender difference and others do not. Where a difference occurs, it is always the boys who are more active. There are virtually no data on adults, but our own findings with college students (EASI-II) reveal no gender differences. It remains moot whether men are more active than women.

How do these results bear on the origin of gender differences? The crucial fact is the *first appearance* of such differences. Almost without exception, no gender difference is found before four years of age. Clearly, if the gender difference is innate, it does not appear at birth or as soon as activity can be measured. Nor do differences appear for the first time around puberty, which means that they are not associated with hormonal changes. In brief, the timing of the first appearance of gender differences in activity argues against their being inherited.

The explanation must reside in culturally shaped gender roles. In our society, boys start playing "boys' games" and girls start playing "girls' games" during the fourth year of life. The boys' games are more vigorous, more rough-and-tumble, and more violent. Boys are permitted to be aggressive with one another; girls are discouraged. These differences *in child rearing* appear to be reflected in subsequent gender differences in activity. Boys engage in more vigorous sports and games, and they fight more than girls. This would account for the greater activity of boys during childhood and adolescence.

However, adults spend less time in active sports and vigorous games. These trends would lessen the gender difference in activity and eventually eliminate it. Are men more active than women? Only in the sense that men are larger and stronger and so can take jobs as lumberjacks, stevedores, and miners. We suggest that when the gender difference in size is controlled, men are no more active than women. It would be interesting to test this hypothesis with actometers. Would a middle-class business man really move more than his suburban wife? Would his office activities burn up more energy than her housework, cooking, and looking after the children? We doubt it. In brief, we read the evidence as suggesting that the gender difference in activity may be attributed to gender role training in early childhood; the difference is transient and disappears in adulthood. We also suggest that differences among cultures in gender-related activities will bear this out.

TABLE 7.1 GENDER DIFFERENCES IN ACTIVITY

1. *Studies with ANY subjects 4 yr and younger*

Measure	Number of subjects		Age	Differences	Reference
	Males	Females			
Ratings of head movements	24	19	First 4 days of life	None	Campbell, 1968
Observational ratings	14	15	1 – 3 mo	None at 3 wk or at 3 mo	Moss, 1967
Locomotion	91	89	3 – 13 mo	None at 3, 8, or 13 mo	Kagan, 1971
Ratings of vigorousness of play	32	33	13 mo	Boys played more vigorously with toys	Goldberg & Lewis, 1969
Rating of gross activity	45	46	3 yr	None	Nelson, 1931
Global score based on ratings of hand, arm, leg, and global movement during free play	17	16	27 – 59 mo	None before 4 yr of age. Boys more active at 4 yr of age	Goodenough, 1930

152

Measure	N	N	Age	Sex differences	Reference
Ratings of overall amount of behavior, tempo, and vigor	16	16	2 – 5 yr	None	Murphy, 1962
Rating of vigor in free play	16	16	40 mo	None	Fales, 1937
Observational ratings in free play	43	31	1 – 10 yr	None before 6 yr of age Boys more active from 6 to 10 yr	Battle & Lacey, 1972
Parental ratings of activity on the Werry-Weiss-Peters Activity Scale	26	17	3 – 5 yr	None	Willerman & Plomin (unpublished)
Parental ratings of the activity scale of the EASI Temperament Survey	140	116	55-mo average	None	Buss, Plomin, & Willerman, 1973

2. Studies with subjects 5 yr and older

Measure	N	N	Age	Sex differences	Reference
Actometer and teacher ratings	20	20	5 – 6 yr	None for the actometer Boys more active on teacher ratings	Loo & Wenar, 1971
Self-report and teacher ratings	199	207	7 – 10 yr	Boys more active on both measures	Walker, 1967

TABLE 7.1 (CONTINUED)   GENDER DIFFERENCES IN ACTIVITY

| Measure | Number of subjects | | Age | Differences | Reference |
	Males	Females			
Ratings of "restless-inactive" from interviews of the Berkeley Guidance Study	45	40	5 – 16 yr	None	Bronson, 1966
Ballistograph	50	50	14 – 18 yr	Males more active than females	Wolfensberger et al., 1962
EASI–II	162	207	College students, 18.5-yr average	None	Buss & Plomin (unpublished)
12 mechanical measures of voluntary tempo	20	20	21-yr average	None	Harrison, 1941

EMOTIONALITY

Expressiveness

It is widely believed that women are more emotional than men. The substance of this assertion depends on what the term *emotional* means. If it means the *expression of affect*, there is some truth to the belief that women are more emotional in America. They are allowed—even encouraged—to be more affectionate toward one another and toward men. In our culture at least, men generally do not hug or kiss one another as signs of friendship or love; women do. And women may cry when unhappy or when sympathizing with another's misery, as at the movies when watching sentimental pictures (sometimes called "women's movies"). Men are required to keep a stiff upper lip and to fight back tears or any other "signs of weakness."

It might be argued that this gender difference in expressing affect is a fundamental one that merely reflects the biological differences between males and females. This view neglects obvious differences from one culture to the next. In France, Italy, and other European countries men hug and kiss one another, and they are not ashamed to weep openly. Such overt affect may seem unmanly to ourselves and others of the "frozen-faced" Anglo-Saxon tradition, but the *fact* of male sentiment being expressed gives the lie to the notion of a *biological* difference in *expressiveness*.

Rationality

The term *emotional* may also mean *nonrational* or irrational. There is a cultural stereotype—fostered by men and accepted by many women—that women make their decisions mainly on the basis of feelings, intuitions, and sentiments. Men, it is argued, base their decisions on cold logic and hard fact. The "evidence" for these assertions is anecdotal, and we know of no reliable data to sustain them.

As far as we can discern, the explanation for the belief in women's irrationality lies in *attribution*. First, in our culture men are trained to give a logical account of their activities and choices. When asked why he acted the way he did, a man is likely to come up with a reasonable answer. The answer may be the truth or a lie or any combination of the two, but it tends to be logical. *Men are trained to supply rational attributions for their behavior.*

Women are not so constrained. They are allowed (even encouraged) to attribute their choices to affect, sentiment, and other nonlogical reasons. This is part of the traditional feminine role. If a woman reports that she has acted on the basis of hard fact and reason, she is regarded by men as cold, tough, bitchy, and unfeminine. Traditional men like their women soft, sentimental, somewhat illogical, and intellectually inferior. Women are of course none of these things *intrinsically*, but they may *act* appropriately to conform to the traditional woman's role. The truth, in our view, is that men are not more logical but better at rationalizing and intellectualizing.

Gender Roles

Is there a logical or empirical basis for *innate* gender differences in emotionality? We could find none and therefore contend that any differences that do exist may be attributed to gender role training. It follows that there should be variations from one culture to the next in the degree and kind of such differences between men and women. There should also be wide variations within each gender in adherence to traditional roles, especially in these days of challenge to traditional roles.

If our position is correct, there should be no difference between male and female infants in distress. Distress occurs early in life, long before the young child becomes aware of its gender. Mothers may treat male infants differently than girl infants, but gender role training does not begin in earnest until the second year of life. It is during the second year of life that the child walks, starts to speak, and develops a variety of gross instrumental behaviors. Such instrumentality is necessary for the differentiation of anger from the more primitive distress.

We assume that gender role training in emotionality focuses on anger and fear. Boys are allowed to become angry but not fearful; girls are allowed to be afraid but not angry. These differences are relative; boys are allowed fear if the threat is sufficient, and girls are allowed anger if the provocation is sufficient. But in general, fear is a more feminine emotion, anger a more masculine emotion.

This difference is merely one aspect of the larger pattern of gender roles. Girls are allowed to be passive and dependent; that is, they are permitted to retain the subordinate role of the child. A young child is relatively helpless in the face of threat or challenges to his poorly developed instrumentality. He must depend on adults for security, defense, and most of the instrumental acts necessary for survival. The traditional feminine role in our culture sustains this pattern, and women are encouraged to depend on men as they once depended on parents. This is not to say that traditional women are without power, but their means of manipulation—indirect appeals and negativism, rather than direct challenges—are those of a subordinate in relationship to a controlling figure.

The angry woman presents a challenge to a man, and the traditional man resents challenges from a woman. Anger in older girls and women may be punished physically but more often by the denial of resources and by a loss of affection. The latter is crucial, for a basic motivation for traditional women is to be loved and admired. Fearful women may be protected and lóved by traditional men; angry women, never.

The traditional male role is symmetrically opposite; fear is suppressed and anger allowed. Boys are supposed to be adventurous, self-reliant, and courageous. Courage and sense of adventure cannot become manifest in a safe environment. Only by taking risks and facing threats can a boy demonstrate the virtues appropriate to his gender role. Bravery is a source of esteem for males; cowards are sneered at or pitied. To be afraid is to be a sissy. Thus boys are taught to inhibit fear.

They are also taught to compete head on. Challenges are met directly, usually with aggression. Given the directness, challenge, and instrumentality that define the male role, it is no surprise that boys are quick to anger. Ask any parent about a typical negative interaction between daughter and son: the daughter taunts and teases her brother, using verbal acts of at least some subtlety; the brother typically responds with anger and physical aggression.

The self-reliance of the male role cannot help but push boys toward anger. Boys are trained to be independent and therefore chafe easily when restricted or forced to comply. In terms of Brehm's formulation (1966), we expect more *reactance* from males than from females. Boys will be more negativistic, rebellious, and quarrelsome.

In short, gender role training most affects the emotions of fear and anger: girls are more fearful and less prone to anger than boys. This hypothesis has a number of implications, all of which can be verified empirically.

1.   Boys engage in more frequent displays of temper, as for example, quarrels.

2.   Girls have more fears and more intense fears than boys.

3.   Concerning the heritability of emotionality, if it is separated into fear and anger components, the longitudinal course of the two should differ between the genders. Girls are allowed to remain fearful, and for them the heritability of fear should hold up better than that for anger. If anger is suppressed in girls, variations in child rearing should play a large role. This means that the heritability of anger for girls should diminish with increasing age. The pattern for boys is precisely opposite. Their fear is suppressed, and variations in the extent of suppression should diminish the heritability of fear, at least with respect to anger, which is given a freer rein.

Research Findings

What are the *facts* about gender differences in emotionality? They are summarized in Tables 7.2 to 7.4, which are divided into sections on distress, fear, and anger.

DISTRESS

When crying, fussing, or irritability is observed, the results are mixed. Most of the studies found no differences between boys and girls. Two studies on *neonates* reported more emotionality in *boys* (Smith, 1936; Moss, 1967), but two reported no gender difference (Birns, 1965; Kessen et al., 1961). Of the remaining investigations on children only one (Goldberg & Lewis, 1969) found a gender difference: *girls* cried more when obstructed by a barrier. The only study of distress in adults found mixed results on autonomic reactivity (Vandenberg et al., 1965). When this group of studies is taken as a whole, it sustains our assumption that there are no gender differences in distress (and, by implication, our assertion that there are no innate gender differences in emotionality).

FEAR

We have argued that as gender role training proceeds, it should produce a difference between boys and girls in degree of fear and number of fears. During the preschool years, gender role training has not proceeded far enough to have a strong impact on emotionality. The first two fear studies in Table 7.3 are consistent with this view. Jersild and Holmes (1935) found a significant difference only for fear of strangers (not replicated by researchers who study attachment), and Hattwick (1937) found no gender difference.

During the school years and into adulthood, the pattern is mixed; some studies report that girls are more fearful, others not. Many researchers have used self-report anxiety questionnaires, which raises a problem of interpretation. These questionnaires contain items that relate not only to fear but also to autonomic and bodily reactions to threatening situations. We expect girls to be more fearful than boys but not more autonomically reactive. With anxiety questionnaires containing both kinds of items, it is not surprising that gender differences have been found in only a little over one half the studies.

On the other hand, research with college-age subjects has used purer measures and yielded clear results. Women show greater galvanic skin response than men to the threat of shock (Berry & Martin, 1957). The incidence of fears has been studied systematically by behavior modification therapists, using several different fear surveys. In many behavior modification studies, only women are used because of the preponderance of women over men who have intense fears. Table 7.3 includes only one behavior modification study of gender differences—the one with the largest sample (Grossberg & Wilson)—and the greater fearfulness of women was significant. And a more recent paper concludes:

> The finding of higher scores of females on all 16 fear factors is consistent with previous research on the Fear Survey Schedule and indicates the basic importance of the sex differences in the expression of fears. [Adams & Rothstein, 1971, p. 365]

In brief, the fear research in Table 7.3 yields the following developmental picture:

1.   There is essentially no gender difference during the preschool years.
2.   During the school years, there is some evidence that girls are more fearful, but the results are far from conclusive.
3.   College-age (and presumably, older) women have a greater number and a greater intensity of fears than do men.

ANGER

Anger presents conceptual and methodological problems because of its association with aggression. Two basically different kinds of aggression have been distinguished (Buss, 1961). *Instrumental aggression* involves punishing another person in order to attain an extrinsic reward, such as a toy, money, or status. In this respect, it is like any other instrumental response, and the aggressor is rarely angry. Thus emotionality does not enter into instrumental aggression.

Angry aggression, in contrast, involves an enraged aggressor, whose reward is the pain and suffering of his victim. The usual antecedent is an attack, a threat, or, less frequently, a frustration. Clearly, with other things equal, the more emotional the person, the more likely he will engage in angry aggression. So angry aggression would appear to be an excellent index of anger, but there is a complication. Angry persons often do not aggress. Rather, they suppress, inhibit, or divert their rage, and it is not expressed in punitive acts. Therefore angry aggression is at best a very rough measure of anger.

Virtually all the research on anger in Table 7.4 used quarrels, conflicts, and other aggressive behavior. We have included these studies not because they are entirely appropriate (some mix instrumental with angry aggression; others fail to take account of anger without aggression) but because they are the only ones available. The earliest investigator (Goodenough, 1931) used the best measure, angry outbursts involving displays of undirected energy. For the one- to two-year range there were no gender differences, but in the three- to eight-year

TABLE 7.2 GENDER DIFFERENCES IN DISTRESS

Measure	Number of subjects		Age	Differences	Reference
	Males	Females			
Frequency of crying	25	25	First 5 days of life	None	Kessen, Williams, & Williams, 1961
Rating of reaction to loud tone and cold disc	15	15	4 and 5 days old	None	Birns, 1965
Ratings of crying in darkness during flash of light	10	10	8 days old	Boys cry more than girls	Smith, 1936
Ratings of crying, fussing, and irritability	13	12	3 wk and 3 mo old	Boys cry, fuss,* and are more irritable* than girls at both 3 wk and 3 mo	Moss, 1967
Frequency of crying during testing situations	31	30	Birth to 1 yr	None	Bayley, 1932
Crying during barrier frustration	32	32	13 mo	Girls cry more than boys in reaction to frustration	Goldberg & Lewis, 1969

160

	N		Age	Sex differences	Reference
Frequency of crying during play	17	12	18 mo to 4 yr	None	Brackett, 1934
Ratings of "ease of crying" during free play	283	296	2 – 4 yr	None	Hattwick, 1937
Ratings of fussing, screaming, and whimpering by 21 children by their teacher and another 27 children by their mothers	48 total		3 – 5 yr	None	Rickets, 1934
Ratings of interview data of the Berkeley Guidance Study of reactivity and emotional lability	45	40	5 – 16 yr	None at any age	Bronson, 1966
Autonomic reactivity (heart rate, GSR, and breathing rate) to a flash of light, a bell, and a falling hammer	(N varied)		Adult	Males generally more reactive for heart rate* and GSR; but females tended to be more reactive in breathing	Vandenberg et al., 1965

*$p < .05$

161

TABLE 7.3 GENDER DIFFERENCES IN FEAR

Measure	Number of subjects		Age	Differences	Reference
	Males	Females			
Number of fears of the child as rated by his parents	56	47	Birth to 5 yr	None	Jersild & Holmes, 1935
Fearfulness of children as rated by their nursery school teacher				None	
Ratings of fearfulness during experimental tests (being left alone, darkened room, strange persons, loud sound, snake, large dog)				On 6 of 8 tests, girls were more fearful only in fear of strangers	
Rating of fear during free play	283	296	2 - 4 yr	None	Hattwick, 1937
Self-report and teacher ratings of fearfulness	199	207	7 - 10 yr	Girls more fearful than boys*	Walker, 1967

162

Measure			Age	Results	Reference
Ratings of fearfulness and anxiety from interview data of the Berkeley Guidance Study	45	40	5 – 16 yr	None	Bronson, 1966
Review of 25 studies of anxiety scales, primarily the Children's Manifest Anxiety Scale and the Taylor Manifest Anxiety Scale				In 14 studies, girls and women were more anxious; in the remaining 11 studies no gender differences	Maccoby, 1966
GSR reactivity to shock	50	60	College age	Women more reactive	Berry & Martin, 1957
Wolpe-Lang Fear Survey	203	302	College age	Women had more fears and classical phobias than men	Grossberg & Wilson, 1965

*$p < .05$

TABLE 7.4 GENDER DIFFERENCES IN ANGER

Measure	Number of subjects Males	Females	Age	Differences	Reference
Number of aggressive acts against peers during outdoor free play	30	25	2½ yr	Boys more aggressive than girls*	Pederson & Bell, 1970
Rating of "aggressive behavior" during free play	283	296	2 – 4 yr	Boys more aggressive than girls*	Hattwick, 1937
Rating of frequency and duration of emotional outbursts	25	20	1 – 8 yr	1 – 2 yr: none 3 – 8 yr: boys have more frequent outbursts than girls	Goodenough, 1931
Conflict behavior during free play	30	24	2 – 4 yr	At 2 yr: none At 4 yr: Boys involved in more conflicts than girls	Jersild & Markey, 1935
Conflict behavior during free play	17	16	2 – 5 yr	None	Roff & Roff, 1940
Number of quarrels and rating of quarrelsomeness	21	19	2 – 5 yr	Boys have more quarrels and are more quarrelsome than girls	Green, 1933a, b

Study	N	Age	Finding	Reference
Reanalysis of Green's data			2 - 3 yr: none in number of quarrels or quarrelsomeness 4 - 5 yr: boys have more quarrels* and are more quarrelsome* than girls	Dawe, 1934
Self-report and teacher ratings of aggressiveness	199 207	7 - 10 yr	Boys more aggressive* than girls	Walker, 1967
Ratings of tantrums from interview data of the Berkeley Guidance Study	45 40	5 - 16 yr	None at any age	Bronson, 1967

*$p < .05$

range boys had more temper outbursts than girls. Similar developmental differences were found in several other studies, with boys surpassing girls in anger at roughly three to four years of age. Bronson (1966) found no gender differences. However, tantrums may be too infrequent in children older than five years to provide a useful index of anger.

In short, boys show more anger than girls starting at three to four years, whereas the greater fear of girls does not start until middle childhood. Boys continue to be more aggressive into adulthood, as reflected in the pattern of more aggression in men than woman (e.g., Buss & Durkee, 1957).

These conclusions are based on measures that combined instrumental and angry aggression. The Buss-Durkee Inventory contains an Irritability scale that is a reasonable measure of temper. On this scale, there are no gender differences. The means for men are roughly the same as those for women over three samples of college students and three samples of psychiatric patients (see Buss, 1961, pp. 176–179).

These findings suggest that women become as angry as men, but women do not express their anger as frequently in aggression (the aggression scores of the Buss-Durkee and similar questionnaires are always higher for men than for women). Thus the self-report data of adults are consistent with our formulation: men and women do not differ in arousability, including the tendency to become enraged, but women are taught to inhibit *expressions* of anger, whereas men are allowed to ventilate their anger.

SOCIABILITY

Women appear to be more sociable than men, and their personal interactions are different. Thus college women score slightly but consistently higher on the Sociability scale or the EASI. As is documented below, women are closer and more personal in their contacts with others, and we know about men's and women's sociability from research on gender roles. Of all the temperaments, sociability is the most central to masculine and feminine roles, for it involves social interaction. We refer to *traditional* gender roles, for these are the model behaviors that allow us to characterize men and women generally. There are strong currents of change, and the descriptions may not apply in a generation or two, but they do apply today.

Masculine and Feminine Roles

The traditional masculine role emphasizes the individual achievement and independence of action and judgment. The notion of "rugged individualism" may be a myth, but it is a myth that partly defines the ascribed masculine role,

TABLE 7.5   THE IRRITABILITY SCALE OF THE BUSS—DURKEE INVENTORY

---

1.   I lose my temper easily but get over it quickly
2F. I am always patient with others
3.   I am irritated a great deal more than people are aware of
4.   It makes my blood boil to have somebody make fun of me
5F. If someone doesn't treat me right, I don't let it annoy me
6.   Sometimes people bother me just by being around
7.   I often feel like a powder keg ready to explode
8.   I sometimes carry a chip on my shoulder
9.   I can't help being a little rude to people I don't like
10F. I don't let a lot of unimportant things irritate me
11. Lately, I have been kind of grouchy

---

and so it is one determinant of men's behavior. The traditional male role also emphasizes getting along in groups, especially submerging one's own selfish interests in favor of group goals. Thus men's gregariousness is channeled into participation in primary groups that have a specific work or recreational purpose:

> Men engage in collective instrumental action more often than women. Relations between men are governed by two apparently contradictory orientations: solidarity and peership, on the one hand, and competition for jobs, prestige, competence, and women, on the other. These tendencies are regulated by norms governing their appropriateness. The norms make it clear whether the goal of solidarity or of competence takes precedence in a particular situation. [Holter, 1970, p. 236]

This quotation highlights men's ambivalence in primary groups. Their self-esteem and status depend mainly on individual achievement and success in competition. These factors are squarely opposed by desires to work and play with others (especially men) and to be liked and respected as a "member of the team." It follows directly from our theory that a man's sociability temperament will help determine how he resolves the conflict. More sociable men tend to renounce selfish ambitions for group goals; their sociability forces them to value affiliation and group respect more than status achieved at the cost of rejection by the group. Less sociable men are not as deterred by the threat of rejection and should therefore be more ready to give up group goals for individual ones. The outcast wealthy man who "laughs all the way to the bank" should, in terms of our theory, be less sociable in temperament.

The traditional feminine role involves less individual achievement and more dependence on men. Primary groups—work or recreational—are not as important for women *as groups*. For example, in a men's bridge club, the emphasis is on sharpening card-playing skills, competing, and on winning. In the typical women's bridge club, the skillful and competitive aspects are less important, and the game is more of an excuse for meeting new persons, seeing old friends, and exchanging gossip. This is not to say that men do not gossip or that women do not compete and acquire skill at bridge, but the differences between men's and women's bridge clubs illustrate a general norm: men's primary groups emphasize the function or purpose of the group, whereas women's primary groups emphasize personal interaction (much as in a dyad).

In their relationships with others, women are traditionally more tender, sympathetic, and understanding. In comparison to men, they look at the other person more often, and speak of more personal topics. It is crucial for the traditional woman to be liked and admired for her appearance and pleasant behavior. And her response to others is complementary: warm, receptive, and giving of attention, praise, affection, and nurturance. If there is a conflict between individual status and being liked and accepted, she tends to resolve it by renouncing the struggle for status. In a traditional marriage, the woman sacrifices her career or vocation for that of her husband. She is left with the options of making a career of home and family and of obtaining vicarious satisfaction from her husband's vocational success (for example, being the wife of a physician or a well-known politician). Most men's identities require individual achievement and primary group membership, whereas most women's identities require offering and receiving attention, affection, and understanding:

> Realistically, most women participate in the success of men in their roles as wives, and for most women that appears to be enough. Simultaneously women have also internalized a set of discretely feminine values which receive less public attention and reward. They conceive of their achievements differently than men, and they evaluate their success as persons in terms of feminine criteria as well as the more obvious masculine values. Women do not perceive rearing children as a secondary accomplishment and they do perceive themselves as successful when they enjoy love (and power and status) from their husbands and children and when they give love and support. They conceive of this as their major function, and their success in affiliative relationships defines their personal success. [Bardwick, 1971, p. 145]

Although gender roles are changing, most men and women still adopt traditional roles. This means that the norms spelled out above hold for most persons. For men, group solidarity and individual achievement are primary, dyadic interaction secondary. For women, close personal relationships are primary, and group solidarity and individual achievement are secondary. In strictly *social* terms, women are more oriented toward individuals, and men are more oriented toward groups of persons. In terms of our perspective on sociability as involving attention, affection, and help, women not only express their sociability differently than men but are also more sociable.

What is the explanation for these gender differences? One approach suggests that they are innate—built into the "wiring diagrams" of men and women. The alternative approach suggests that they are learned during socialization. Thus there are two theories of gender differences in sociability, one emphasizing biology and the other emphasizing socialization.

Biogrammar

The term *biogrammar* was coined by Tiger and Fox (1971) to refer to the rules—analogous to rules of syntax—that underlie the behavior of animals and man. They assume that the differences between men and women are (1) the product of natural selection, and (2) part of a basic primate pattern, with some uniquely human addition. The flavor of their approach can be sensed from a few selected quotations:

> The point is not that man has shed or risen above his primate nature, but simply that he is a unique primate with a unique primate nature. [p. 8]

> At first glance the bewildering variety of customs suggests that humans can invent any kind of culture with any kind of process. But on closer scrutinizing it turns out that while the variations are almost endless, the themes are restricted in number, and are, in all cultures, the fixed points on which the system turns. The story can be told in many different ways, but the plot and the characters remain the same. [pp. 10–11]

> In sum: we behave culturally because it is in our nature to behave culturally, because natural selection has produced an animal that has to behave culturally, that has to invent rules, make myths, speak languages, and form men's clubs. . . . [p. 20]

The last phrase is especially appropriate to our topic. Tiger and Fox believe that men and women behave differently because they are wired to do so. The basic pattern was laid down during the evolution of primates, and innate gender differences were enhanced by early man's hunting behavior. To the argument that man is now no longer a hunter but a farmer and manufacturer, Tiger and Fox reply:

> We remain Upper Paleolithic hunters, fine-honed machines designed for the efficient pursuit of game. Nothing worth noting has happened in our evolutionary history since we left off hunting and took to the fields and the towns—nothing except perhaps a little selection for immunity to epidemics, and probably not even that. "Man the hunter" is not an episode in our distant past: we are still the hunter, incarcerated, domesticated, polluted, crowded, and bemused. [p. 21]

Finally, Tiger and Fox (1971) speculate about the topic of this section, gender differences in social interaction:

> ... in general, females occupy themselves with interpersonal matters involving face-to-face encounters and focusing upon subjects that have to do with the bearing, nurturing, and training of the young, and with the establishment and management of dwellings and other immediate surroundings. By contrast, males involve themselves with groups and activities that extend directly to the whole community. [p. 104]

As they point out, this description roughly fits traditional male and female roles. Their theoretical contribution is to insist that this is the basic primate pattern, supplemented only by the division of labor involved in hunting by groups of men. Tiger and Fox thus provide a rational basis for regarding gender differences in sociability as being innate: a history of such differences that extends back through early man (the hunter) to our primate forebears. These enduring, adaptive tendencies should surely be inherited, and evidence for inheritance would provide an empirical basis for the notion of a *primate biogrammar*. But there are other ways of testing the theory: universality and time of appearance.

UNIVERSALITY

If Tiger and Fox are correct, gender differences in sociability should be species-wide. Differences among cultures should be minimal, and the basic primate pattern should prevail in all cultures. This hypothesis is difficult to test. There are some data from anthropological research, but they are little more than rough descriptions and case illustrations. There are variations in gender roles within societies and from one society to the next, but the general stereotypes appear in all societies. So the issue remains unresolved.

There is also a clear implication of an *enduring* pattern of gender roles, one that does not change over generations or even millenia. Tiger and Fox believe that human nature was laid down hundreds of thousands of years ago, and it has not changed since then. This contention flies in the face of the many changes in gender roles during the last 100 years and also the current turmoil in pursuit of more radical changes. Again, data are sparse and subject to varying interpretations. Can women's traditional role change when child care is available and physical strength is no longer crucial? The results of a recent cross-cultural study have been interpreted in the affirmative:

> For me, the important implication of the differences between American sex stereotypes and child-rearing orientation as compared with those of the European

nations studies is that there *can* be differences, differences that begin to abandon the narrow definitions of sex roles held over from harsher and less civilized times. [Block, 1973, p. 520]

The second corollary of the Tiger-Fox theory is that gender differences in kind of interaction are inherited. The inheritance may be sex-linked, which suggests a pattern of father-daughter and mother-son correlations. Another possibility is that the gender differences are sex-*related,* as in baldness. Men's baldness is due to a genetic disposition that is potentiated by male sex hormones, and a similar pattern might prevail for gender differences in sociability. There is only very indirect evidence on this point (see below) and no evidence suggesting sex-linked inheritance.

If the gender differences are innate, their first appearance should be genetically determined. The most straightforward hypothesis is that gender differences in sociability will appear as soon as they can be assessed: during infancy or, at the latest, in the nursery school period.

Of course, sex hormones may play an important role, and the developmental timing of gender differences offers indirect evidence of hormonal involvement. If gender differences do not appear until puberty, sex hormones may be involved.

Socialization

There is extensive literature on the acquisition of gender roles (see Maccoby, 1966; Goslin, 1969; Bardwick, 1971), and we merely sketch the high points. From early childhood, the toys and games of boys are different from those of girls. There are gender differences in toys and games in all cultures, and it could be argued that they merely reflect innate, universal differences. But the *kinds* of gender differences vary considerably, making the biological hypothesis tenuous. For example, in Western societies girls play with dolls but boys do not; in most technologically backward societies dolls are less prevalent and, where present, are not limited to girls.

Children are furnished with appropriate gender models: mothers and fathers, older brothers and sisters, and the heroes of literature, history, and sports. In traditional terms, most boys want to grow up to be athletes, firemen, or astronauts; most girls want to be actresses, nurses, or mothers. When children imitate the gender-appropriate models, they are strongly rewarded; otherwise, they are unrewarded or even punished. A girl is chided for being a tomboy, and a boy is attacked verbally or physically for being a sissy. When a parent is absent—through either death or divorce—there is often a problem in the children's gender role identification (Biller, 1971). There are few data about the effects of inappropriate role models and virtually none on incorrect shaping procedures, but the general consensus is that their effects are strong (Maccoby & Masters, 1970; Block, 1973).

All these influences push boys and girls in the direction of the traditional gender roles of the society. In America, this means that boys become instrumental and achieving, and they direct their social tendencies mainly toward primary groups. Girls become expressive and nurturant, and they direct their social tendencies mainly toward dyadic interactions.

Socialization theory is not easy to test because it has so many implications. We shall discuss the three most important ones.

CULTURAL DIFFERENCES

Socialization theory takes a position directly opposite to that of biogrammar theory. The former suggests that there are clear variations among different cultures and that the variations are most striking when "modern" and "primitive" cultures are compared. But even contemporary Western cultures show differences, and it has been found that American child rearing emphasizes competition among boys more than does European child rearing (Block, 1973).

Socialization theory suggests that time periods as short as a generation should make a difference, and a few hundred years should see marked changes in the pattern of gender differences. Again, there is no way of checking this hypothesis. There have certainly been changes over time, and the present generation has accelerated the speed of change. It could be argued, however, that these are minor variations of no great significance, slight variations in the way different actors play the same part.

IMPACT OF SOCIALIZATION

We mentioned earlier that parental absence (especially the father) affects the gender-related behavior of the children. But it could be argued that such absence represents a major deviation of the "normally expected environment" of the child. Innate characteristics occur only in the usual species-wide context, which for children is a complete family. Also, as noted earlier, there are no unequivocal data on the effects of inappropriate role models or shaping.

TIME OF APPEARANCE

According to socialization theory, gender differences in social behavior should appear only after gender role training begins. Unfortunately, the theory is less

TABLE 7.6 GENDER DIFFERENCES IN SOCIABILITY DURING INFANCY

Measure	Number of subjects Males	Females	Age	Differences	Reference
Pupil dilation to social vs. nonsocial stimuli	(30)		1, 2, and 4 mo	None at any age	Fitzgerald, 1968
Smiling Eyes on mother	(30)		0 – 3 mo	None At 3 wk, boys looked at mother more than girls; none at 3 mo	Moss, 1967
Ratings during play with mother present	33	32	13 mo	Girls return to mother faster, more often, and touch mother more	Goldberg & Lewis, 1969
Ratings of "cuddling"	(37)		0 – 18 mo	None	Schaffer & Emerson, 1964
Preference for cuddly toys or toys with face-like features	40	40	13 mo	None, but in two experiments, girls prefer cuddly toys more	Jacklin, Maccoby, & Dick, 1973

TABLE 7.7 GENDER DIFFERENCES IN SOCIABILITY DURING THE PRESCHOOL PERIOD

Measure	Number of subjects		Age	Differences	Reference
	Males	Females			
Ratings of nurturance and dependency	19	22	3 – 4 yr	None	Hartup & Keller, 1960
Ratings of interactions with mothers for warmth, dependency, and independence	21	19	3 – 5 yr	None	Hatfield et al., 1967
11 wk of observations during free play	(39)		2 – 4 yr	For 2-yr-olds: none For 4-yr-olds: boys more frequently interacted with others	Hagman, 1933
Ratings of sociability, affection, and interest in group	(132)		1 – 5 yr	None	Berne, 1931

Observations of number of children played with and number of strong friendships	21	19	2 – 5 yr	None	Green, 1933 (a)
Analysis of talking and drawing	20	20	2 – 4 yr	Girls mention persons and draw persons more often than boys	Goodenough, 1957

175

TABLE 7.8 GENDER DIFFERENCES IN SOCIABILITY IN LATER CHILDHOOD—ADOLESCENCE

Measure	Number of subjects Males	Females	Age	Differences	Reference
Teachers' ratings of gregariousness	(102)		6 – 7 yr	Boys more gregarious than girls	Digman, 1963
Self–report and teachers' ratings of "socialness"	199	207	7 – 8 yr	None	Walker, 1967
Sociometric rating of friendliness	(1429)		6 – 10 yr	Girls friendlier than boys	Tuddenham, 1952
Teachers' ratings of need for nurturance	(48)		5 – 14 yr	Girls have a greater need at all ages	Sanford et al., 1948
Social orientation self–report	33	16	10 – 12 yr retested at 16 – 18 yr	None at 10 – 12 yr; girls were more socially oriented at 16 – 18 yr	Carlson, 1965
Self–report of interest in interpersonal relations	(36)		7 – 16 yr	Girls reported more interpersonal interest	Winker, 1949

Interview	1045	2005	11 – 18 yr	Boys instrumental, vocation important; girls expressive, stress personal relations, intimacy	Douvan & Adelson, 1966
Asked what their biggest problem is	(4000)		10 – 19 yr	Girls were concerned with more interpersonal problems	Adams, 1964
Observations during free groupings in high school	27	27	14 – 18 yr	Boys seek wider range of companions	Wellman, 1926

177

TABLE 7.9   GENDER DIFFERENCES IN SOCIABILITY IN ADULTS

Measure	Number of subjects Males	Number of subjects Females	Age	Differences	Reference
Preference for sending personal vs. task oriented messages in an experimental group	48	48	Adult	Women prefer sending personal messages	Exline, 1962
Visual interaction in experimental groups	48	48	Adult	Women look at people more	Exline, 1963
Maintaining eye contact with interviewer	40	40	Adult	Women maintain eye contact longer	Exline et al., 1965
Typewriting interaction between two individuals	43	43	Adult	Women asked more intimate questions and disclosed more about themselves	Sermat & Smyth, 1973
Self-report of social orientation	(1300)		Adult	Women more socially oriented	Bennett & Cohen, 1959

Edwards Personal Preference Schedule Need for nurturance and need for affiliation	Adult	Women have greater need for nurturance and affiliation than men	Spangler & Thomas, 1962
Sociability Scale of the EASI Temperament Survey	Adult	Women consistently more sociable than men	Buss et al., 1973

specific about the precise time. It might be as early as the nursery school period if the training were intense and the appropriate behaviors easy to acquire.
At first glance, this possibility is slight, for social behaviors are acquired slowly
relative to other instrumental acts. A more likely period is late childhood—
grammar-school years of ages six to 12. Additional gender role training should
enhance the differences, so that with each passing year, they become more distinct.

Research Findings

The time of first appearance of gender differences in sociability is an important
issue for biological and socialization theories. The appropriate data are
presented in four tables: one each for infancy, preschool age, later childhood
and adolescence, and adulthood.

Only one study reported a gender difference in infancy (see Table 7.6).
Goldberg and Lewis (1963) found that among 13-month olds, girls appeared
more attached to their mothers. It is difficult to square this study with all the
other research on infants, which reveals no difference between males and females. Of special interest was Fitzgerald's (1968) use of pupillary dilation as
an objective measure of interest in social stimuli (woman's face, mother's face)
versus nonsocial stimuli (checkerboard, triangle). The infants showed more
interest in (more pupillary dilation to) the social than the nonsocial stimuli,
but there were no gender differences at one, two, or four months of age.

The results for the preschool period are essentially the same (see Table 7.7).
In one study, four-year old *boys* were more sociable (Hagman, 1933), but in
another *girls* drew more persons and talked more about people, which are indirect indices of sociability (Goodenough, 1957). The remaining research
found no gender difference, and this appears to be the safest conclusion to
draw from the evidence on preschool children.

Gender differences appear unequivocally during later childhood, and they
are more stable in adolescence (see Table 7.8). At the risk of overinterpreting
the data, we suggest that the differences fit the pattern described earlier. Boys
were found to be more sociable than girls in two studies (Digman, 1963; and
Wellman, 1926). In both instances boys were seeking a wider range of acquaintances, a tendency consistent with the male predilection for primary
groups in preference to dyads. In the six studies that found girls to be more sociable, it was in the direction of nurturance, interpersonal interest, and intimacy. This fits the female pattern of seeking the closeness of dyads in
preference to the wider, looser bonds of primary groups.

By adulthood, the pattern is firmly established, and all the evidence shows
women to be more sociable. We believe that the male preference for primary
groups does not show up simply because it is not examined. The adult re-

search is more experimentally oriented, and the greater intimacy of women emerges clearly, as reflected in greater eye contact and more personal messages.

How do these data bear on theories of gender differences? Gender differences certainly do *not* appear as early as they can be measured, which weakens biological theory. But perhaps clear differences do not emerge until early puberty. This means that they may be linked to the upsurge of sex hormones, which is consistent with the biological hypothesis.

Concerning socialization theory, it assumes that gender role training should produce differences in sociability by later childhood. Such differences do begin to emerge in late childhood, but the precise time period is uncertain (see Table 7.8). During the progression from childhood to adolescence to adulthood, males and females diverge more and more in sociability. This increment in gender differences is precisely what socialization theory predicts. Thus socialization theory is supported by the developmental data, and the best that can be said for biological theory is that the hormonal hypothesis has not been ruled out.

CONCLUSIONS

We found no evidence for a gender difference in impulsivity. Of course, the status of impulsivity as a temperament is doubtful, and we cannot be sure precisely what impulsivity is. We do know that it must be some combination of inhibitory control, decision time, persistence, and sensation seeking, and there is no male-female difference in any of these variables. Males might differ from females on any of these factors, whether or not the impulsivity is an inborn disposition. So we must conclude that there is no gender difference in impulsivity.

Gender differences are well established for the other three temperaments, at least for Americans. Boys are more active than girls, and women are both more fearful and more personally interactive than men. Our examination of the first appearance of these sex differences led us to conclude that they are caused by socialization practices. Boys are encouraged to play more vigorous games than girls, which can account for the fact that boys are more active. If this is true, boys and girls should be equal in activity when play is excluded. Similarly, when adult physical games are excluded, men should be more active than women. And cultural patterns should reveal that in some societies men are less active than women, and in others men and women are equally active. None of these three implications has been examined, but all three follow directly from the notion that socialization practices account for the greater activity of males in our society.

We also assume that the greater fearfulness of women and their stronger interpersonal ties both derive from gender role training. If this is true, there should be variations from one society to the next in both fearfulness and sociability. It also follows that as societies evolve, gender differences in personality dispositions should also change. Consider the *avant garde* end of the distribution of American women. As they become more liberated from older, stereotyped sex roles, they are eliminating many of their fears, identifying more strongly with peer groups, and engaging in more active sports (both amateur and professional). These trends are moving them closer to the traditional masculine role (courage, strong group ties, and physical activity), thereby narrowing gender differences in emotionality, sociability, and activity.

At first glance, our stand on these issues might appear paradoxical. We assert that there are inherited personality dispositions but at the same time deny inborn gender differences. Perhaps the paradox is more apparent than real, for the assertion of inborn gender differences requires additional data beyond those needed to sustain the presence of temperaments. There must be facts showing that infant boys and girls differ in temperament as soon as it can be measured. Or adolescent males and females must suddenly become different in temperament, reflecting the impact of hormonal differences. Or there should be direct evidence of the presence of a sex-linked trait (such as color blindness): a quantitative excess of males in such proportion that the involvement of the XX versus XY chromosomal pairs appears necessary. Any of these—first appearance in infancy, first appearance in adolescence, or appropriate sex ratios—would make a case for the genetic hypothesis. But where such data are available, they are opposed to the genetic hypothesis. So we must conclude that the gender differences in three temperaments are caused by the same socialization practices that produce other kinds of sex-role divergence.

Our stance is a conservative one. In the past, acquired sex roles have been given the status of inherited dispositions. The notion that women are *temperamentally* different from men has been used to justify bigotry and denial of opportunity. Given the sexism that pervades most societies, it seems fairest to be conservative in seeking the causes of gender differences in personality dispositions. This holds even when the personality dispositions are inborn. In our view, the distribution of temperaments is the same for both males and females in any given population. Socialization practices then selectively reinforce one direction or another and produce divergence between men and women.

CHAPTER

COMBINATIONS
OF
TEMPERAMENTS

Each of the previous four chapters described a temperament, stated the evidence for regarding it as a temperament, and discussed theoretical implications. Although it was necessary to discuss each temperament separately to understand it better, we acknowledge that temperaments do not occur in isolation but in combinations. Theoretically, all combinations of two, three, or four temperaments *might* occur, but this does not mean that they exist in nature. And not all the combinations that do exist are likely to be identified because there has been so little research on temperaments.

We shall focus on those combinations that have been identified by researchers and clinicians. An example of a combination identified by researchers is *introversion-extraversion*, which comprises sociability and impulsivity; a clinical example is *hyperkinesis*, which combines activity and impulsivity. It should come as no surprise that the temperaments are closely linked with adjustment. A child who is high on both impulsivity and emotionality, for example, is likely to have problems in adapting to pressures for control of affect.

183

The basic assumption of this chapter is that temperament theory offers an explanation of some commonly seen patterns of behavior. Four temperaments are clearly insufficient to account for the many patterns of personality, but this point is relevant only when the temperaments are considered singly. *Combinations* of temperaments yield a larger number of patterns, which is more consistent with the variety observed in everyday life. This is not to say that temperaments, singly or in combination, offer a *complete* explanation of personality patterns, only that they offer a new way of accounting for a significant portion of the variance.

In attempting to identify meaningful combinations of temperaments, we have made the simplifying assumption that the continuous distribution of each temperament can be split in half to yield those above average and those below average on each temperament. For present purposes, an average amount of temperament is ignored.

The exposition is divided into combinations of two temperaments and combinations of three temperaments; many more of the former have been identified. In each instance, if a temperament is ignored, it is assumed to be unimportant in identifying the pattern. Thus introversion-extraversion is defined by a combination of sociability and impulsivity. An extravert (high on both sociability and impulsivity) may be more or less active, but the amount of activity temperament does not bear on introversion-extraversion.

COMBINATIONS OF TWO TEMPERAMENTS

Activity and Impulsivity

A person who is high in both activity and impulsivity suffers from a problem that can be described in terms of an automobile metaphor: not only does he have an extremely powerful engine (activity) that requires very strong brakes, but the brakes are insufficient (impulsivity). This syndrome has been identified clinically under the names *hyperactivity* and *hyperkinesis*. We prefer the latter term because it does not equate the problem solely with an excess of activity.

The hyperkinetic child is not merely overactive; he is excessively active in contexts that require relative immobility, quiet, and focused attention. The problem is not so much one of excessive motion per se as a lack of control. A high-active child who is average or below in impulsivity will not be seen as hyperkinetic. He will be able to suppress temporarily his rapid tempo, delaying the explosion of energy until a more appropriate time. The impulsive child simply cannot command such control over his level of activity.

Hyperkinesis is a serious childhood problem, one that has been studied intensively (see Fish, 1971; Kenny et al., 1971; and Werry & Sprague, 1970). It wanes with maturity as children slowly attain control. They learn not only to suppress motility in places such as the schoolroom and library but also to organize their activity into socially acceptable channels and to miniaturize it, progressing from bounding around the room to restless fiddling with clothes, hair, or pencils. For many hyperkinetic children, however, *distractibility* remains a serious problem even into adolescence, and many hyperkinetic boys become delinquents when they reach adolescence (Weiss et al., 1971). These facts are consistent with the view that the core problem is one of control (impulsivity) rather than solely of excessive energy (activity).

Temperament theory may contribute to a better understanding of hyperkinesis, which includes not only children high in two temperaments but also children of very low intelligence and those with at least minimal brain damage. Surely it would help to separate hyperkinetic children into two types. One type includes children with various biological deficits (organic brain damage, etc.); the excessive, uncontrolled activity is merely symptomatic of an underlying neurological disorder. The other type consists of biologically normal children who are temperamentally active and impulsive; they may need special handling because of their personality dispositions, but ordinarily they should not be referred to clinics. Perhaps this distinction will help to disentangle the mixed results obtained when amphetamines are administered to "hyperactive" children (Fish, 1971).

The metaphor of too much engine and not enough brakes also fits the description of *mania*. This is an adult disorder marked by incessant overactivity and hasty, impetuous behavior. There is an established hereditary component (see Buss, 1966, for relevant literature), and perhaps what is inherited is a combination of two temperaments, activity and impulsivity.

This discussion of mania and hyperkinesis bears on the issue of whether impulsivity is a temperament. As we noted in Chapter 6, the case is weak. But hyperkinesis is coming to be considered primarily a problem of impulse control, not of excessive activity. The paradoxical finding that hyperkinetic children are helped by a *stimulant* drug (amphetamine) is turning out to be not a paradox at all. Amphetamine and kindred stimulants help the child to focus his attention and perhaps to exercise greater control over his own behavior. So, insofar as such drugs work, they appear to affect impulsivity, not activity. No one suggests that hyperkinesis is learned early in childhood, and there is general agreement that it is a constitutional problem. Furthermore, the inheritance of mania has been established. These facts and interpretations suggest that we should not foreclose the possibility that impulsivity is a temperament.

Activity and Emotionality

The combination of high activity and low emotionality describes a classic American hero: the strong, silent man who gets the job done with a minimum of fuss and bother. This description is not fictional; there are persons who fit it. They are much sought after by the military, and they are especially valued in the fields of business, engineering, and the space programs. Their lack of emotionality tends to render them relatively unflappable, and their high level of activity guarantees productivity. Such persons can be relied on to get the job done.

The opposite pattern—*low activity and high emotionality*— would seem to be maladaptive. It appears to be characteristic of neurotic or agitated depressives, whose lack of coping behavior is accompanied by intense fears of dying or of being abandoned. It is sheer speculation to suggest that this combination of temperaments underlies agitated depression, but the notion is testable and should be checked out.

Activity and Sociability

These two temperaments are correlated, and the reasons for the correlation were discussed earlier. In spite of the correlation, there are persons who are high in one and low on the other. The pattern of *high activity and low sociability* is frequent enough to identify a particular kind of person. Such a person directs his energies into solitary activities, avoiding social interaction whenever possible. In track he runs the marathon or the cross-country race rather than the more crowded sprints. He prefers the solitude of his own lathe to an assembly line, of his own desk to an open office, or of the woods and farm to the city. He is best fit to be a pioneer, pushing into uncharted regions and using his abundant energy to master a relatively unpopulated environment. He is a loner with energy to burn, and we would be surprised if every reader did not know at least one or two persons that fit this description.

More frequent and certainly more noticeable is the combination of *high activity and high sociability*. Such a person uses his exuberant energy to attend many meetings, make new friends, form new groups, and organize those around him into more coherent assemblies. His need for action is strong, but it can be tempered by his need for people. Thus on a mountain-climbing adventure, he will want to push on when others are exhausted but will do so only if others can be convinced. Such a person is usually well adjusted and liked by others. One danger is that he might easily become meddlesome and intrusive. It is difficult to maintain privacy when such a person is around because he finds it difficult to understand why people want to rest or to be alone, or both. Again, this is no fictional description, and the reader should be able to furnish examples from among his acquaintances.

Emotionality and Impulsivity

High emotionality would seem to predispose a person toward maladjustment. Whether it is fear or anger, the emotion needs to be controlled. High emotionality intensifies the problem of control, and control is the crucial issue for the temperament of impulsivity. Thus when high emotionality combines with either extreme of impulsivity, adjustment problems become more likely.

One combination has been clearly identified for women: *high emotionality (fear) and high impulsivity*. Such a person tends to be childish, complaining, impetuous, seductive, and possessed of numerous bodily complaints. The syndrome is called *hysteria*, and it is far more prevalent among women than among men.

When the combination of high emotionality and high impulsivity occurs in men, the problem is more of controlling anger. Such men are truculent, troublesome, and difficult to control. Their fiery nature usually brings them into conflict with others, often the law. It may appear paradoxical that the same temperamental pattern renders a woman neurotic and a man incendiary, but we believe that the difference is nicely explained by gender role training in emotionality (see Chapter 7).

The combination of high emotionality (fear or rage) and low impulsivity may well fit another kind of maladjustment: psychosomatic problems. Temperament cannot supply a complete explanation for such bodily disturbances, if indeed a full explanation is possible at present, but this particular temperamental pattern does describe many psychosomatic patients. On the one hand, they tend to be fearful or, alternatively, easily moved to rage. On the other hand, they are restrained, cautious, and overinhibited. It has been speculated that they quickly prepare for violent action (the emotions underlying flight or fight) but then do not act. This is precisely the behavior of a person of high emotionality (fearful or easily angered) and low impulsivity (cautious, inhibited).

The last combination of emotionality and impulsivity consists of persons *low on both*. They ordinarily do not suffer from maladjustment. Quite the contrary, they can usually find a neat niche in society and fit it beautifully. They should be easy to socialize because there is little emotionality to control and a strong inhibitory mechanism to use if needed. Such persons tend to learn all the "externals" needed for coping with the exigencies of everyday life. They tend to be neat, orderly, cautious, and inhibited; they make good librarians and accountants. The problem—if there is a problem—is that they may lack the sparkle and zest that mark persons with at least average emotionality or impulsivity. The low emotional, overinhibited person may not cause trouble for society or for himself, but he might bore you to death.

Emotionality and Sociability

A very sociable person, by definition, needs the things that only others can furnish, and he has a strong desire to be with others. A highly emotional person, by definition, is easily aroused, and the major emotion is often fear. A person who is *high in both emotionality and sociability* tends to be socially anxious. He is strongly motivated to seek the company of others but is inhibited by strong fear. The apprehension may concern rejection, ridicule, or shame, but whatever its specific content, the fear does retard social interaction. Such persons usually show paradoxical social behavior over time. They initially appear cool, reserved, and unsociable, but this bland unconcern for others presumably overlays an intense ambivalence: a conflict between a desire to socialize and a fear of possible aversive consequences. With the passage of time, the fear usually habituates. With increasing knowledge of the other and deepening friendship, the socially anxious person discovers that there is nothing to fear. This removes the negative end of the ambivalence, allowing the strong need for others to become manifest. Thus the paradox of initial shyness and reserve that is followed by close friendship and relaxed socializing may be attributed to the combination of two temperaments: high emotionality and high sociability.

The combination of *high emotionality (fear) and low sociability* may portend difficulties in adjustment. The low sociability means that others have little to offer and there is no reason to seek their presence. The high emotionality means that the aversive aspects of social interaction become magnified. Thus others are not a source of reward and they are to be feared. The likely outcome is a tendency to be not only shy but also seclusive and isolated. This pattern of behavior has been called *schizoid* because it is typical of the unsocial tendencies seen in many schizophrenics.

Sociability and Impulsivity

The combination of these two temperaments comprises the best known and most researched pattern of personality. The person who is high in both sociability and impulsivity is called an extravert, and the person who is low in both is called an introvert. These patterns have been described repeatedly in the literature:

> The typical extravert is sociable, likes parties, has many friends, needs to have people to talk to, and does not like reading or studying by himself. He craves, takes chances, often sticks his neck out, acts on the spur of the moment, and is generally an impulsive individual. He is fond of practical jokes, always has a ready answer, and generally likes change; he is carefree, easygoing, optimistic, and "likes to laugh and be merry." He prefers to keep moving and doing things, tends to be aggressive and loses his temper quickly; altogether his feelings are not kept under tight control, and he is not always a reliable person.
>
> The typical introvert is a quiet, retiring sort of person, introspective, fond of books rather than people; he is reserved and distant except to intimate friends. He tends to plan ahead, "looks before he leaps," and mistrusts the impulse of the moment. He does not like excitement, takes matters of everyday life with proper seriousness, and likes a well-ordered mode of life. He keeps his feelings under close control, seldom behaves in an aggressive manner, and does not lose his temper easily. He is reliable, somewhat pessimistic and places great value on ethical standards. [Eysenck & Rachman, 1965, p. 19]

Eysenck (1947, 1957, 1967, 1970) has developed a comprehensive theory of introversion-extraversion, which attempts to integrate a variety of personality, clinical, and experimental findings. His theory and his research have generated much controversy, especially concerning the relationship of experimental data to theory. Most of these issues, although of considerable importance for the study of personality, are not relevant to the topic at hand, the descriptive aspects of introversion-extraversion. Our discussion is limited to these aspects of introversion-extraversion: measures of it, whether it is unitary or dual, and whether sociability and impulsivity are best combined or kept separate.

MEASURES

The primary measuring tools have been self-report questionnaires, either the Maudsley Personality Inventory (Eysenck, 1959) or its revision, the Eysenck Personality Inventory (Eysenck & Eysenck, 1963b). Eysenck's first self-report questionnaire, consisting of 39 items of neurotic symptoms, was administered to 700 hospitalized neurotics. One factor derived from an analysis of these data was dysthymic versus hysteric symptoms. Eysenck (1947) concluded that "the dysthymic-hysteric dichotomy [is] closely related to Jung's introversion-extraversion dichotomy" (p. 73).

In 1953, Eysenck hypothesized and found introversion-extraversion to be a major second-order factor of Guilford's (1940) personality questionnaire. Guilford's Rhathymia scale loaded most highly on introversion-extraversion, but the General Activity and Ascendance versus Submission scales also contributed to it. Eysenck (1953) concluded that "there is ample evidence to support the view that the R (Rhathymia) scale is a promising measure of extraversion." In 1956, Eysenck eliminated repetitive items from Guilford's Rhathymia scale and used the remaining 24 items as the extraversion scale of his Maudsley Personality Inventory. The five highest-loading extraversion items in this study were the following:

Would you rate yourself as a lively person?

Do you like to mix socially with people?

Are you inclined to be shy in the presence of the opposite sex?

Do you prefer action to planning for action?

Are you inclined to take your work casually, that is, as a matter of course?

Even at this early point in time, the Rhathymia scale included clear sociability items ("Do you like to mix socially with people?"), clear impulsivity items ("Do you prefer action to planning for action?"), and items that involve both sociability and impulsivity ("Would you rate yourself as a lively person?"). In 1964, Eysenck and Eysenck refactored and restandardized the Maudsley Personality Inventory, but the Eysenck Personality Inventory that emerged was essentially the same. Thus introversion-extraversion as measured by either of these inventories is similar to Guilford's Rhathymia scale.

Two Factors

Throughout the considerable work by Eysenck and others, introversion-extraversion has been treated as a unitary dimension, but Carrigan (1960) suggested that at least two factors underlie extraversion. In 1963, Eysenck and Eysenck found two clusters of extraversion items. One cluster was *sociability* (highest-loading item: "are you inclined to keep in the background on social occasions?"); the other cluster was *impulsivity* (highest-loading item: "are you inclined to stop and think things over before acting?"). Eysenck and Eysenck found a correlation of .47 between the 14 highest-loading sociability items and 14 highest-loading impulsivity items. All items loaded at least minimally on a general introversion-extraversion factor. This may be due to the inclusion of many items that involve both sociability and impulsivity, for example:

Do you enjoy practical jokes?

Do you like to play pranks on others?

Do you like to be in a situation with plenty of excitement and bustle?

Of the 14 sociability items and 14 impulsivity items, only 6 items in each cluster had a factor loading above .30 on its respective cluster; that is, the majority of the items were not representative of the appropriate cluster of items, either sociability or impulsivity. The inclusion of low-loading items may have artifically inflated the correlation between sociability and impulsivity in Eysenck and Eysenck's study. These low-loading items appear to involve *both* sociability and impulsivity:

Low-loading "sociability" items

Can you usually let yourself go and have a hilariously good time at a gay (lively) party?

Does your natural reserve generally stand in your way when you want to start a conversation with an attractive stranger of the opposite sex?

Do you enjoy opportunities for conversation so that you rarely miss a chance of talking to a stranger?

Low-loading "impulsivity" items

Would you rate yourself as a happy-go-lucky individual?

Are you ordinarily a carefree individual?

Is your motto to take matters of everyday life with proper seriousness rather than to "laugh and be merry?"

The "sociability" items have an impulsivity component because they ask about inhibitory control. The sociability component in the "impulsivity" items is more speculative: "happy-go-lucky," "carefree," and, "laugh and be merry" are usually placed in a social perspective. We suggest that the inclusion of such items artificially inflated the correlation between sociability and impulsivity in Eysenck and Eysenck's (1963a) study. The same argument applies to the research of Farley (1970), who found an average correlation of .39 between Eysenck's sociability and impulsivity items in five adult samples.

What would happen if we used only the "pure," unconfounded impulsivity items from Eysenck's extraversion scales? The correlations between sociability and impulsivity should drop. This prediction was borne out in a series of studies by Horn at the University of Texas. He analyzed his Maudsley Personality Inventory (MPI) data separately by impulsivity and sociability. Some of the highest-loading sociability and impulsivity items in the Eysenck and Eysenck (1963) study are not on the MPI: and some of the items of the MPI are not in the 1963 study. The MPI items chosen by Horn to represent sociability and impulsivity were the following:

Sociability

  4. Do you usually take the initiative in making new friends?

  9. Would you be very unhappy if you were prevented from making numerous social contacts?

14. Are you inclined to keep in the background on social occasions?

20. Do you like to mix socially with people?

22. Are you inclined to limit your acquaintances to a select few?

36. Are you inclined to keep quiet when out in a social group?

Impulsivity

  1. Are you happiest when you get involved in some project that calls for rapid action?

  5. Are you inclined to be quick and sure in your actions?

12. Do you prefer action to planning for action?

18. Are you inclined to be overconscientious?

34. Would you rate yourself as a happy-go-lucky individual?

42. Are you inclined to take your work casually, that is, as a matter of course?

In a sample of 41 college and 63 college women (Cohen & Horn, 1974), the sociability and impulsivity items correlated .10 for men and .22 for women. In another study (Horn, 1971, unpublished), a correlation of .29 was obtained for 263 junior and senior engineering men. In a third study (Horn, 1972, unpublished) of 42 liberal arts college men and 56 liberal arts college women, the correlations were .20 and .08, respectively. The average correlation between sociability and impulsivity in these three studies was .19 for men and .15 for women.

These items used in Horn's studies are not necessarily the most discriminating sociability and impulsivity items. The items that loaded highest in the sociability and impulsivity clusters in Eysenck and Eysenck's (1963) study were the following:

Sociability

Are you inclined to keep in the background on social occasions?

Are you inclined to keep quiet when out in a social group?

Are you reserved and distant except to intimate friends?

Are you inclined to limit your acquaintances to a select few?

Do you usually take the initiative in making new friends?

Do you like to mix socially with people?

Impulsivity

Are you inclined to stop and think things over before acting?

Are you given to acting on impulses of the moment which later land you in difficulties?

Do you often act on the spur of the moment without stopping to think?

Would you describe yourself as an easy-going person not concerned to be precise?

Do you prefer action to planning for action?

Do you tend towards a rather reckless optimism?

Although these items appear to be better measures of sociability and impulsivity, the latter is a very complex personality disposition. The impulsivity items from Guilford's Rhathymia scale are primarily measures of decision time, with a secondary emphasis on boredom-sensation seeking. We suggest that more can be learned about the relationship between sociability and impulsivity if *all* components of impulsivity are considered (see Chapter 6).

A recent study (Plomin, in preparation) examined the *impulsivity* factor that has been found among the extraversion items of Eysenck's questionnaires. The *impulsivity* factor which contained items like, "I would rate myself as a lively individual," was labeled *liveliness*, which is closer to the original Rhathymia scale of Guilford. The *liveliness* factor correlated .59 with the sociability scale of EASI-III. It did not correlate significantly with any of the EASI impulsivity components except sensation seeking ($r = .27$). So it appears that even the so-called impulsivity component of extraversion does not adequately sample the components of impulsivity.

SOCIABILITY VERSUS IMPULSIVITY

We suggest that there are strong reasons for keeping sociability and impulsivity separate. Even when sociability items are confounded with impulsivity, as on the standard measures of introversion-extraversion, the correlation between sociability and impulsivity is low. When "cleaner" items are written (as in our own temperament survey), the correlation drops to near zero. This means that any given score on an introversion-extraversion measure consists of an unknown combination of sociability and impulsivity. As a consequence, quite different persons might obtain the same score. Consider two very different kinds of persons, both of whom are "ambiverts."

The first kind is *low in sociability and high in impulsivity*. Such a person tends to be self-centered and unconcerned with the welfare of others. He tends not to offer affection and is somewhat unresponsive to others. It follows that social rewards mean little to him, and therefore it is more difficult to socialize him. This difficulty is compounded by his relative lack of control and his need for excitement. He wants "kicks" but not necessarily from people. A likely source is drugs or possibly the thrill of defying authority or engaging in clandestine activities. Such a person may turn to criminality, for he tends to lack the self-control (impulsivity) or regard for others (sociability) that might otherwise deter him. He shares many features with psychopaths and, given a low level of emotionality, he may be predisposed to become one (see below).

The second kind of ambivert is precisely opposite: *high in sociability and low in impulsivity*. He is affectionate and seeks the company of others. His responsiveness and need for others makes him strongly susceptible to social rewards and punishments and therefore easy to socialize. As we suggested earlier, self-control is one of the major goals of socialization, and it is here that this person has a large advantage. He is temperamentally cautious and restrained, and he prefers familiar surroundings and an organized life. He is not very fond of surprises and abhors chaos and unplanned activities. Because of his strong sense of order and control (low impulsivity) and his strong sense of loyalty and concern for others (high sociability), he makes a splendid organizational man.

Let us return now to introversion-extraversion and consider what a middle score on such an inventory might mean. A person attaining a middle score might be high in sociability and low in impulsivity; he would be easy to socialize and would probably be a model citizen in the community. Or a middle score might represent a person low in sociability and high in impulsivity; he would be difficult to socialize and might well be on the criminal fringe of society. Lastly, a middle score might represent a person who is average in both sociability and impulsivity, and he would be different from the first two. Thus the same score might be attained by three very different persons, a possibility that might account for some discrepancies in the literature.

Another strong reason for keeping sociability and impulsivity separate concerns inheritance. There is some evidence that introversion-extraversion has an inherited component. Eysenck (1956b) measured introversion-extraversion with self-ratings, teachers' ratings, projective techniques, and sociometric ratings. The correlations were .50 for identical twins and −.33 for fraternal twins. Shields (1958, 1962) used an early version of the Maudsley Personality Inventory and found correlations of .42 for identical twins and

−.17 for fraternal twins; for another set of separated identical twins the correlation rose to .61. Other studies have confirmed the role of heredity in introversion-extraversion (see Carter, 1933a, 1935; Newman et al, 1937; Wilde, 1964; and Vandenberg, 1967), but in all this research sociability and impulsivity were not analyzed separately.

In a more recent study with the Eysenck Personality Inventory, the sociability and impulsivity items were scored separately by Canter (1969). Her twin data showed that sociability was heritable but impulsivity was not. The identical twin correlation for sociability was .51, and the fraternal twin correlation was .26. For impulsivity, the correlations were −.03 and −.26. These findings were corroborated in a subsample of identical twins who had been separated for at least five years. The correlation for sociability was .91. For impulsivity, the correlation was .20. These results are consistent with our own research (Buss et al., 1973) which showed strong support for the inheritance of sociability but mixed findings for impulsivity. However, a recent study by Eaves and Eysenck (unpublished) of a large sample of adult twins and another study by Eaves (1973) suggested that both impulsivity and sociability are inherited. Even in these two studies, the correlation *between* impulsivity and sociability was attributed more to the environment than to genes. By implication what is inherited are the specific traits of impulsivity and sociability, not a general trait of extraversion. No correlations were reported and the method of analysis was too complex to be discussed here.

The arguments for keeping sociability and impulsivity separate may be summarized briefly. The two dimensions of personality do not correlate with one another when care is taken to write unconfounded items. There are two different kinds of ambiverts, one highly socialized and the other relatively unsocialized or difficult to socialize. Sociability has a strong inherited component, but there is a real question whether impulsivity has an inherited component. This is perhaps not surprising in light of the way impulsivity is usually measured and the issue of its various aspects (see Chapter 6). In brief, whatever theoretical arguments that can be mustered for a dimension of introversion-extraversion, there are compelling descriptive and genetic arguments for separating it into its two components, sociability and impulsivity.

THREE TEMPERAMENTS

Our theory of temperament did not *introduce* each of the four temperaments. Each of them has been studied previously as a trait, a factor, or a dimension of personality. The novelty in our theory is the establishment of criteria for selection, the choice of four particular temperaments, an analysis of the nature of these temperaments and their developmental course. Until now, no one has specified activity, emotionality, sociability, and impulsivity as temperaments, and therefore no one has examined combinations of any three of them. In any event, combinations of three involve a high degree of complexity, which means that such patterns would be difficult to discern and isolate from the variety of personalities that confront the investigator.

Our analysis yields only two patterns involving three temperaments, psychopathy and aggressiveness. In addition, the notion of *arousal* appears to involve three of the four temperaments, and so it is discussed here.

Psychopathy

Although clinicians disagree on details, there is a consensus about the major features of psychopathy: a deficit in inhibitory control, a lack of concern about or response to others, and a low level of anxiety (see Buss, 1966). Translated into temperamental terms, this description yields a pattern of *high impulsivity, low sociability, and low emotionality*. There are many theories of psychopathy, but we believe that this one is most consistent with the facts: psychopaths are born with a specific combination of three temperamental tendencies. The remainder of this section shows how closely descriptions of psychopaths match these three temperaments.

HIGH IMPULSIVITY

The psychopath cannot wait. He must have his pleasure now and cannot abide delay. His time sense is disturbed, and he cannot work toward distant goals. He is at the mercy of his impulses and is susceptible to momentary temptation or escape from aversiveness, regardless of later negative consequences:

> Unlike the normal person, or even the average criminal, the psychopath's adventures often seem purposeless. Even his crimes are rarely planned. He robs a store in a whim of the moment, not after careful consideration. He flits from woman to woman with volatile passion, never feeling a prolonged attraction. [McCord & McCord, 1964, p. 10]

LOW SOCIABILITY

The psychopath has been described as a hollow, isolated person who is extremely self-centered. He cannot share affection, has no loyalty to groups or persons, and does not respond to social reinforcement:

> The psychopath has often been characterized as a "lone wolf." He seems cold and compassionless. He treats people as he does objects: as a means for his own

pleasure. Though he may form fleeting attachments, these lack emotional depth and tenderness. . . . [McCord & McCord, 1964, p. 15]

The low level of sociability may bear on the psychopath's impulsivity. A sociable child, being sensitive to social reward and punishment, is strongly susceptible to the efforts of socializing agents. If the child is impulsive, the impulsivity becomes socialized; that is, he learns inhibitory control and also when it is appropriate to let loose. The unsociable, impulsive child does not readily learn either the necessary discriminations or a minimal amount of inhibitory control because he resists the efforts of socialization agents. He neither responds to others nor cares for the rewards of personal interaction. Thus he is doubly immature: unsociably self-centered and impulsively lacking in control.

LOW EMOTIONALITY

Another reason for the psychopath's resistance to socialization may be his low level of emotionality. It is generally assumed that anxiety is necessary for avoidance learning, at least in the early phases of such learning. There have been a number of studies on this topic, and after reviewing the literature, Hare (1970) concluded:

It appears that psychopaths do not develop conditioned fear responses readily. As a result, they find it difficult to learn responses that are motivated by fear and reinforced by fear reduction. The fact that their behavior appears to be neither motivated nor guided by the possibility of unpleasant consequences, particularly when the temporal relationship between behavior and its consequences is relatively great, might be interpreted in this way. (p. 93)

The notion that psychopaths are unemotional can be tested more directly. One aspect of emotionality is autonomic responsivity. Psychopaths should be lower on autonomic reactivity than normal persons. Again, Hare's review of the evidence is supportive:

During periods of relative quiescence psychopathic subjects tend to be hypoactive on several indices of autonomic activity, including resting level of skin conductance and automatic variability ("spontaneous" fluctuations in electrodermal and cardiac activity). Although these findings must be interpreted with caution, they are at least consistent with most clinical statements about the psychopath's general lack of anxiety, guilt, and emotional "tension."
The situation with respect to autonomic responsivity is more complex. Nevertheless, it appears that psychopaths may give relatively small electrodermal responses to "lie detection" situations and to situations that would ordinarily be considered stressful. They may also exhibit rapid electrodermal recovery at the termination of stressful situations. (1970, p. 57)

The issue of emotionality has come up *within* psychopathy. Psychopaths have been divided into a *primary* type who are not anxious and a *secondary* type who are anxious (Karpman, 1941). The secondary type have also been called neurotic psychopaths, and some clinicians refuse to include them under the heading of psychopathy. In any event, the amount of anxiety (in terms of our temperaments, the amount of emotionality) is a major determiner of galvanic skin response (GSR) conditioning and avoidance learning. Lykken (1957) divided psychopaths into primary and secondary types on the basis of scores on an anxiety inventory. Both groups were compared with normal subjects in GSR conditioning and avoidance learning. In both tasks normal subjects learned fastest, secondary psychopaths next, and primary psychopaths last. On the reasonable assumption that normal persons were the most realistic and would be most fearful of the electric shock used in the research, it follows that the more anxious the subject was, the faster he learned. This research further solidifies the hypothesis that psychopaths are low in anxiety (they learned most slowly) and, by inference, low in emotionality.

Aggressiveness

The tendency to aggress is regarded by most ethologists as an instinct. Diamond (1957), noting its prevalence among animals and men, labeled it a temperament. We acknowledge the ubiquity of aggression but suggest that these are three reasons for rejecting aggressiveness as a temperament.

First, it does not meet the crucial empirical criterion of temperament—evidence of its heritability. It must be admitted that research on this point is sparse, but we know of no published research demonstrating a genetic component in human aggressiveness.

Second, when ethologists or other behavioral researchers discuss aggression, they implicitly refer to *males*. In most species it is the males who fight with one another, and in virtually all primate species it is the males who protect the troop. In animals, testosterone has been causally linked with aggressiveness (Clark & Birch, 1945); there is no similar evidence in humans, but boys are generally more aggressive (physically) than girls, and men are more aggressive than women. These human gender differences in aggression appear to be caused by gender role training (see Chapter 7), and thus we see no need to involve temperament as an explanation.

Third, aggressiveness can be explained in terms of a combination of three temperaments: activity, emotionality, and impulsivity. Aggressiveness does not originate in a particular combination of these temperaments in the sense that extraversion consists of high sociability and impulsivity. Rather, each of the three temperaments contributes to aggressiveness in a way that probably summates, so that a person *high in activity, emotionality, and impulsivity* is likely to be aggressive.

HIGH ACTIVITY

The highly active person, by definition, makes more responses, rushes more, and is more energetic and intense in his behavior. He is likely to show considerable initiative and compete strongly with others, activities that may bring him into conflict with others. Thus his greater output of behavior should involve him in more frequent instrumental aggression instigated by himself as a competitor or by others who are resisting his efforts.

The intensity and fast tempo of his behavior should involve him in more aggression for two reasons. First, he is something of an irritant to others because of his speed and incessant push of behavior. When others become sufficiently annoyed, they become aggressive, and the active person may be forced to retaliate merely to defend himself. Second, aggression is itself an intense response, and it has been viewed as merely ordinary behavior that is amplified—the high magnitude theory of aggression (Bandura & Walters, 1963). In these terms anyone who tends to respond with greater intensity is likely to be more aggressive. Thus there are several reasons for a highly active person being more *instrumentally* aggressive.

HIGH EMOTIONALITY

High emotionality leads to greater aggressiveness mainly in men. As we suggested in Chapter 7, boys are encouraged (or not actively discouraged) to ventilate anger in the form of aggression, whereas girls are allowed to express fear but not anger. This means that for the traditional man, high emotionality has been channeled mainly into rage, and he is likely to be high in *angry aggression*. If his gender role training is inadequate or if he tends to be unmasculine (in traditional terms), the high emotionality might be channeled into fear. Such fear would inhibit angry aggression, and therefore high emotionality would lead to *less*, not more aggression.

The situation for women is reciprocal. Given high emotionality, it is directed toward fear in traditional homes; fear inhibits angry aggression, and the outcome is a *less* aggressive woman. On the other hand, if a highly emotional girl is trained to be a "liberated women," the emotionality might well be directed toward rage; in this event, she would become *more* aggressive.

In brief, high emotionality leads to greater aggressiveness (specifically angry aggression) only when socialization directs it toward anger. This means that for persons with traditional gender roles, high emotionality leads to more aggressiveness in men and less aggressiveness in women.

HIGH IMPULSIVITY

The highly impulsive person has trouble in controlling both his emotions and his wants. If he becomes angry, he will tend to express the rage rather than inhibit it. Therefore he is likely to engage in more angry aggression. If he is competing with others or pursues a goal that can be accomplished only by aggressing, he will tend not to inhibit the aggression. Therefore he is likely to engage in more *instrumental* aggression.

Thus the highly impulsive person suffers double jeopardy in that he is more susceptible to both angry and instrumental aggression. His uncontrolled temper means more frequent violent ourbursts of aggression. His inability to delay gratification means more frequent aggression both when it is sanctioned (competition) and when it is not (crime).

THE COMBINATION

For expository purposes, we have overemphasized the connection between each of the three temperaments and aggression. Other things equal, the more active person is expected to be more aggressive, and so should the more emotional person or the more impulsive person. Of course, things are rarely equal, and so the correlation between any single temperament and aggression may be low. Of the three temperaments involved (activity, emotionality, and impulsivity), impulsivity should have the highest correlation with aggressiveness simply because it leads to both angry and instrumental aggression. When all three temperaments are taken into account, each would presumably add variance, and a composite score should correlate reasonably well with aggressiveness.

These predictions were tested on 162 college men and 207 college women. They were administered the EASI-II and the Buss-Durke Inventory (Buss & Durkee, 1957). The latter consists of seven scales of aggressiveness. Two were selected for present purposes: the verbal aggression and the physical aggression scales. The correlations between them and the four temperaments of the EASI-II are presented in Table 8.1. These correlations are roughly in accord with our predictions. For women the correlations between three of the temperaments and aggression are low but significant, and for men the same pattern emerged but only two of the four were significantly related to aggression. The correlations for sociability were close to zero. The correlations for impulsivity were the highest, and the multiple correlations between the temperaments and aggressiveness reached an acceptable level. We must add that all scales involved in these correlations were very short. The temperament scales were five items each, and the aggression scales numbered 10 (physical) and 13 (verbal) items. Presumably, with longer scales, reliability would be increased and the

TABLE 8.1   CORRELATIONS BETWEEN THE TEMPERAMENTS AND AGGRESSION
(Buss–Durkee Scale)

	Verbal aggression		Physical aggression	
	Men (162)	Women (207)	Men (162)	Women (207)
Emotionality	.13	.14*	.09	.14*
Activity	.17*	.23*	.16*	.18*
Sociability	−.02	.23*	.05	.02
Impulsivity	.32*	.32*	.24*	.20*
Multiple correlation	.33*	.37*	.24*	.27*

*p<.05

correlations would rise. But in any event, these data do support the notion that activity, emotionality, and especially impulsivity contribute to aggressiveness.

AROUSAL

Arousal is an important issue in personality, especially as it relates to temperament, but it is a tricky concept because of its inclusiveness. We say that someone is aroused when he is excited, tense, or overactive, but arousal also refers to internal states of the body, specifically the nervous system. With so many referants for the term, it is not surprising that the concept of arousal has contributed as much to misunderstanding as to understanding of behavior. It may help to distinguish three different kinds of arousal, especially because one kind of arousal may occur in the absence of the other two.

BEHAVIOR

Observe a person jumping up and down, waving his hands, shouting or screaming, flailing about, dashing to and fro, speaking very rapidly, or struggling with great force; all these suggest high behavioral arousal. All such acts are also examples of high vigor or rapid tempo, and these are indicants of activity temperament. Any single incident of great expenditure of energy— either intense activity or rapid movement—suggests high behavioral arousal. Presumably, the tendency to act this way is determined largely by activity temperament.

AUTONOMIC NERVOUS SYSTEM

Consider what happens when a person is about to have a tooth extracted by a dentist. In the waiting room, the patient may start becoming apprehensive as he considers the pain, discomfort, and bleeding that are imminent. His pulse pounds, his face flushes, his breath comes in rapid, shallow bursts, and he starts to sweat. These are all recognizable signs of fear, the physiological preparations for flight from an oncoming noxious stimulus. As such, they indicate strong emotion, and they are also the best indicators of the temperament of emotionality.

CENTRAL NERVOUS SYSTEM

The central nervous system is continually active, both in wakefulness and sleep, but there are wide variations in the level of activity, especially in the brain. Our focus here is on the activity of the cerebral cortex. During waking, this activity varies from slow, steady brain waves that are called the *alpha* rhythm (associated with quiescence) to fast, irregular brain waves (associated with alertness and vigilance). When a person is concentrating very hard on looking through a telescope, playing a difficult passage of music, or solving a tricky mathematics problem (or, alternatively, when his brain waves are fast, shallow, and irregular) we infer that the cerebral nervous system is highly aroused.

There are some persons who become bored very easily and continually seek novelty. Presumably, they prefer a state of high central nervous system arousal, their brains constantly being called on to process new inputs. In neural terms, they seek to abolish the quiescent alpha rhythm and to instigate the more rapid rhythms associated with cortical excitement. Such persons are called sensation seekers, and as we saw in the last chapter, sensation seeking may well be an important aspect of the temperament of impulsivity.

Certainly not all cortical arousal can be linked to sensation seeking, which is merely one aspect of impulsivity and perhaps not a central aspect. Nevertheless, there is some indirect supporting evidence. Psychopaths, whose impulsivity is proverbial, tend to have peculiar and deviant patterns of brain waves. There is some evidence that they are cortically *under*aroused, and presumably, they seek external stimulation and excitement to pep up the cerebral cortex (see Hare, 1970, Chapter 5, for details). There is more to psychopathy than impulsivity and the evidence is far from certain, but it does suggest that impulsivity may be a determinant of central nervous system arousal.

TEMPERAMENTS AND AROUSAL

Thus the three aspects of arousal are apposite to three of our temperaments (sociability is not relevant here). We suggest that activity level is the major determinant of the tendency to be behaviorally aroused and that emotionality is the major determinant of the tendency to become emotionality aroused. We also propose a connection between impulsivity and *low* cortical arousal (leading to the continual seeking of a state of higher arousal) but admit that the connection is tenuous.

Activity, emotionality, and impulsivity are not highly correlated, which means that a variety of patterns involving their combinations exist in the population. Two extreme patterns are of interest here because they relate to arousal: persons high on all three temperaments and persons low on all three. A person who is high on activity, emotionality, and impulsivity would be exciting to be around because there would never be a dull moment. His actions would be vigorous and rapid; his general mood would be constantly seeking change and adventure. A person who is low on all three of these temperaments would be comparatively dull. His actions would tend to be slow and lethargic; his general mood would be calm, stable, and unperturbed; and he would constantly seek the haven of conformity and routine. In metaphorical terms, the person low on all three temperaments would bore you to death, whereas his opposite number would drive you crazy.

MOOD

Mood is a background variable. It refers to one's general state of being over a limited period of time: hours or days but probably not weeks and certainly not months or years. Mood concerns *affect*: happy-sad, calm-anxious, friendly-grouchy, optimistic-pessimistic, etc. As such, it must in part be determined by the everyday events of living. It is affected by physiological variables that influence biological functioning, such as amount of sleep the night before, present state of health, and heat and humidity in the surroundings. It is affected by the rewards and punishments that impinge on all of us: success-failure, acceptance-rejection, friendliness-hostility from others, and in general, the good and bad things of life.

If these external variables were the sole determinants of mood, it would be of little interest to personality researchers, but mood would also seem to be determined by stable personality characteristics, especially temperaments. An emotional person, by definition, becomes upset more easily and so is likely to be "down" in mood. An active person keeps moving and so does not remain long in a melancholy mood; there is a correlation between activity and elation in the way we describe one another (Buss & Murray, 1965). A sociable person tends to be more outgoing and involved with others and therefore less preoccupied with his troubles; his mood is likely to be "up." Finally, an impulsive person is likely to be at the mercy of his own inner urges and so is unable to control feelings of irritability, sadness, or pessimism; other things equal, his mood should be "down." In brief, if we assign a good mood to the high end of the scale, we predict positive correlations between mood and both activity and sociability, and negative correlations between mood and both emotionality and impulsivity.

We tested these predictions in a seven-day study of mood with college students, 96 men and 71 women. On the first day there was a group administration of EASI-II, and each subject was given a set of mood rating sheets. Each sheet consisted of 12 mood items to be described shortly. They were to be rated on a scale of 1 (hardly at all) to 5 (a lot). The ratings were to be made the last thing at night and mailed the following morning. This procedure was followed for seven days, and we used the average mood ratings for the seven-day period.

The items are shown in Table 8.2, which is divided into three sections. All items are presented the way they were to the subjects; note that some items are reversed so that a good mood is not represented consistently on the right or left

TABLE 8.2 DAILY RATING SHEET OF MOOD ITEMS

---

1. Loaded on general factor;
no *a priori* confound with temperaments

```
    Depressed. . . . . . . . . . . . happy
    Felt hemmed in, constrained. . . felt free, unconstrained
    Felt pessimistic, cynical. . . . . .felt optimistic
    Couldn't think clearly. . . . . felt very clearheaded
    Touchy, easily hurt. . not affected by slights from others
    Felt confident of self. . . . felt unconfident of self
```

2. Loaded on general factor;
a priori confound with temperaments

```
    Listless didn't feel
    like doing anything. . . . . . . full of energy
    Felt loose, calm, relaxed. . . . . .felt tense,
                                   strained, knotted up
    Felt like being alone. . . . . . felt very sociable
    Alert, responsive. . . . . . sluggish, unresponsive
```

3. Did not load on general factor

```
    Felt very attractive. . . . . felt very unattractive
    Daydreaming, musing mood. . . . . down-to-earth,
                                   matter-of-fact mood
```

---

side of the page (this avoided a possible response set). Of the 12 items, selected after reviewing previous mood research, 10 loaded on a general factor. The remaining two (in Section 3 of the table) were not used in computing correlations with the temperaments. We were concerned that there might be a built-in relationship between mood and temperament because certain items tapped directly into temperament. For example, "felt like being alone" would appear to describe the usual tendency of a low-sociable person. To eliminate this possible confound, we removed four items that loaded on the general factor; they are listed in Section 2 of the table. This left six items that loaded on the general factor and did not appear to have an a priori, built-in relationship with the four temperaments. We arranged the ratings of these six items so that a high rating indicated a good mood, and then we averaged the ratings for all six over the seven days of the study. Finally, the average mood rating was correlated with each of the four temperaments.

The correlations are presented in Table 8.3. None of the correlations is high, which is consistent with the notion that mood is largely determined by external, day-to-day events. But five of the eight correlations are significant, and the other three approach significance. The multiple correlations of the four temperaments with mood are .40 for men and .53 for women. The size of these two correlations means that (1) the temperaments are making somewhat independent contributions to mood; and (2) there is significant input from temperaments into mood. The latter is not surprising in light of the nature of temperament, which, like mood, is involved with the more stylistic and background aspects of personality.

Table 8.3 contains two other facts of some interest. First, the data bear out our predictions on the relationships between individual temperaments and mood: for activity and sociability the correlations are positive, and for emotionality and impulsivity the correlations are negative. Second, the correlations are consistently higher for women, which suggests that women's mood tends to reflect more of their basic personality than does the mood of men.

TABLE 8.3   RELATIONSHIP OF MOOD TO TEMPERAMENT

	Men	Women
Emotionality	−.29*	−.42*
Activity	.18	.23
Sociability	.20*	.28*
Impulsivity	−.17	−.34*
Multiple correlation	.40*	.53*

*$p < .05$

CONCLUSIONS

We have attempted to explain some easily identified personality patterns in terms of combinations to temperaments. Thus high sociability and impulsivity presumably underlie extraversion, and a combination of high impulsivity, low emotionality, and low sociability should influence psychopathy. Our strategy has been to dissect a personality configuration so as to reveal the temperaments that might constitute it. For purposes of exposition, we have ignored the impact of the environment, specifically socialization variables and individual learning.

Temperaments and Environment

Suppose that environmental inputs played no important role in determining the personality patterns described in this chapter. If this were true, inherited endowments (temperaments) would account for all the systematic variance. One way of testing this hypothesis would be to correlate each of the appropriate temperaments with a particular personality pattern being examined—for example, correlate activity, emotionality, and impulsivity with aggressiveness. If only temperaments were important, the multiple correlation would be high, perhaps in the .60 to .80 range (the rest of the variance would be error). We predict that multiple correlations will not attain this magnitude. In other words, we suggest that environmental inputs are important and control enough systematic variance to lower the correlations between temperaments and personality patterns.

Suppose environmental inputs were extremely powerful. They might be strong enough to conceal or even reverse the original personality dispositions. If this occurred, the multiple correlation between combinations of temperaments and personality patterns would be drastically reduced. The expected range would be 0 to .20. We believe that this estimate is too low, which is another way of saying that environmental variables are not strong enough to cancel the effect of temperaments.

The third possibility is that both temperament and environment are important. Presumably, socialization pressure and individual learning would modify the original personality endowment, but only within limits. Thus a child of above average sociability and impulsivity might be shaped to be more extraverted or less extraverted, but he would never become introverted. If both temperaments and environment determine personality configurations, the multiple correlations between any configuration and the corresponding set of temperaments would be neither extremely high nor extremely low; they would be in the moderate range of .30 to .60. In brief, multiple correlations between such patterns as hyperkinesis, psychopathy, and aggressiveness and the appropriate combinations of temperaments yield information about both temperaments and environment.

Utility

It might be argued that our temperament theory has added little to understanding personality patterns: all we have done is to describe a particular personality pattern and then ascribe it to some combination of temperaments. We agree that to "explain" after the fact without spelling out any implications is merely playing verbal games. But we have spelled out the implications of our hypotheses with specific predictions that can be tested. Thus we predicted a temperamental contribution to mood, and the multiple correlations strongly supported this prediction. We predicted that two temperaments would be positively correlated with mood and two would be negatively correlated, and the data confirmed these predictions. We predicted that impulsivity would correlate highest with aggressiveness, that sociability would be unrelated, and that the combined temperaments would show a clear relationship with aggressiveness; all three predictions were confirmed. And the theory leads to testable predictions about the various combinations believed to underlie specific patterns. For example, children identified as hyperkinetic can be assessed to discover whether—as we predict—they are well above average not only in activity but also in impulsivity. Similarly, psychopaths, once identified, could be assessed to discover whether our predicted pattern (high impulsivity, low sociability, and low emotionality) is present. Beyond the specific predictions it makes about particular personality configurations, the theory suggests two areas that might be clarified by examining combinations of temperaments: adjustment and socialization.

Our culture values self-control, order, and conformity. Adjustment to society is usually defined in terms of at least minimal control and compliance. These societal goals pose a special problem for persons who are high in the temperaments of emotionality and impulsivity. High emotionality—whether expressed as fear or rage—can lead to disruption of individual performance or of group interactions. High impulsivity denies or makes difficult achieving the control demanded by society. Thus the person of high emotionality and high impulsivity suffers double jeopardy: the push of fear or rage and the relative inability to control it.

Either of these two temperaments (emotionality or impulsivity) spells adjustment difficulty when combined with the extreme of another temperament (or two). In one way or another they are involved in hyperkinesis, anxiety neurosis, and psychopathy, all of which are serious psychological abnormalities. And presumably they contribute to high aggressiveness, which can lead to adjustment difficulties.

Temperament theory also directs our attention to the more subtle adjustment problem of *strain*. Consider the plight of an extravert whose job is to monitor a radar screen in an underground military installation. His high sociability requires the presence of others, but he is virtually alone; his high impulsivity makes it difficult to tolerate waiting and monotony, but his job involves both. Perhaps this extravert can persist in getting the job done, but only at the expense of a high degree of tension that is properly called strain. His opposite number, the extreme introvert, would undergo similar strain if we were stuck in a job that required much social interaction and spontaneity (for example, master of ceremonies). Our theory predicts that men and women will usually take jobs that are at least not incompatible with their temperament patterns. If they are temperamentally unsuited to the job, the outcome will be a strain that is easily identified as personal unhappiness, dissatisfaction, inefficiency, and discord.

Our theory also attempts to predict which children will prove "difficult" for their parents. We have already suggested that high impulsivity and emotionality tend to cause adjustment problems, but now the focus is on integration with socializing agents. As we mentioned earlier, the child who is high-impulsive and low-sociable should prove difficult to socialize. He suffers from a relative lack of control (impulsivity), and achieving self-control is one of the major goals of socialization. Furthermore, social rewards mean little to him (low sociability), making it more difficult for parents to shape his behavior. His opposite number—the low-impulsive, high-sociable child—should be easy to socialize and be seen by his parents as "a good child." In brief, the child's temperaments will in part determine the process and outcome of socialization, and they will in part determine how his parents rear him. These topics are the focus of the next chapter.

CHAPTER

┌─────────┐
│   │
│   9   │
│   │
└─────────┘

PARENT-CHILD
INTERACTION

Temperaments are not immutable. The evidence reviewed in previous chapters builds a case for the inheritance of the EASI temperaments. But this same evidence demonstrates that genetic factors cannot account for all the variance. Environmental factors are also important. In our view, temperaments predispose an individual to a limited range of a phenotype, but the interaction between the temperament and environment, especially during the critical developmental years, determines where the phenotype falls within this range. The purpose of this chapter is to examine theoretically and empirically one aspect of this interaction, that between child-rearing practices and temperament.

A child's personality is shaped by many different influences during development. His immediate family nurtures him, offers him attention and affection, teaches him to comply with their own needs, and prepares him for the demands that society will make. As the child enters the world beyond his own home, he is increasingly affected by the actions of friends, teachers, and a variety of authority figures (babysitters, policemen, physicians, and caretakers). He is also affected by his own experiences in play, games, school, and television. Because our focus is on temperament, we cannot discuss all the environmental determinants on personality and must restrict ourselves to the most important ones. The environmental influences on personality development that have received the most attention are child-rearing practices of the parents. Child-rearing practices seem to be a reasonable starting point in studying the interplay between temperament and environment. The child's interaction with his parents is not only primary in the sense of occurring early and lasting throughout childhood, but it is also the most pervasive. Not all children have siblings or nonparental caretakers, but all have parents. Thus, although there are other determinants of the child's personality, we shall discuss only the parent-child interaction.

The term *interaction* is meant to be taken literally in the sense that each affects the other. Much of the research on children is guided by the implicit assumption that parental behavior is the independent variable and child behavior, the dependent variable. We suggest that this assumption omits the other half of the interaction: children affect the behavior of their parents. A highly active child may require more parental supervision or control than a lethargic child, and a sociable child may elicit (and reward) more attention and affection than an unsociable child. Of course, the parental influence on children is also important. However, the child is *not* a blank slate on which the parent writes. Rather, the child has his own initial dispositions, which may blunt, enhance, or otherwise modify the way his parents act toward him. Our interest is in how temperament affects both parties in the parent-child interaction.

CHILD-REARING PRACTICES

The parent plays several roles in relation to his child, and the importance of any given role varies with the child's increasing maturity. The first role, that of caretaker, is forced on the parent by the infant's helplessness. The very young child must be fed, kept warm and clean, and given at least minimal attention and stimulation. As the child develops his abilities and skills, he needs less and less caretaking, and the importance of this role diminishes.

The child's ability to locomote and manipulate forces the parent to become a controller. Now the child must be kept out of mischief, warned of hot stoves and dangerous perches, and closely watched around city traffic and swimming pools or lakes. This role is marked by a high frequency of three parental words: "No," "Don't," and "Bad." All this starts during the second year of life, when the child acquires rudimentary control over locomotion and manipulation. Such achievements also mark the beginning of *socialization*, in which the parent's role is to prepare the child to meet the requirements of society.

These involve the learning of rules and codes of morality, and such conduct training continues until adulthood. The parent also helps his child move toward self-help and self-control (bowel and bladder training, tolerating delay, etc.). The parents are not the only ones who help the child to learn what is expected and what is forbidden, but they are the major socializing agents throughout childhood.

In brief, parents play these roles: caretaker, controller, and socializing agent. In these roles—especially the last two—parents vary considerably in how they behave toward the child. Some parents are relaxed and confident, others tense and apprehensive; some are restrictive and rule-oriented, others permissive and inconsistent; some are overindulgent, others harsh. Presumably, these variations have some impact on the child's personality.

When two persons live together for any length of time, they develop strong affective ties, both positive and negative. Most close relationships consist of a mixture of love and hate, and the parent-child pair is no exception. The parent also plays an *affectionate* role with his child, and the love is offered in two contexts. The first is the love that any parent has for his own child; the child is esteemed merely because he is *progeny*, and there are no strings attached. The second context is training, in which love is offered *conditionally*. The child is rewarded for self-control or achievement by parental affection, and punished for loss of control or failure by loss of love. In both contexts the parents vary in the amount and frequency of love they offer. They also vary in the amount of hostility toward the child.

The various parental roles may be categorized under two headings. The first is *nurturance*, in which the parent cares for and protects the child, and initiates socialization (or neglects the child). The second is *affection*, in which the parent displays love (or hate) toward the child.

Dimensions of Child-rearing Practices

A theoretical analysis of parental roles may aid understanding the complexities of parent-child interactions, but it is no substitute for knowledge about how parents actually rear their children. During the past few decades, researchers have accumulated many facts about maternal practices because mothers are ready and willing to answer the relevant questions, and they are available. Fathers are more elusive, and we know less about their child-rearing practices. In addition, most of our knowledge comes from interviews of mothers and questionnaires filled out by them. Direct observation in the home would be an excellent supplement to these methods, but it is rarely possible. Observing mothers and children under relatively controlled conditions is more practical, and it has yielded valuable information (Schaefer & Bayley, 1963). With this warning about the diverse ways data have been collected, let us describe the major dimensions of child-rearing practices.

Maccoby and Masters (1970) compiled a list of dimensions of parental behavior that have been found in factor analyses:

Warmth (versus hostility or rejection)

Permissiveness (versus restrictiveness)

Child-rearing anxiety

Sex anxiety

Inhibitory demands and discipline

Responsible child-rearing orientation

Physical punishment

Dependency encouragement

Democratic attitudes

Authoritarian control

Punishment (versus nonpunishment)

General family adjustment

Several of the factors refer to similar behavior, and some are specific to particular child behaviors (for example, sex anxiety). Schaefer (1959) suggested that the first two factors on the list, which he renamed *love-hostility* and *control-autonomy*, would account for most child-rearing practices. Schaefer found the love and control factors in ratings of observations of the interaction between mothers and their one- to three-year-old children, in ratings of interviews with mothers of 9- to 14-year-old children, and in self-report data from mothers who responded to the Parental Attitude Research Instrument (Schaefer & Bell, 1958). These dimensions have been confirmed by other researchers (Sears et al., 1957; Milton, 1958; Hatfield et al., 1967). The dimensions were independent (see Figure 9.1). On the hostility-love dimension, the love end is defined by positive evaluation of the child, expression of affection, and egalitarianism; the hostility end is defined by ignoring the child, being punitive and irritable, and seeing the child as a burden. Concerning the autonomy-control dimension, the autonomy end involves permissiveness; the control end includes such diverse parental behaviors as anxiety, intrusiveness, protectiveness, demand for achievement, and concern about health—all involving either restrictive or demanding behavior by the parent.

These two dimensions are recognizable as essentially the same ones that emerged from our analysis of parental roles. The hostility-love dimension is essentially the same as *affection*, which we suggest would characterize any en-

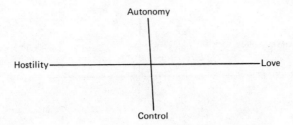

Figure 9.1. Two dimensions of childrearing practices (Schaefer, 1959).

during relationship. And the autonomy-control dimension is nothing more than parental *nurturance*, which involves caring for, watching over, and socializing the child.

The autonomy-control dimension has been researched and discussed for many decades, and there have been heated debates about the virtues and faults of permissiveness, schedules, discipline, type of punishment, and so on. Baumrind (1966) has suggested that the dimension could be pegged by three modal types of parental practices: *permissive, authoritative,* and *authoritarian*:

> The *permissive* parent attempts to behave in a nonpunitive, acceptant, and affirmative manner toward the child's impulses, desires, and actions. [p. 889]
>
> The *authoritative* parent attempts to direct the child's activities in a rational, issue-oriented manner. She encourages verbal give and take, shares with the child the reasoning behind her policy, and solicits his objections when he refuses to conform. [p. 891]
>
> The *authoritarian* parent attempts to shape, control, and evaluate the behavior of the child in accordance with a set standard of conduct, usually an absolute standard, theologically motivated and formulated by a higher authority. She values obedience as a virtue and favors punitive, forceful measures to curb self-will at points where the child's actions or beliefs conflict with what she thinks is right conduct. [p. 890]

These descriptions reveal that Baumrind's control dimension also includes elements of the hostility-love dimension: permissive and authoritative parents are at least minimally on the love end, and authoritarian parents are on the hostility end. We suggest that Baumrind's and Schaefer's schemata can be merged into a single model (see Figure 9.2). The permissive parent exercises minimal control and is at least a little loving; the authoritative parent blends control with affection; and the authoritarian parent is both controlling and hostile (punitive). The fourth kind of parent—as suggested by this analysis— would be annoyed by the child and would see him as a burden (hostility) and would therefore furnish little attention or discipline (autonomy); the appro-

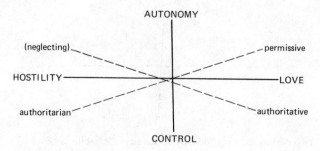

Figure 9.2. A merger of Schaefer's model (capital letters) with Baumrind's model (lowercase letters).

priate label is *neglecting*. Concerning the model in Figure 9.2, Schaefer's axes derive from factor analyses, and the axes that link Baumrind's types do not. So we shall use Schaefer's two dimensions, referring to them as the *love* and *control* dimensions.

Determinants of Child-rearing Practices

INITIAL PRACTICES

During the first year of a child's life, the parents are largely caretakers, but they increasingly become controllers and socializing agents, and they are *always* involved in affectional relationships. What determines their *initial* parental child-rearing practices?

The primary determinant of initial parental practices appears to be previous learning. During their own development parents are exposed to parental models, and they acquire child-oriented responses by imitation. There may be direct teaching of parental practices, and in many families girls are instructed in various aspects of the mother's role. And there are the secondary sources of knowledge: books, magazines, newspapers, television, radio, and motion pictures, all of which suggest, directly or indirectly, how children should be managed.

A less potent but important determinant of initial parental practices is the parents' temperament. A highly active parent is likely to intrude considerably into the child's life, investing the relationship with the same vigor he devotes to all activities. It follows that he will tend to control the child more and probably push the child toward high-energy and achievement-related behavior. The lethargic parent, on the other hand, has less energy to spare on the child and therefore may tend to be less controlling and demanding, and perhaps even neglectful.

The effect of emotionality on parental practices depends on whether fear or rage is preeminent. The fearful parent may be unsure and apprehensive about rearing the child and this may have implications for parental control. Unfortunately, it seems possible that parental fear may lead to either undercontrol or overcontrol because the fearful parent may abdicate control or may lean toward excessive protection and restriction. Research will have to answer this question. The angry, irritable parent tends to have temper outbursts, which may communicate hostility and rejection to the child.

Impulsivity appears to have less relevance for child-rearing practices. Presumably, a highly impulsive parent would vacillate and show inconsistency in his interactions with the child. He might swing from autonomy to control or from affection to rejection in an apparently random pattern. The low-impulsive parent would presumably seek order and stability; he would therefore exercise considerable control in the context of a no-nonsense, get-the-job done approach to child-rearing.

The most important temperament for child-rearing appears to be sociability. The highly sociable person, by definition, seeks relationships and offers affection. Thus a highly sociable parent would be loving and would at least lean away from punitiveness (to avoid rejecting the child and being rejected by the child). He might also demand affection from the child, especially if other sources of affection were scarce. The low-sociable parent would not offer love easily or freely and would be amenable to punishing or neglecting the child. The child-parent bond would be less rewarding for him, and he might consider the child as something of a burden.

The expectation that sociability is an important determinant of child-rearing practices has some support (Zuckerman & Oltean, 1959). Parents of college students filled out the Parental Attitude Research Instrument (Schaefer & Bell, 1958) and a variety of personality inventories. The *love* dimension of the parental attitudes questionnaire was found to correlate .67 with the affiliation scale (a rough measure of sociability) of the Edwards Personal Preference Inventory. Our interpretation of this correlation is that the parental temperament of sociability *determines* the extent to which parents are affectionate toward their children.

DIRECTION OF EFFECTS

Presumably, parents' previous learning and their temperaments continue to influence their child-rearing practices until their children attain maturity. But with the birth of a child, a new determinant begins to affect child-rearing practices, *the child's own behavior*. It is accepted as a truism that parents shape and modify the behavior of their children, but the idea that children also alter the behavior of their parents rarely has been considered by theorists or researchers. A paper by Bell (1968) signaled an important new perspective on the parent-child relationship: that each affected the behavior of the other. This perspective led directly to a new way of regarding the autonomy-control dimension of child-rearing practices:

> Two types of parent control repertories must be differentiated. *Upper-limit control* behavior reduces and redirects behavior of the child which exceeds parental standards of intensity, frequency, and competence for the child's age. *Lower-limit control* behavior stimulates child behavior which is below parental standards. In other words, parental control behavior, in a sense, is homeostatic relative to child behavior. [p. 88]

Bell illustrated his thesis with examples bearing directly on temperament. Thus extremely active children elicit upper-limit control from parents, and lethargic children elicit lower-limit control.

An example from research with abnormal children helps to drive the point home. It is widely believed that maternal possessiveness predisposes children to schizophrenia, but it could equally be argued that mothers of deviant children are merely *responding* to their children's abnormality. Mothers of schizophrenic, brain-injured, mentally retarded, and normal children were administered the Parental Attitude Research Instrument (Klebanoff, 1959). The mothers of all three groups of abnormal children reported being more possessive than the mothers of normals. As maternal overprotection clearly cannot cause brain damage or retardation, Klebanoff concluded that mothers confronted with disturbed behavior in their children tend to develop similar attitudes regardless of the nature of the disturbance. Thus the child's behavior might be a cause as well as an effect.

Rheingold (1969) has gone a step further and asserted that the infant socializes others more than he is socialized:

> The infant modulates, tempers, regulates, and refines the caretaker's activities. He produces delicate shades and nuances in these operations to suit his own needs of the moment. By such responses as fretting, sounds of impatience or satisfaction, by facial expression of pleasure, contentment, or alertness he produces elaborations here and dampening there. [p. 785]
> The infant also amplifies the dimension of tenderness and compassion characteristic of most mature adults. Caring for a helpless organism gives them an awareness of their own usefulness in the eyes of the world. Their concern for the infant is generalized to a concern for all living persons, large and small, here and away. [p. 786]

Without endorsing all of Rheingold's rhetoric, we agree that young children can modify adults' behavior toward them.

The child can affect parental practices in the three ways described in the first chapter: as a background stimulus object, setting the tone for interactions with parents; as an initiator, stimulating or programming child-rearing practices; or as a reinforcer, rewarding or not rewarding the efforts of his parents. The first, setting the tone, may be the least important but is nonetheless intuitively evident when one is confronted with a pouting, whining child as compared to a smiling, affectionate child.

The child can also elicit new or different behavior from his parents as Bell (1968) has suggested. The relatively inert child may goad the parent into stimulating him, and the excitable, uncontrolled child may force the parent to damp his behavior. Thus, regardless of the child-rearing practices that the parent is ready to initiate (because of previous learning and parental temperament), he may have to abandon them in favor of practices that are responsive to the child's behavior.

The third way the child affects parental practices is through *feedback*. The feedback may be immediate, direct, and affective. The child may be either contented and happy in the face of the parental practice, or frustrated and annoyed. Presumably, smiling strengthens the parental behavior, and crying weakens it. Thus the child's immediate affective response may serve as a reward or punishment, thereby altering parental behavior.

The feedback may also be more subtle and less immediate. Parental practices may be successful in achieving control, socializing the child, and keeping the child reasonably content, or they may be unsuccessful. If parental practices succeed, they should be strengthened; if they fail, they should be weakened. Thus as a major determiner of the *outcome* of parental practices, the child plays a role in modifying them.

The child's temperament is likely to be a major contributor to feedback. The highly sociable child is more responsive and offers more positive affective feedback than the low-sociable child. And the highly impulsive or highly emotional child is less likely to develop the self-control that is a major goal of parental child-rearing practices, which means that the practices will receive less long-run reinforcement. These examples are meant only as illustrations, and the role of the child's temperament will be spelled out in more detail in the next section, which deals with the interaction between the child's temperament and parental practices. The determinants of parental practices are summarized in Table 9.1.

TEMPERAMENT AND THE PARENT-CHILD INTERACTION

We can now present a more complete model of the parent-child interaction as it relates to temperament (see Figure 9.3). The determinants of parental learning have been discussed in detail, and our present focus is on the three

TABLE 9.1 DETERMINANTS OF CHILDREARING PRACTICES

Previous learning of the parent

Modeling
Shaping
Mass media

Parental temperament

Emotionality
Activity
Sociability
Impulsivity

Child's temperament

Setting the tone of interactions
Initiating behavior
Reinforcement

processes involving the child's temperament: how the effect of parental practices is modified by the child's temperament, the impact of the child's temperament on the parents, and the child's modeling of the parent.

The two dimensions of parental practices—love and control—may not be equally relevant to all of the child's temperaments. The love dimension is clearly more important for sociability, and the control dimension is more important for emotionality and impulsivity. The permissiveness end of the control dimension presumably has no impact on the child's temperament. The permissive parent grants the child considerable autonomy, and under this regime the child's initial dispositions are likely to show up clearly in behavior and remain stable over time.

The child's temperament can elicit new parental behaviors or changes in child-rearing practices. The principal direction of change in the parent is toward more control over the child, especially limiting behavior. It is usually the "troublesome child" who forces the parent to take special pains, and the trouble typically concerns the child's excessive impulsivity or emotionality. Parents vary considerably in how much turmoil and behavioral excess they will tolerate, and a major determinant of such tolerance is parental temperament. Therefore, we shall discuss the child's eliciting behavior in relation to his parents' temperaments.

The last process in the parent-child interaction is modeling (see Figure 9.3). Imitation learning has been documented (see Bandura & Walters, 1963), and it is well known that young children tend to model themselves after their parents. Our concern is with the temperamental aspects of modeling. The degree of similarity between the child and his parents is an important determinant of modeling. One reason for this is that a child wishes to be like, and identifies more with, persons who are similar (for example, boys with fathers and girls with mothers). A more important reason is that the child will already be disposed to behave like a parent whose temperament is similar (for example, a temperamentally high-active child already has the propensity and energy level to copy the behavior of a high-active parent). This means that for each temperament, we must take into account temperamental matches and mismatches between parents and children. Remember that temperaments have an inherited component, which means that children are more likely than not to resemble their parents in temperament.

In summary, the parent-child interaction has three components: parental child-rearing practices, the impact of which is in part determined by the child's temperament; the eliciting effects of the child's temperament, which are in part determined by parental temperament; and modeling, the extent of which is partly determined by parent-child similarity in temperament.

Before discussing research, we need to make one more point. The four temperaments are not equally acted on during the course of development. Society, through various socializing agents, pays minimal attention to variations in activity level; in general, a child must be either hyperactive or extremely lethargic to warrant special attention and strong pressure for change. Emotionality receives more attention in most cultures, and there is pressure for control of affect, especially the expressive aspects. The extremes of sociability are also subjected to attempts at modification, and both the social isolate and the intrusive, love-demanding child are pressured to change their behavior. Finally, a major aspect of socialization is the development of tolerance for frustration, delay of gratification, and general self-control; in temperamental

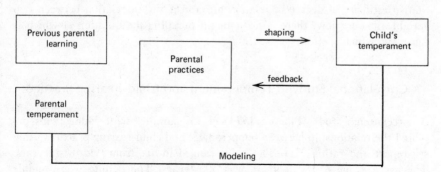

Figure 9.3. The parent-child interaction.

terms, this is reflected in the diminution of impulsiveness that characterizes most maturing children. Thus a rough ranking of the temperaments from least to most pressure by parents and other socializing agents is activity, emotionality, sociability, and impulsivity.

RESEARCH ON THE MODEL OF PARENT-CHILD INTERACTION

Our model has generated a number of hypotheses about the relationship between temperament and child-rearing practices. Virtually none of these hypotheses can be checked against known facts because research on children's personality has neglected temperament. Our most important hypotheses involve statements about the effects of practices on temperament and the effects of temperament on practices. These can be tested only by *longitudinal research*, in which time sequences allow inferences about cause and effect. The personality of children has been studied developmentally, but previous studies have contributed very little to knowledge about temperament because usually they have not assessed temperament. Consider two major studies in this area, those of Kagan and Moss (1962) and Schaefer and Bayley (1963). Kagan and Moss measured several different aspects of personality, but the closest they came to temperament was a measure of reaction to frustration. Schaefer and Bayley assessed several temperaments, but activity and emotionality were studied only during the first year of life. They measured sociability longitudinally and found that at each time period it correlated with parental child-rearing practices.

Before risking the huge expenditure of time and energy involved in longitudinal research, it is necessary first to establish that the hypothesized relationships exist, regardless of the direction of effects. Such research, which we shall call *correlational*, is accomplished more easily because it involves measurements at only one point in time. It does, nevertheless, provide a quantitative estimate of degree of relationship and if the correlation between two variables is very low, there is no point in pursuing the question of which is cause and which is effect.

A Correlational Study of Temperament and Child-Rearing Practices

A correlational study (Plomin, 1974) of 137 families with young twins explored the relationship between temperament and child-rearing practices using self-report and rating data. The twins ranged in age from two to six years. The average age of the mothers was 30.5 years. The families were middle class: the average total family income was nearly $14,000 and the average maternal education was nearly two years of college.

Both parents rated themselves, their spouse, and both of their twins on the EASI-III (Appendix 2). They also rated themselves and their spouse on a child-rearing questionnaire constructed to measure the love and control dimensions discussed above. Four items were written to measure the love dimension and eight items were written to measure the limiting and demanding aspects of control. The items are listed in Table 9.2. A factor analysis of the child-rearing questionnaire indicated that the love dimension items were factorially distinct, and the factor representing items from the control dimension consisted of limiting and demanding control items. The a priori limiting and demanding control scales correlated about .70, suggesting that parents who are controllers tend to use both types of control. The factor analyses were similar for the mothers' and fathers' self-reports and ratings of their spouse. The correlations between the items from the love and control factors were not completely ortho-

TABLE 9.2   CHILDREARING PRACTICES QUESTIONNAIRE

Love dimension

I tend to lavish warmth and affection on my child*
When angry I sometimes tell my child that I don't love him/her
I am more or less reserved toward my child (reverse)*
I express my affection to my child more than most parents*

Limiting control

It is very important to me to teach my child obedience to
authority**
I rarely try to impose my will on my child to make him/her
conform (reverse)
I encourage my child to control himself without my supervision**
Children the age of my child need a strong restraining hand

Demanding control

More than most parents, I expect a lot from my child
I encourage my child to set goals for himself/herself**
I don't mind pushing my child a little to get him/her to do
things he/she should**
What my child does with his/her free time is mainly up to
him/her (reverse)

---

* Items used in the factored love scale
**Items used in the factored control scale

gonal. For the parents' self-report data, the correlation between the love and control dimensions was .20 and for the parents' ratings of their spouse, the correlation was .28.

Two other psychometric issues merit attention: test-retest reliability and rater agreement. A subsample of 32 mothers was retested after a two- to three-month interval on their self-reports of child rearing. The test-retest correlation was .60 for the love dimension and .43 for the control dimension. Because both spouses rated themselves and their spouse, it was possible to estimate rater agreement by correlating the parents' self-reports with their spouses' ratings of them. Wives' ratings of their husbands agreed more with the self-reports of their husbands (.40 for the love dimension and .39 for the control dimension) than the husbands' ratings of their wives agreed with the self-reports of their wives (.39 and .25, respectively). Although neither the reliability nor rater agreement on child-rearing practices was overwhelming, the questionnaire appeared acceptable for this preliminary exploration.

The EASI-III was more satisfactory in terms of these psychometric properties. The average test-retest correlations for the mothers' self-reports on the eleven subscales of the EASI was .79 and the average rater agreement was .51. For the children's version of the EASI-III the average test-retest correlation was .72, but the rater agreement was not as good, .36 on the average.

CHILD-REARING PRACTICES AND THE TEMPERAMENT OF CHILDREN

Contrary to our expectations, the temperament of children showed little relation to child-rearing practices. None of the correlations was high, and few were significant. No relationships were consistent for both self-report and rating data, and for both mothers and fathers. We do not attempt to interpret the few marginally significant correlations because four significant correlations can be expected by chance out of 88 correlations (between mothers' and fathers' self-reports and ratings on 11 EASI scales vs. two child-rearing scales).

CHILD-REARING PRACTICES AND THE TEMPERAMENT OF PARENTS

There was somewhat more relationship between parental temperament and child-rearing practices. Sociability of parents was positively related to the love dimension of child rearing and, to a lesser extent, to the control dimension. Activity was related to the control dimension. Vigorously active mothers exercised more control over their children. For the husbands, the tempo component of activity was a better predictor of control. Both parents reported that they were less controlling—and to some extent, less loving—if they were fearful (the fear scale of emotionality) and impulsive (the persistence scale of impulsivity). These relationships held, for the most part, for both the self-report and rating data, and they correspond to some of our predictions.

TEMPERAMENT OF CHILDREN AND PARENTS

Although the EASI-III items are similar for the adult and children versions, the meaning of an item may differ substantially when a 30-year-old adult is rated as compared to a four-year-old child. Despite this problem, correlations between the EASI of parents and their children shed some light on the combined influence of genetic factors and modeling. For the parents' EASI self-reports correlated with the parents' ratings of their children's EASI, all the correlations were positive, and nearly all the correlations were positive for the parents' ratings of the spouse also. The highest parent-child correlations were obtained for emotionality (especially the fear component), sociability, and the sensation-seeking and persistence components of impulsivity. Although the correlations were clearly higher than those between child rearing and temperament, the *highest* parent-child correlation was only .41 and the *average* correlation was .17 between the mothers and their children and .10 for the fathers.

The data for the mother-child correlations showed some agreement with the father-child data. For the self-report data, the rank-order correlation between the mother-child correlations and the father-child correlations for the 11 EASI subscales was .27. For the ratings by the spouse, the rank-order correlation was .48. These correlations were deflated considerably by one comparison, that of general emotionality. In both the self-report and rating data, the second highest parent-child correlation for the mothers was general emotionality; for fathers, it was the lowest. This suggested a strong maternal effect for general emotionality. Excluding general emotionality, the agreement between the rank ordering of the mother-child and father-child correlations was .53 for the self-report data and .64 for the cross-rating data.

CONCLUSIONS

Any conclusions must be tentative for several reasons: (1) this was the first attempt to study the relationship between temperament and child rearing; (2) we studied preschool twins; and (3) the data were self-reports and ratings. Any of these limitations may have affected the results.

Our theory led us to consider the environmental factors that may interact with temperament during development. A reasonable starting point was child-rearing practices, but the data of the study suggest that child rearing may not be an important influence in the development of temperament. Perhaps the love and control dimensions are more important for the development of non-temperamental traits. Perhaps other aspects of child rearing are more important for the development of temperaments. The factor analytic work discussed earlier indicated that the love and control dimensions of child rearing account for much parental behavior. So, if our findings are generalizable the question becomes, which environmental factors account for the environmental variance of the temperaments? One possibility that we must be willing to consider is that there are *no* broad systematic environmental influences in personality development. The environmental variance may come about as the child makes his idiosyncratic way through the world, experiencing many slightly different situations. This counterintuitive and rather radical conclusion was reached in a recent book by Loehlin and Nichols (in press):

> In short, we seem to see environmental effects in the personality area which operate almost randomly with respect to the sorts of variables psychologists (and other people) have traditionally deemed important in personality development. . . . The major, consistent directional factors in personality are the genes, and that the important environmental influences are highly variable situational inputs. This need not imply actual randomness in the environment, of course. If the ways in which environment affects personality are sufficiently complex, contingent, and subtle, they will appear random to an analysis such as ours.

This is a strong challenge, and, in light of the data just presented, it should not be ignored. It is hard to believe that there is little or no parental input into the child's personality. A reasonable working hypothesis is that there is a strong input but the psychologists have not yet discovered the relevant variables. But we should also remember that this is in effect a promissory note, and the indebtedness eventually must be paid off.

CHAPTER

$$\boxed{10}$$

CONCLUSIONS

This chapter is not a summary but a discussion of some broader issues concerning temperament and personality. There have been previous theories of temperament and in Chapter 1 we promised to discuss them here. There are several substantive issues that bear directly on built-in personality dispositions: their inheritance, how many dispositions there are, and their nature. Finally, there are implications for the study of personality development.

PREVIOUS THEORIES OF TEMPERAMENT

Sheldon

Ask a psychology graduate student to associate a name to the word *temperament*, and he is likely to say "Sheldon." Ever since the appearance of *Varieties of Temperament* (1942), Sheldon's name has been linked with the constitutional approach to personality. Actually, his major contribution was to insist that there are three basic body types, each with its own corresponding temperament. The body types are essentially fat, muscular, and lean, and the associated personality types are viscerotona, somatotonia, and cerebrotonia, respectively. Sheldon reported very high correlations between body type and personality type, but there were possible confounds. The worst confound was that the same person who estimated body type also evaluated personality.

Subsequent research by other investigators corrected this basic flaw, and the correlations between body type and personality fell to lower levels (Davidson et al., 1957; Walker, 1962; and Cortes and Gatti, 1965). But the correlations did hold up, and evidently there is a relationship between body build and personality. Part of this relationship is built in and therefore of no consequence. For example, the personality type of the fat person contains such items as love of physical comfort, love of eating, socialization of eating, and pleasure in digestion. That fat persons eat more is true but trivial. Of greater importance are personality characteristics that do not derive from body build. For example, fat persons are more sociable than muscular persons, and thin persons are less sociable. At present no one can explain this relationship between sociability and body type, and it remains an intriguing fact.

What about Sheldon's formulation as a theory of temperament? He did not establish that his personality types were inherited, and their factorial unity is questionable. He had nothing to say about the nature of the temperaments (they are a hodgepodge of traits) or about their developmental course. And he did not spell out their implications for personality except to suggest that body build is an important variable.

Thomas, Chess, and Birch

The *development* of personality is the focus of the temperament theory of Thomas et al. (1968, 1970). They suggest that there are nine inborn characteristics, present at birth, that are the building blocks of personality:

1. Level and extent of motor activity.
2. Rhythmicity or regularity of functions (eating, eliminating, etc.).
3. Acceptance or withdrawal from a new person or object.
4. Adaptability to changes in the environment.
5. Threshold or sensitivity to stimuli.
6. Intensity or energy level of responses.
7. General mood or disposition.
8. Distractibility.
9. Span of attention and persistence.

These nine features are presumably the "origins of personality," which is the title of one of their papers. They assessed these nine characteristics in children soon after birth, and then traced the youngsters until 10 years of age. Thomas et al. claim that the individual differences held up over the years, with children continuing to manifest their temperamental traits over the years. There is also some evidence that children with "difficult" temperaments (moody, overly sensitive, etc.) tended to develop behavior problems later in childhood.

In brief, Thomas et al. present a temperament theory that starts out with nine tendencies present at birth and traces these tendencies as they develop throughout childhood. The theory has value as a temperamental approach to the development of personality, and there are some data to sustain it. But the theory does have problems. There is no evidence of factorial unity, and the reader can easily see that several of the nine features listed above probably belong to a single factor: sensitivity to stimuli, intensity or response, and general mood would seem to be intercorrelated. Thomas et al. present no data bearing on the relationships among the nine factors, and we must wonder whether a smaller number of variables would account for most of the variance.

A second problem concerns the developmental course of the temperaments. It is hard to see how some of the behaviors falling under a temperament during infancy belong together with behaviors listed under the same temperament at the age of 10 years. For example, under Distractibility, the following behaviors indicate a child who is not distractible: at two months, will not stop crying when diaper is changed and fusses after eating even if rocked; and at 10 years, can read a book while television set is at high volume and does chores on schedule. We are asked to accept on faith that both sets of behaviors, at two months and at 10 years, are indications of low distractibility. But on the face of it the behaviors are not at all comparable, and there is a real question of whether the two months' items really tap distractibility. We suggest that Thomas et al. need to provide evidence that they are measuring the same temperament in late childhood that they are in infancy.

Perhaps the most serious problem with this theory is its failure to establish that the personality features it specifies are really inherited. The fact that individual differences are present at birth is consistent with inheritance but does not prove the point. It has yet to be established through behavior genetics research that the nine features of Thomas et al. are inherited. We have no doubt that some of them are inherited because they overlap our own temperaments. We suggest that of their nine personality dispositions, the only ones that will prove to be heritable are those that are the same as or overlap our temperaments. Furthermore, we believe that a factor analysis would reveal that most of their nine features would boil down to a smaller number of factors. with most of the variance being accounted for by a version of our four temperaments. This suggestion is speculative but testable.

Diamond

Theories do not spring full blown from the foreheads of theorists, and we must acknowledge our indebtedness to Diamond (1957). It was Diamond who insisted that we should take the comparative approach and learn from the personality dispositions of our mammalian and primate forebears. He formulated four temperaments shared by man and animals close to man: fearfulness, aggressiveness, affiliativeness, and impulsiveness. *Fearfulness* includes both a physiological tendency to become aroused and a behavioral tendency to cower, freeze, and avoid dangerous situations. *Aggressiveness* is simply the tendency to fight, whether in attacking or defending against attack. *Affiliativeness* refers to seeking contacts with others and avoiding solitude. *Impulsiveness* has two components: inhibitory control and level of activity or energy expenditure.

This brief description shows the similarities between our theory and Diamond's, and we gratefully admit to borrowing from him. But our theory is different on several counts. Only one of our temperaments is the same as his: our sociability is essentially the same as his affiliativeness, although we included warmth as part of the temperament. We have no temperament of aggressiveness, and there are three reasons for this. First, there is no clear evidence that aggressiveness is inherited. Second, we believe that the anger component in aggressiveness is better viewed as having differentiated from the more primitive emotionality temperament present at birth—distress. Third, insofar as there is a temperamental input into aggressiveness, it would appear to derive from three different temperaments: activity, emotionality, and impulsivity, with the last-named being the most important (see Chapter 8).

Our impulsivity temperament is different from Diamond's. His includes activity level; ours does not. We believe that the factorial evidence leans in our direction: activity and impulsivity, when measured without confounds, are factorially different, and the correlation between the factors is low. Also, as we saw in Chapter 6, impulsivity is somewhat more complex than simply inhibitory control.

Our emotionality temperament is also different from Diamond's. His includes only fearfulness, whereas ours starts out with a generalized distress and differentiates into fear and anger. And there is some evidence from self-report and rating research that our position is correct.

This last point raises the further issue of data. Diamond's theory appeared slightly less than 20 years ago, and there was little evidence bearing on temperaments. The absence of data at the time Diamond formulated his theory cannot be blamed on Diamond, and perhaps the following decade was not the appropriate time for his theory to be taken up. But the fact remains that his theory did not generate any research, and so it has remained merely a set of speculations. Neither he nor anyone else has collected data bearing on heritability or factorial unity, and we suggest that there are problems in both areas. Aggressiveness does not appear to be heritable, nor is it likely to show factorial unity. Impulsivity appears to consist of several different dispositions, and its inheritance is still an open question. In summary, Diamond's theory must be considered a fascinating set of speculations, but it lacks any confirming data and it has not led to any subsequent research.

Eysenck

Whatever else may be said about Eysenck's personality theory, it is opposite to Diamond's in that it has led to an outpouring of research. Eysenck's approach may have led to more research than any other theory in the area. Further, unlike the first three theories mentioned, Eysenck's is supported by at least some evidence of heritability. His theory is also valuable in the way it integrates experimental laboratory research with personality dispositions. Above all, the theory has set forth explicit predictions and so is eminently testable.

But our concern is with temperament and Eysenck's theory has several problems. Its best known variable is *extraversion*, a composite of sociability, impulsivity, and perhaps several other components. We discussed extraversion in detail in Chapter 8 and so need only remind the reader of our conclusions. Sociability and impulsivity are quite independent when assessed in an unconfounded way. Sociability appears to be a clear and unitary factor with excellent evidence for its heritability; impulsivity appears to be a mixed bag of variables, with equivocal evidence for its heritability. Persons high in sociability and low in impulsivity would seem to be entirely different in personality (and easy to socialize) from persons low in sociability and high in impulsivity (who are hard to socialize). In brief, the dimension of extraversion is best divided into its major components, sociability and impulsivity.

The other relevant factor is *neuroticism*, which bears a passing resemblance to our temperament of emotionality. But neuroticism is different in several ways. Its heritability is open to question, as we documented in Chapter 4, and the reason is not hard to find. Neuroticism refers not only to a tendency to become distressed easily (inherited) but also a combination of acquired fears and worries. In any given person, a high score on the neuroticism scale would reflect an unknown combination of the learned and inherited components.

Another problem concerns the way both neuroticism and extraversion are defined. Part of the problem lies in the items that make up the self-report inventory. For example, the neuroticism scale includes, "Are you daydreams frequently about thing that can never come true?" and "Are you inclined to ponder over your past?" What have these to do with items that refer to distress and nervousness, such as, "Have you often lost sleep over your worries?" and "Would you rate yourself as a tense or high strung individual?" Inclusion of both kinds of items in a single scale has to make us wonder precisely what *neuroticism* means. Another part of the problem lies in the mixture of self-report inventory items with experimental laboratory measures and demographic variables (years of education, for example). Eysenck claims that his various factors (neuroticism, extraversion, etc.) emerged from correlation matrices involving these three sources of data (self-reports of personality, laboratory measures such as reaction time, and demographic variables). One of the defects of Eysenck's theory *as a theory of temperament* is this mixture of diverse components. The mixture may be acceptable for his original theoretical goals, but it is not if the goal is a theory of temperament. In brief, these comments apply only insofar as Eysenck's theory is regarded as a temperament theory: its factorial unity is questionable and the heritability of the variables is in doubt. In addition, Eysenck has nothing to say about the developmental course of either extraversion or neuroticism.

INHERITANCE

In discussing four previous theories of temperament, we sought evidence about their inheritance. Heritability is a central issue for temperaments because it is what distinguishes them from other personality dispositions. Having inquired about the inheritance of temperaments postulated by others, we must in fairness ask about our own four temperaments.

There is good evidence that activity, emotionality, and sociability have a genetic component; the evidence for the inheritance of impulsivity is equivocal. We feel reasonably safe in our conclusion about the heritability of the first three temperaments because the evidence converges from several sources. Monozygotic twins tend to be more alike in these three temperaments than are dizygotic twins. Children tend to resemble their parents in these temperamental dispositions. Also, there are marked individual differences in these temperaments immediately after birth or as soon as the dispositions can be measured. Newborn infants clearly differ in emotionality both physiologically and behaviorally. Individual differences in activity and sociability appear later in infancy, probably because some maturation is necessary before they can clearly be seen. (The same is evidently true for intelligence, which cannot adequately be measured until some time after infancy.)

It might be argued that each kind of evidence can be explained in nongenetic terms. The greater similarity of monozygotic twins might be due to some artifact such as their being treated more alike by parents and others (although there is evidence against this assumption). Resemblance between parents and their children might come about through imitation and shaping. And the individual differences present at birth or soon after might be caused by the events of fetal development or the birth process itself. In brief, each of the three kinds of data bearing on the inheritance of temperaments might be explained in nongenetic terms. But note that each explanation is ad hoc and accounts only for one set of data. There is one explanation that accounts for all three sets of data: that at least three personality dispositions are inborn. So on the grounds of parsimony and generality, we prefer to interpret the evidence as being consistent with the notion of temperaments.

But we do not mean to overstate the case. We are aware of the methodological problems of twin studies, ratings, and self-reports. In much of the research, the samples are small, and the correlations vary considerably from one study to the next. As measures are refined and improved, and as the methods of behavior genetics progress, the quantitative estimates of heritability of temperaments should stabilize. Perhaps this book will stimulate the needed research. We believe that previous research supports the heritability of at least three of the temperaments, but we must agree that more documentation is needed.

HOW MANY TEMPERAMENTS?

Our theory assumes that there are four temperaments, but there is nothing magical about the number *four*. (Theoretically, *three* may well be the magic number, as in the holy trinity or in id-ego-superego). Perhaps there are really only three temperaments; perhaps there are more than four.

The Cases for Three Temperaments

Impulsivity may not be a temperament. There is a serious question about its factorial unity, and its heritability is still in doubt. If impulsivity is not a built-in personality disposition, how can we explain the individual differences that exist in quickness of reaction versus reflectivity and planning? The answer clearly lies in early environmental training. There is a strong push during socialization for children to control their behavior, specifically, to inhibit immediate responding and delay gratification. If an adult is still impulsive, it follows that there has been a failure of socialization. There is the further implication that an impulsive adult, having been incompletely socialized, lacks guilt, altruism, and other tendencies that are strongly reinforced by socializing agents. What we are pointing out is that if a strictly environmental account of impulsivity does not have testable implications it is not a worthwhile hypothesis. At present the evidence for a strictly environmental explanation of impulsivity is lacking. So we are confronted with the dilemma of choosing between a temperament hypothesis that is only equivocally supported and an environmental hypothesis that as yet has no evidence for it.

Given this choice, we prefer the temperament hypothesis, at least for the present. In effect, we are issuing a promissory note that more positive evidence will be forthcoming. If subsequent research does not sustain impulsivity as a temperament, it will be dropped from the list. If the present evidence is read more skeptically, perhaps impulsivity should be dropped now. If this is done, then there are only three temperaments. Thus one case for three temperaments is to exclude impulsivity and stick to activity, emotionality, and sociability.

A quite different case can be made for three temperaments by retaining impulsivity but combining it with one or more of the remaining temperaments. Thus activity and impulsivity could be combined into a single temperament along the lines sketched out by Diamond (1957). A person high on this temperament would be energetic, fast-moving, sensation seeking, and stimulus bound. He would be galvanized into action by each new stimulus and so would display little persistence or inhibitory control. We agree that there are such persons but assume them to be a combination of high activity and high impulsivity.

If activity and impulsivity belong together as a single temperament, they should be highly correlated. In fact, they were highly correlated in EASI-I, but this was due to the confound of two items concerned with restlessness. If two persons differ in activity level and they are both required to sit quietly, the more active one will tend to fidget and move about more; this restlessness will be viewed as impulsivity as well as activity. So there is a built-in confound between activity and impulsivity in the set of behaviors called restlessness. When this item was eliminated in EASI-II, the correlation between activity and impulsivity disappeared (see Table 2.11). In brief, activity and impulsivity are not correlated and so must be retained as distinct temperaments.

There is a better case for combining impulsivity with emotionality. A person high on this temperament would be excitable, easily upset, and generally uncontrolled in his affect. If he tended in the direction of being neurotic, he would have severe fears and would be unable to control his expressions of fear or his desire to escape from and avoid the feared situations. Again, we agree that there are such persons but maintain that they are a combination of emotionality and impulsivity.

If emotionality and activity belong together as a single temperament, they should be highly correlated. In fact, in the several versions of the EASI the correlations averaged about .30. This is a definite relationship but far below that needed to combine the two dispositions into a single temperament. Consider vigor and tempo, which are the components of activity temperament, These two correlate in the sixties and seventies, and when they are both assessed, a single factor emerges. Now contrast the data for emotionality and impulsivity. First, the correlation is much lower, roughly .30. Second, there is virtually no item overlap on the factor analyses of the several versions of the EASI. So there are no compelling facts that would lead us to combine emotionality with impulsivity to form a single temperament.

If this is our position, how do we explain the .30 correlation between the two? The explanation was suggested in our first account of the temperaments in Chapter 1. In metaphorical terms, emotionality is a kind of *motor* in that the person is aroused, distressed, and excited, in brief, in a state of intense motivation. In the same terms, impulsivity is a kind of brakes (actually, a lack of brakes) in that control is (or is not) exercised over impulses to respond to either internal motives or external stimuli. If one person expresses more affect than the next, he will be seen not only as more emotional but also as more impulsive. We see no way out of this confound and suggest that it is built into the way we are. So our explanation of the .30 correlation between emotionality and impulsivity is that the former involves a stronger motive force and the latter involves resistance or lack of resistance to such force. A moderate correlation between them is therefore inevitable but not sufficient grounds for combining them into a single entity.

The Cases for More Than Four Temperaments

One logical argument for postulating inborn personality dispositions is the concept of intelligence. Virtually all psychologists agree that there is an innate component in intelligence, and this consensus is based on a solid body of evidence: the similarity of twins, the similarity of parents and their children, the early appearance of individual differences, the stability throughout childhood, and the relative resistance to change by environmental contingencies. If there is an inborn disposition relating to cognitive ability (intelligence), should there not be other inborn dispositions relating to personality? Our answer has been to postulate four temperaments, but perhaps there are more.

What are the possibilities? Diamond (1957) has suggested aggressiveness because of the prevalence of individual differences in the tendency to attack across a wide range of animal species. By the same token, dominance might be proposed as a temperament. Several other possibilities have been suggested by Thomas et al. (1963). They involve combinations or components of our four temperaments plus two distinct temperaments: rhythmicity and adaptability. Rhythmicity refers mainly to regular cycles of sleep-wakefulness, hunger-satiation, etc. These are entirely appropriate to infancy, but they are hard to isolate in older children and adults. Adaptability is such a generalized concept that it is difficult to pin down.

Regardless of whether the disposition lasts throughout childhood or is hard to pin down, it must be shown to be heritable if it is to be regarded as a temperament. None of the four dispositions mentioned—aggressiveness, dominance, rhythmicity, or adaptability—has been shown to be heritable. If such evidence appears, the dispositions should be seriously considered as temperaments. So at present there is no empirical basis for adding any new temperaments.

But perhaps there is a logical case for adding to the list. We know that personality is a complex entity and that there are many kinds of persons. Are four temperaments sufficient to deal with the many different kinds of personalities seen in the population? Our answer has two parts. First, temperament theory is not intended to explain *all* aspects of personality, only those aspects that derive from inborn dispositions. We freely admit that many aspects of personality are acquired wholly through experience, modeling, and shaping. We see no way to account for individual differences in guilt, self-esteem, or systematic bigotry in terms of temperamental tendencies. So, the first part of our answer is that temperament theory attempts to account for a more limited range of behavior than all the individual differences in personality.

Second, although there are only four temperaments, they presumably occur in different combinations. Assume for the moment that we can assign persons to one of three places on a quantitative dimension of each temperament: high, average, and low. This works out to 54 separate patterns of combinations of two temperaments, and the permutations for combinations of three or four temperaments are very large. We are not suggesting that every possible combination of temperaments actually exists in the population, but clearly there are enough combinations to account for the variety of personalities that exists in the population.

It would serve no useful purpose to spell out descriptions of all the possible combinations of temperaments, but in Chapter 8 we described some salient and important ones. For illustrative purposes, let us mention two combinations of activity and emotionality. Compare a person high on both temperaments with one who is high on activity but low on emotionality. In the face of stress or danger, both persons would respond with vigorous, fast-moving activity. But whereas the low-emotional person would presumably engage in efficient, instrumental acts, the high-emotional person would engage in wild, undirected behavior. The total energy output would be the same in both persons, but the unemotional person would function better in the face of stress. This account is speculative, but it can be tested. It is designed to show that combinations of temperaments can explain (or predict) specific behaviors in a wide variety of contexts.

THE NATURE OF THE TEMPERAMENTS

In attempting to specify the nature of the temperaments, we have analyzed each into two or more components. We regard activity as consisting of two closely related aspects, quickness of movement and amplitude of response. Our own research agrees with evidence of others: tempo and vigor are highly correlated. As mentioned earlier, when they are included in the same inventory, they emerge as a single factor.

We have analyzed emotionality into autonomic and behavioral components. This follows traditional usage by psychologists, but an empirical case has not yet been made. There is no negative evidence; there is simply no evidence at all. Our theory points to a needed area of research: joint measurement of physiological and behavioral aspects of emotion to determine their relationship. If our assumptions are correct, the correlation should be highest in infancy and then drop during childhood under the impact of behavioral shaping and modeling of the expressive (behavioral) aspects of emotionality.

The division of sociability into need and warmth appears to be novel but it, too, is untested. Need appears to be easy to measure through self-reports and ratings, and so it has been assessed often. Warmth should not be measured through self-report because social desirability would be too strong, and it is hard to measure in ratings because of its subjectivity. For example, if a person smiles frequently, this is a good indication that he is warm. But the smile may be frozen and superficial, as in the smile of a professional model or of a maitre d'hotel. So the rater would have to allow for the role being played, the formality of the context, etc. Nevertheless, difficult as it is to rate warmth, it must be done and correlated with the need to be with others. Otherwise, we shall never discover whether our assumption of their close relationship is true.

What are the components of impulsivity? We suggest that there are two basic components, both involving inhibition or lack of it. The first concerns inhibition of motivations to act, such as hunger, thirst, sex, or any of a list of primary or secondary drives. The second concerns response to external stimuli: a fast reaction, as opposed to a delayed, planned reaction. From these two components, we derive two others, persistence and sensation seeking (or its opposite, boredom). But we must admit that our assumptions lack an empirical base. Our first attempt to assess these four components in EASI-III (see Appendix 2) have not yielded consistent findings; at present all we can do is to state our assumptions. It may turn out that there are four different temperaments of impulsivity, or two, or one, or perhaps there is no temperament called impulsivity.

The term *nature of the temperaments* can have another meaning. In discussing our theory with others, we have sometimes been asked, "What are the temperaments, really?" On elucidation, this question turned out to be a query about the biological substrate of the temperaments. We could offer speculations about three of the temperaments. Activity might reside in some basic vegetative process such as the underlying metabolic rate of the body. Emotionality might originate in the limbic-midbrain-hypothalamic system that is presumed to control the autonomic nervous system and the expressive components of emotion. Impulsivity might derive from the complex interaction between the cerebral cortex and the reticular formation. Sociability appears to have no biological substrate that we can see.

But these are the sheerest, gossamer hypotheses, and we do not take them seriously. Some scientists find it hard to believe that there are inborn behavioral dispositions, and they are more comfortable with purely biological mechanisms. The name for this approach is *reductionism*. This is not the place to discuss reductionism, except to point out that we cannot see where it would lead in the present instance. We would welcome any knowledge about the biological substrates of behavior—any behavior, including temperamental dispositions. But extant theories deal with a conceptual nervous system, as opposed to a real nervous system; in our view, they do not add to our understanding of personality. For example, intelligence has been found to be a useful and relevant concept, but at present no one has any testable notion about its underlying biological substrate. In brief, we suggest that the issue of the nature of temperaments is best construed in terms of their behavioral components rather than their ostensible biological underpinnings.

THE DEVELOPMENT OF PERSONALITY

Our theory has profound implications for the study of personality development. We read the current theorizing and research on personality development as being one-sided in that it overemphasizes the environmental determinants of behavior. It is not that parental inputs, peer influences, and the experiences of everyday life are unimportant in influencing personality, but that these determinants are not the only ones. We suggest that it is foolhardy to ignore the personality dispositions that are built into each of us. As Diamond wrote,

> A crucial problem in the study of personality is to determine what are the most fundamental respects in which individuals differ from each other. All attempts to do this on the basis of observation of adult human behavior, no matter how sophisticated in either a statistical or clinical sense, have the common failing that they are unable to distinguish between the essential foundations of individually and its cultural elaborations. [pp. 4–5]

We suggest that the essential foundations of individuality are the four temperaments of our theory. Presumably what is inherited is a tendency to occupy one part of the dimension of each of the four temperaments. Thus a high-active child tends to be somewhere above the average in tempo and vigor. The initial *range* of his activity level might be somewhat broad, but it is narrowed during development (see Figure 10.1). The initial inherited potential is molded by life experiences that select the part of the range most appropriate to family, subculture, peers, etc. Although the *origin* of the temperament is inheritance, its final *outcome* depends on modification by the environment.

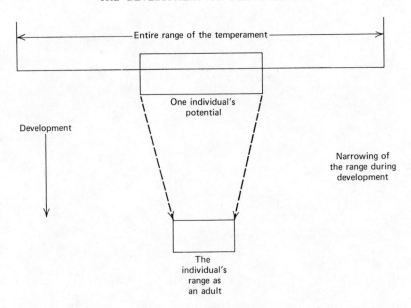

Figure 10.1.   Modification of temperament.

The child is not merely the passive recipient of environmental shaping. Our theory assumes an *interaction* between the child and the forces that mold his personality. He is an *initiator* who in part makes his own environment. He is a *reinforcer*, selectively rewarding or punishing agents in his environment for the way they behave toward him. And he is a *responder*, who modifies the *impact* of the environment on his personality. This is a considerably more complex model of personality development than that of the child as a blank slate on which the environment writes. But we suggest that it is a truer picture of what actually happens. There have been decades of research guided by the simplistic model of a passive child who is molded by his environment. Have the time and effort expended been rewarded by significant increments in knowledge and understanding? Most psychologists would say no. Perhaps it is time to adopt the more complex model, to concentrate on built-in personality dispositions, and to keep them separate from the dispositions that are wholly learned.

APPENDICES

APPENDIX 1   INTRACLASS CORRELATIONS OF INDIVIDUAL ITEMS OF THE EASI-I

A *priori* Scale Assignment	Correlations			
	Boys		Girls	
	MZ	DZ	MZ	DZ
Emotionality				
Child cries easily	.56	.10	.47	.23
Child has a quick temper	.34	.10	.40	.70
Child gets upset easily	.64	.10	.66	.00
Child is easily frightened	.58	.11	.70	.00
Child is easygoing or happy-go-lucky	.46	.00	.38	.00
Activity				
Child is off and running as soon as he wakes up in the morning	.88	.41	.86	.00
Child is always on the go	.48	.02	.72	.01
Child cannot sit still long	.76	.25	.65	.27
Child prefers quiet games such as coloring or block play to more active games	.77	.00	.21	.03
Child fidgets at meals and similar occasions	.67	.38	.68	.31
Sociability				
Child makes friends easily	.74	.26	.47	.00
Child likes to be with others	.61	.27	.29	.05
Child tends to be shy	.57	.10	.51	.00
Child is independent	.58	.25	.44	.24
Child prefers to play by himself rather than with others	.55	.10	.73	.46
Impulsivity				
Learning self-control is difficult for the child	.75	.55	.83	.69
Child tends to be impulsive	.81	.00	.68	.39
Child gets bored easily	.83	.13	.49	.59
Child learns to resist temptation easily	.72	.35	.70	.52
Child goes from toy to toy quickly	.82	.44	.83	.62

EMOTIONALITY

General

I frequently get upset
I am almost always calm--nothing ever bothers me (reverse)
I get excited easily
I am somewhat emotional
I often feel like crying (child often cries)

Fear

I am easily frightened
I often feel insecure
I tend to be nervous in new situations
I have fewer fears than most people my age (reverse) (... than most children that age)
When I get scared, I panic

Anger

When displeased, I let people know it right away
It takes a lot to get me mad (reverse)
I am known as hot-blooded and quick-tempered
I yell and scream more than most people my age
There are many things that annoy me

ACTIVITY

Tempo

I usually seem to be in a hurry
For relaxation I like to slow down and take things easy (reverse)
I like to be off and running as soon as I wake up in the morning
I like to keep busy all the time
My life is fast paced (most of my child's activities are fast paced)

Vigor

I like to wear myself out with exertion
I often feel sluggish (reverse)
I often feel as if I'm bursting with energy (child often appears to be bursting with energy)
When I do things, I do them vigorously
My movements are forceful and emphatic

SOCIABILITY

I make friends very quickly
I am very sociable

I tend to be shy (reverse)
I usually prefer to do things alone (reverse)
I have many friends

IMPULSIVITY

Inhibitory control

I have trouble controlling my impulses
Usually I can't stand waiting
I can tolerate frustration better than most (reverse)
I have trouble resisting my cravings (for food, cigarettes, etc.) (child has trouble resisting temptation)
I like to spend my money right away rather than save it for long-range goals (child finds self-control easy to learn)

Decision time

I often say the first thing that comes into my head
I often have trouble making up my mind (reverse)
I like to plan things way ahead of time (reverse)
I often act on the spur of the moment
I like to make detailed plans before I do something (reverse)

Sensation seeking

I generally seek new and exciting experiences and sensations
I'll try anything once
I sometimes do "crazy" things just to be different
I'm happiest in familiar surroundings (reverse)
I get bored easily

Persistence

I generally like to see things through to the end (reverse)
I tend to hop from interest to interest quickly
I tend to give up easily
Unfinished tasks really bother me (reverse)
Once I get going on something I hate to stop (reverse)

---

*
 For an extended discussion of factor analyses, intercorrelations, and other data concerning EASI-III see Plomin, 1974. Details for each temperament are presented in Chapters 3 to 6.
**
 The children's version of EASI-III uses the same items (with exceptions noted) worded in the third person; for example, the first item is "Child frequently gets upset."

BIBLIOGRAPHY

Adams, J. P. Adolescent personal problems as a function of age and sex. *Journal of Genetic Psychology*, 1964, **104**, 207–214.

Adams, J. and Rothstein, W. The relationship between 16 fear factors and psychiatric states. *Behavior Research and Therapy*, 1971, **9**, 361–365.

Alexander, A. and Osborne, R. Psychophysiological aspects of adaptation in twins. Paper presented at the *Third Annual Meeting of the Behavior Genetics Association*, 1973.

Allport, G. W. *Pattern and Growth in Personality*. New York: Holt, Rinehart and Winston, Inc., 1961.

Aronfreed, J. and Reber, A. Internalized behavior suppression and the timing of social punishment. *Journal of Personality and Social Psychology*, 1965, **1**, 3–16.

Ax, A. F. The physiological differentiation between fear and anger in humans. *Psychosomatic Medicine*, 1953, **15**, 433–442.

Bandura, A. Social learning theory of identificatory processes. In D. A. Goslin (Ed.), *Handbook of Socialization Theory and Research*. Chicago: Rand McNally, 1969, pp. 213–262.

Bandura, A. and Walters, R. *Social Learning and Personality Development*. New York: Holt, Rinehart and Winston, Inc., 1963.

Bardwick, J. *Psychology of Women*. New York: Harper & Row, 1971.

Barker, R. G., Dembo, T., and Lewin, K. Frustration and regression: An experiment with young children. *University of Iowa Studies in Child Welfare*, 1941, **18**, 1–314.

Barratt, E. S. Factor analysis of some psychometric measures of impulsiveness and anxiety. *Psychological Reports*, 1965, **16**, 547–554.

Battle, E. and Lacey, B. A context for hyperactivity in children over time. *Child Development*, 1972, **43**, 757–773.

Baumrind, D. Effects of authoritative parental control on child behavior. *Child Development*, 1966, **37**, 887–907.

Bayes, M. A. Behavioral cues of interpersonal warmth. *Journal of Consulting and Clinical Psychology*, 1972, **39**, 333–339.

Bayley, N. A study of the crying of infants during mental and physical tests. *Journal of Genetic Psychology*, 1932, **40**, 306–329.

Bayley, N. *Bayley Scales of Infant Development*. New York: Psychological Corp., 1969.

Bell, R. Q. Relations between behavior manifestations in the human neonate. *Child Development*, 1960, **31**, 463–477.

Bell, R. Q. A reinterpretation of the direction of effects in studies of socialization. *Psychological Review*, 1968, **75**, 81–95.

Bem, D. J. *Beliefs, Attitudes, and Human Affairs,* Belmont, Calif.: Brooks-Cole, 1970.

Bennett, E. M. and Cohen, L. R. Men and women: Personality patterns and contrasts. *Genetic Psychology Monographs,* 1959, **59,** 101–155.

Berlyne, D. F. *Conflict, Arousal, and Curiosity.* New York: McGraw-Hill, 1960.

Berne, E. V. An experimental investigation of social behavior patterns in young children. *University of Lower Studies in Child Welfare,* 1931, **4,** whole number 3.

Bernreuter, R. G. *The Personality Inventory.* Palo Alto, Calif.: Stanford University Press, 1935.

Berry, J. and Martin, B. GSR reactivity as a function of anxiety instructions and sex. *Journal of Abnormal and Social Psychology,* 1957, **54,** 9–12.

Biller, H. B. *Father, Child, and Sex Role.* Lexington, Mass.: Heath, 1971.

Birns, B. Individual differences in human neonates' responses to stimulation. *Child Development,* 1965, **36,** 249–256.

Block, J. Monozygotic twin similarity in multiple psychophysiologic parameters and measures. In J. Wortis (Ed.), *Recent Advances in Biological Psychiatry,* Vol. IX. New York: Plenum Press, 1967.

Block, J. H. Conceptions of sex role: Some cross-cultural and longitudinal perspectives. *American Psychologist,* 1973, **28,** 512–526.

Brackett, C. W. *Laughing and Crying of Preschool Children.* New York: Columbia Teachers College, 1934.

Brehm, J. W. *A Theory of Psychological Reactance.* New York: Academic Press, 1966.

Bridger, W. and Birns, B. Experience and temperament in human neonates. In G. Newton and S. Levine (Eds.), *Early Experience and Behavior.* New York: Charles Thomas, 1968.

Bridges, K. Emotional development in early infancy. *Child Development,* 1932, **2,** 324–341.

Bronson, W. Central orientations: A study of behavior organization from childhood to adolescence. *Child Development,* 1966, **37,** 125–155.

Bronson, W. C. Adult derivatives of emotional expressiveness and reactivity-control: developmental continuities from childhood to adulthood. *Child Development,* 1967, **38,** 801–817.

Brown, A., Stafford, R., and Vandenberg, S. Twins behavioral differences. *Child Development,* 1967, **38,** 1055–1064.

Buss, A. H. *The Psychology of Aggression.* New York: Wiley, 1961.

Buss, A. Two anxiety factors in psychiatric patients. *Journal of Abnormal and Social Psychology,* 1962, **65,** 426–427.

Buss, A. H. *Psychopathology.* New York: Wiley, 1966.

Buss, A. and Durkee, A. An inventory for assessing different kinds of hostility. *Journal of Consulting Psychology, 1957,* **21,** 343–349.

Buss, A. H. and Gerjuoy, H. The scaling of terms used to describe personality. *Journal of Consulting Psychology,* 1957, **21,** 361–369.

Buss, A. H. and Murray, E. N. Activity level and words connoting mood. *Perceptual and Motor Skills,* 1965, **21,** 684–686.

Buss, A., Plomin, R., and Willerman, L. The inheritance of temperaments. *Journal of Personality,* 1973, **41,** 513–524.

Caldwell, B. M. and Herscher, L. Mother-infant interaction during the first year of life. *Merrill-Palmer Quarterly,* 1964, **10,** 119–128.

Campbell, D. Motor activity in a group of newborn babies. *Biology of the Neonate,* 1968, **13,** 257–270.

Canter, S. In G. Claridge, S. Canter, and W. I. Hume (Eds.), *Personality Differences and Biological Variations*. New York: Pergamon Press, 1973.

Carlson, R. Stability and change in the adolescent's self-image. *Child Development*, 1965, **36**, 659–666.

Carrigan, P. M. Extraversion-introversion as a dimension of personality: A reappraisal. *Psychological Bulletin*, 1960, **57**, 329–360.

Carter, H. D. Twin-similarities in personality traits. *Journal of Genetic Psychology*, 1933a, **43**, 312–319.

Carter, H. D. A preliminary study of free association: Twin similarities and the technique of measurement. *Journal of Psychology*, 1933b, **6**, 201–215.

Carter, H. D. Twin-similarities in emotional traits. *Character and Personality*, 1935, **4**, 61–78.

Carter, H. D. Resemblance of twins in speed of association. *Psychological Bulletin*, 1939, **36**, 641.

Cattell, R. B. *Description and measurement of personality*. Yonkers-on-Hudson, New York: World Book, 1946.

Cattell, R. B. *Handbook for the IPAT Anxiety Scale*. Champaign, Ill.: Institute for Personality and Ability Testing, 1957.

Cattell, R. B., Blewett, D. B., and Beloff, J. R. The inheritance of personality: A multiple-variance analysis of approximate nature-nurture ratios for primary personality factors in Q-data. *American Journal of Human Genetics*, 1955, **7**, 122–146.

Cattell, R., Saunders, D. R., and Stice, G. *Handbook for the Sixteen Personality Factor Questionnaire*. Champaign, Ill.: Institute for Personality and Ability Testing, 1957.

Cattell, R. B., Stice, G. F., and Kristy, N. A first approximation to nature-nurture ratios for eleven primary personality factors in objective tests. *Journal of Abnormal and Social Psychology*, 1957, **54**, 143–159.

Clark, G. and Birch, H. G. Hormonal modification of social behavior. *Psychosomatic Medicine*, 1945, **7**, 321–329.

Cohen, D., Dibble, E., Grawe, J., and Pollin, W. Separating identical from fraternal twins. *Archives of General Psychiatry*, 1973, **29**, 465–469.

Cohen, D. and Horn, J. Extraversion and performance: A test of the theory of cortical inhibition. *Journal of Abnormal Psychology*, 1974, **83**, 304–307.

Comrey, A. L. Factored homogeneous item dimensions in personality research. *Educational and Psychological Measurement*, 1961, **21**, 417–431.

Cortes, J. B. and Gatti, F. M. Physique and self-description of temperament. *Journal of Consulting Psychology*, 1965, **29**, 432–439.

Cromwell, R. L., Baumeister, A., and Hawkins, W. F. Research in activity level. In N. R. Ellis (Ed.), *Handbook of Mental Deficiency*. New York: McGraw-Hill, 1963, pp. 632–663.

Davidson, M., McInnis, R., and Parnell, R. The distribution of personality traits in seven-year-old children: A combined psychological, psychiatric, and somatotype study. *British Journal of Educational Psychology*, 1957, **27**, 48–61.

Dawe, H. C. An analysis of two hundred quarrels of preschool children. *Child Development*, 1934, **5**, 139–157.

Derner, G., Aborn, M., and Canter, A. The reliability of the Wechsler-Bellevue subtests and scales. *Journal of Consulting Psychiatry*, 1950, **14**, 172–179.

Diamond, S. *Personality and Temperament*. New York: Harper and Brothers, 1957.

Digman, J. Principal dimensions of child personality as inferred from teacher's judgements. *Child Development*, 1963, **34**, 43–60.

Douvan, E. and Adelson, J. *The Adolescent Experience.* New York: Wiley, 1966.

Duffy, K. E., Jamison, K., and Comrey, A. L. Assessment of a proposed expansion of the Comrey Personality Factor System. *Multivariate Behavioral Research,* 1969, **4,** 295–307.

Eaves, L. J. The structure of genotypic and environmental covariation for personality measurements: An analysis of the PEN. *British Journal of Social and Clinical Psychology,* 1973, **12,** 275–282.

Eaves, L. and Eysenck, H. J. The nature of extraversion: a genetical analysis. Unpublished, 1974.

Edwards, A. L. *Edwards Personal Preference Schedule.* New York: Psychological Corporation, 1954.

Ellis, N. and Pryer, R. Quantification of gross bodily activity in children with severe neuropathology. *American Journal of Mental Deficiency,* 1959, **63,** 1034–1037.

Emmerich, W. Continuity and stability in early social development. *Child Development,* 1964, **35,** 311–322.

Escalona, S. and Heider, G. *Prediction and Outcome.* New York: Basic Books, 1959.

Escalona, S. and Leitch, M. Early phases of personality development: a non-normative study of infant behavior. *Monograph of the Society for Research in Child Development,* 1952, **17,** No. 1.

Exline, R. V. Effects of need for affiliation, sex, and the sight of others upon initial communications in problem-solving groups. *Journal of Personality,* 1962, **30,** 541–556.

Exline, R. V. Explorations in the process of person perception: Visual interaction in relation to competition, sex, and need for affiliation. *Journal of Personality,* 1963, **31,** 1–20.

Exline, R. V., Gray, D., and Schuette, D. Visual behavior in a dyad as affected by interview content and sex of respondent. *Journal of Personality and Social Psychology,* 1965, **1,** 201–209.

Eysenck, H. *Dimensions of Personality.* London: Kegan, Paul, Trench, Trubner, 1947.

Eysenck, H. *The Structure of Human Personality.* London: Methuen, 1953.

Eysenck, H. The questionnaire measurement of neuroticism and extraversion. *Revista de Psicologia,* 1956a, 113–140.

Eysenck, H. J. The inheritance of intraversion-extraversion. *Acta Psychologica,* 1956b, **12,** 95–110.

Eysenck, H. *The Dynamics of Anxiety and Hysteria.* New York: Praeger, 1957.

Eysenck, H. *The Maudsley Personality Inventory.* London: University of London Press, 1959.

Eysenck, H. J. *The Handbook of Abnormal Psychology.* New York: Basic Books, 1961.

Eysenck, H. *The Biological Basis of Personality.* Springfield, Ill.: Charles C Thomas, 1967.

Eysenck, H. *Readings in Extraversion-Introversion:* Volume 1: *Theoretical and Methodological Issues.* New York: Wiley-Interscience, 1970.

Eysenck, S. B. and Eysenck, H. J. On the dual nature of extraversion. *British Journal of Social and Clinical Psychology,* 1963a, **2,** 46–55.

Eysenck, H. J. and Eysenck, S. B. *Manual for the Eysenck Personality Inventory.* San Diego: Educational and Industrial Testing Service, 1963b.

Eysenck, H. J. and Prell, D. B. The inheritance of neuroticism: An experimental study. *Journal of Mental Science,* 1951, **97,** 441–465.

Eysenck, H. and Rachman, S. *The Causes and Cures of Neurosis.* San Diego, Cal.: Robert Knapp, 1965.

Falconer, D. S. *Introduction to Quantitative Genetics.* New York: Oliver and Boyd, 1960.

Fales, E. A comparison of the vigorousness of play activities of preschool boys and girls. *Child Development,* 1937, **8,** 144–158.

Farley, F. H. Social desirability and dimensionality in the sensation-seeking scale. *Acta Psychologica,* 1967, **26,** 89–96.

Farley, F. H. Further investigation of the two personae of extraversion. *British Journal of Social and Clinical Psychology,* 1970, **9,** 377–379.

Farley, F. H. and Farley, S. V. Impulsiveness, sociability, and the preference for varied experience. *Perceptual and Motor Skills,* 1970, **31,** 47–50.

Farnsworth, P. R. A genetic study of the Bernreuter Personality Inventory. *Journal of Genetic Psychology,* 1938, **52,** 3–13.

Fenigstein, A. Gender differences in the effect of rejection by a group. Unpublished, University of Texas at Austin.

Firestone, I. J., Kaplan, K. J., and Russell, C. J. Anxiety, fear, and affiliation with similar-state versus dissimilar-state others: Misery sometimes loves nonmiserable company. *Journal of Personality and Social Psychology,* 1973, **26,** 409–414.

Fish, E. The 'one-child, one drug' myth of stimulants in hyperkinesis. *Archives of General Psychiatry,* 1971, **25,** 193–203.

Fitzgerald, H. D. Automatic pupillary reflex activity during early infancy and its relation to social and nonsocial visual stimuli. *Journal of Experimental Child Psychology,* 1968, **6,** 470–482.

Foshee, J. Studies in activity level: I. Simple and complex task performance in defectives. *American Journal of Mental Deficiency,* 1958, **62,** 882–886.

Foulds, G. A. Temperamental differences in maze performance. Part I. Characteristic differences among psychoneurotics. *British Journal of Psychology,* 1951, **42,** 209–217.

Fouts, G. T. and Click, M. M. The effects of live and TV models on observational learning in introverted and extroverted children. Paper presented to the Society for Research in Child Development, Philadelphia, 1973.

Freedman, D. G. An ethological approach to the genetic study of human behavior. In S. Vandenberg (Ed.), *Methods and Goals in Human Behavior Genetics.* New York: Academic Press, 1965, 141–161.

Freedman, D. G. An evolutionary approach to research on the life cycle. *Human Development,* 1971, **14,** 97–99.

Frischeisen-Kohler, I. The personal tempo and its inheritance. *Character and Personality,* 1933, **1,** 301–313.

Gewirtz, J. and Baer, D. Deprivation and satiation of social reinforcers as drive conditions. *Journal of Abnormal and Social Psychology,* 1958, **56,** 49–56.

Goldberg, S. and Lewis, M. Play behavior in the year-old infant: Early sex differences. *Child Development,* 1969, **40,** 21–31.

Goodenough, F. L. Interrelationships in the behavior of young children. *Child Development,* 1930, **1,** 29–47.

Goodenough, F. L. *Anger in Young Children.* Minneapolis: University of Minnesota Press, 1931.

Goodenough, E. W. Interest in persons as an aspect of sex differences in the early years. *Genetic Psychology Monographs,* 1957, **55,** 287–323.

Goslin, D. A. (Ed.) *Handbook of Socialization Theory and Research.* Chicago: Rand McNally, 1969.

Gottesman, I. Heritability of personality: A demonstration. *Psychological Monographs,* 1963, **77,** whole No. 572.

Gottesman, I. I. Genetic variance in adaptive personality traits. *Journal of Child Psychology and Psychiatry*, 1966, **7**, 199–208.

Gough, H. G. *Manual for the California Psychological Inventory*. Palo Alto, Cal.: Consulting Psychologists Press, 1957.

Gough, H. G. and Heilbrun, A. *The Adjective Check List Manual*. Palo Alto, Cal.: Consulting Psychological Press, 1965.

Green, E. Friendships and quarrels among preschool children. *Child Development*, 1933a, **4**, 237–252.

Green, E. Group play and quarreling among preschool children. *Child Development*, 1933b, **4**, 302–207.

Grinder, R. E. Parental child-rearing practices, conscience, and resistance to temptation of sixth grade children. *Child Development*, 1962, **33**, 803–820.

Grossberg, J. and Wilson, H. A correlational comparison of the Wolpe-Lang Fear Survey and Taylor Manifest Anxiety Scale. *Behavior Research Therapy*, 1965, **3**, 125–128.

Guilford, J. P. *An Inventory of Factors STDCR*. Beverly Hills, Cal.: Sheridan Supply Co., 1940.

Guilford, J. P. *Personality*. New York: McGraw-Hill, 1959.

Guilford, J. P. and Zimmerman, S. Fourteen dimensions of temperament. *Psychological Monographs*, 1956, **70**, whole No. 417.

Hagman, E. P. The companionships of preschool children. *University of Iowa Studies in Child Welfare*, 1933, **7**, whole No. 4.

Hall, E. *The Hidden Dimension*. New York: Doubleday and Co., Inc., 1966.

Hamilton, M. The assessment of anxiety states by rating. *British Journal of Medical Psychology*, 1959, **32**, 50–59.

Hare, R. D. *Psychopathy: Theory and Research*. New York: Wiley, 1970.

Harlow, H. The formation of learning sets. *Psychological Review*, 1949, **56**, 51–65.

Harrison, R. Personal tempo and the interrelationship of voluntary and maximal rates of movement. *Journal of General Psychology*, 1941, **24**, 343–379.

Hartrup, W. W. and Keller, E. D. Nurturance in preschool children and its relationship to dependency. *Child Development*, 1960, **31**, 681–689.

Hartshorne, H., May, M., and Maller, J. B. *Studies in Service and Self Control*. New York: MacMillan, 1929.

Hatfield, J. S., Ferguson, L. R., and Alpert, R. Mother-child interaction and the socialization process. *Child Development*, 1967, **38**, 365–414.

Hattwick, L. A. Sex differences in behavior of nursery school children. *Child Development*, 1937, **8**, 343–355.

Herron, R. E. and Ramaden, R. W. Continuous monitoring of overt human body movement by radio telemetry: A review. *Perceptual and Motor Skills*, 1967, **24**, 1303–1308.

Hess, E. H. Attitude and pupil size. *Scientific American*, 1965, **212**:46–54.

Holter, H. *Sex Roles and Social Structure*. Oslo: Universitetforlaget, 1970.

Horn, J. Unpublished, University of Texas at Austin, 1971 and 1972.

Jacklin, E., Maccoby, E., and Dick, A. Barrier behavior and toy preference: Sex differences (and their absence) in the year-old child. *Child Development*, 1973, **44**, 196–200.

Jackson, D. N. *Personality Research Form Manual*. Goshen, N.Y.: Research Psychologists Press, 1967.

Jersild, A. and Holmes, F. *Children's Fears*. New York: Columbia University Teachers College, 1935.

Jersild, A. J. and Markey, F. V. Conflicts between preschool children. *Child Development Monographs,* 1935, whole No. 21.

Johnson, C. F. Hyperactivity and the machine: The actometer. *Child Development,* 1971, **42,** 2105–2110.

Johnson, C. F. Limits on the measurement of activity level in children using ultrasound and photoelectric cells. *American Journal of Mental Deficiency,* 1972, **77,** 301–310.

Jones, A., Wilkinson, H., and Braden, I. Information deprivation as a motivational variable. *Journal of Experimental Psychology,* 1961, **62,** 126–137.

Kagan, J. Developmental studies in reflection and analysis. In A. Kidd and J. Rivoire (Eds.), *Perceptual Development in Children.* New York: International Universities Press, Inc., 1966.

Kagan, J. *Change and Continuity in Infancy.* New York: Wiley, 1971.

Kagan, J. and Moss, H. A. *Birth to Maturity: A Study in Psychological Development.* New York: Wiley, 1962.

Karpman, B. On the need for separating psychopathy into two distinct clinical types: Symptomatic and idiopathic. *Journal of Criminology and Psychopathology,* 1941, **3,** 112–137.

Kelly, E. L. Consistency of the adult personality. *American Psychologist,* 1955, **10,** 659–681.

Kenny, T. J. Characteristics of children referred because of hyperactivity. *Journal of Pediatrics,* 1971, **79,** 618–622.

Kessen, W., Hendry, L., and Leutzendorff, A. Measurement of movement in the human newborn. *Child Development,* 1961, **32,** 95–105.

Kessen, W., Williams, E. J., and Williams, J. P. Selection and test of response measures in the study of the human newborn. *Child Development,* 1961, **32,** 7–24.

Klebanoff, L. B. Parental attitudes of mothers of schizophrenic, brain-injured, and retarded, and normal children. *American Journal of Orthopsychiatry,* 1959, **24,** 445–454.

Korner, A. Individual differences at birth: Implications for early experience and later development. *American Journal of Orthopsychiatry,* 1971, **41,** 608–619.

Korner, A., and Grobstein. Visual alertness as related to soothing in neonates: Implications for maternal stimulation and early deprivation. *Child Development,* 1966, **37,** 867–876.

Lacey, J. I. Psychophysiological approaches to the evaluation of psychotherapeutic process and outcome. In E. A. Rubenstein and M. B. Parloff (Eds.), *Research in Psychotherapy.* Washington, D.C.: American Psychological Association, 1959.

Lacey, J. I., Kagan, J., B. C., and Moss, H. A. The visceral level: Situational determinants and behavioral correlates of autonomic response patterns. In P. H. Knapp (Ed.), *Expression of the Emotions in Man.* New York: International Universities Press, 1963.

Laird, J. D. Self-attribution of emotion: The effects of expressive behavior on the quality of emotional experience. *Journal of Personality and Social Psychology,* 1974, **29,** 475–486.

Lazarus, R. S. *Psychological Stress and the Coping Process.* New York: McGraw-Hill, 1966.

Lipsitt, L. and DeLucia, C. An apparatus for the measurement of specific response and general activity of the human neonate. *American Journal of Psychology, 1960,* **73,** 630–632.

Lipton, E. L. and Steinschneider, A. Studies on the psychophysiology of infancy. *Merill-Palmer Quarterly,* 1964, **10,** 102–117.

Lipton, E. L., Steinschneider, A., and Richmond, J. B. Autonomic function in the neonate: 4. Individual differences in cardiac reactivity. *Psychosomatic Medicine,* 1961, **23,** 472–484.

Loehlin, J. C. and Nichols, R. C. *Heredity, Environment, and Personality: A Study of 850 Twins.* Austin, Tex.: University of Texas Press, in press.

London, H., Schubert, D., and Washburn, D. Increase of autonomic arousal by boredom. *Journal of Abnormal Psychology,* 1972, **80,** 29–36.

Loo, C. and Wenar, C. Activity level and motor inhibition: Their relationship to intelligence-test performance in normal children. *Child Development,* 1971, **42,** 967–971.

Lykken, D. T. A study of anxiety in the sociopathic personality. *Journal of Abnormal and Social Psychology,* 1957, **55,** 6–10.

Maccoby, E. (Ed.), *The Development of Sex Differences.* Palo Alto, Cal.: Stanford University Press, 1966.

Maccoby, E. and Masters, J. Attachment and dependency. In P. H. Mussen (Ed.), *Carmichael's Manual of Child Psychology,* 3rd ed. New York: Wiley, 1970, 159–259.

Maccoby, E., Dowley, E., Hagen, J. W., and Degerman, R. Activity level and intellectual functioning in normal preschool children. *Child Development,* 1965, **36,** 761–770.

Mason, W. A. Determinants of social behavior in young chimpanzees. In A. M. Schrier, H. F. Harlow, and F. Stollnitz, (Eds.), *Behavior in Nonhuman Primates,* Volume 2. New York: Academic Press, 1965, 335–364.

Mason, W. A. Early social deprivation in nonhuman primates: Implications for human behavior. In D. C. Glass (Ed.), *Biology and Behavior: Environmental Influences.* New York: Rockefeller University Press, 1968, 70–101.

McConnell, T. R., Cromwell, R., Bialer, I., and Son, C. Studies in activity level: VII. Effects on amphetamine drug administration on the activity level. *American Journal of Mental Deficiency,* 1964, **68,** 647–651.

McCord, W. and McCord, J. *Origins of Crime.* New York: Columbia University Press, 1959.

McGrade, B. Newborn activity and emotional response at eight months. *Child Development,* 1968, **39,** 1247–1252.

Mehrabian, A. The development and validation of measures of affiliative tendency and sensitivity to rejection. *Educational and Psychological Measurement,* 1970, **30,** 417–428.

Milton, G. A. A factor analytic study of child-rearing behaviors. *Child Development,* 1958, **29,** 381–395.

Mischel, W. Preference for delayed reinforcement and social responsibility. *Journal of Abnormal and Social Psychology,* 1961, **62,** 1–7.

Mittler, P. *The Study of Twins.* Baltimore: Penguin Books, 1971.

Moss, H. A. Sex, age, and state as determinants of mother-infant interaction. *Merrill-Palmer Quarterly,* 1967, **13,** 19–36.

Murphy, L. B. *The Widening World of Childhood.* New York: Basic Books, 1962.

Murray, H. *Explorations in Personality.* New York: Oxford University Press, 1938.

Nelson, J. *Personality and Intelligence.* New York: Columbia Teachers College, 1931.

Newman, J., Freeman, F., and Holzinger, K. *Twins: A Study of Heredity and Environment.* Chicago: University of Chicago Press, 1937.

Nichols, R. C. The resemblance of twins in personality and interests. *National Merit Scholarship Corporation Research Reports,* 1966, **2,** 1–23.

Nichols, R. C. and Bilbro, W. C. The diagnosis of twin zygosity. *Acta Genetica,* 1966, **16,** 265–275.

Nichols, R. C. and Schnell, R. Factor sales for the California Psychological Inventory. *Journal of Consulting Psychology,* 1963, **27,** 228–235.

Owen, D. and Sines, J. O. Heritability of personality in children. *Behavior Genetics,* 1970, **1,** 235–248.

Peacock, L. J. and Williams, M. An ultrasonic device for recording activity. *American Journal of Psychology,* 1962, **75,** 648–652.

Pedersen, F. A. and Bell, R. Q. Sex differences in preschool children without histories of complications of pregnancy and delivery. *Developmental Psychology*, 1970, **3**, 10–15.

Plomin, R. *A Temperament Theory of Personality Development: Parent-Child Interactions.* Dissertation, University of Texas, 1974.

Plomin, R., Willerman, L., and Loehlin, J. Resemblance in appearance and the equal environments assumption in twin studies of personality traits. Submitted to *Behavior Genetics,* 1974.

Porteus, S. D. *The Porteus Maze Test and Intelligence.* Palo Alto, Cal.: Pacific Books, 1950.

Rethlingshafer, D. Relationships of tests of persistence to other measures of continuance of activities. *Journal of Abnormal and Social Psychology*, 1942, **37**, 71–82.

Rheingold, H. L. The social and socializing infant. In D. A. Goslin (Ed.), *Handbook of Socialization Theory and Research.* Chicago: Rand McNally, 1969, 779–790.

Ricketts, A. F. *A Study of the Behavior of Young Children in Anger.* Des Moines: University of Iowa Studies in Child Welfare, 1934, 9, part 5.

Roff, M. and Roff, L. An analysis of the variance of conflict behavior in preschool children. *Child Development*, 1940, **11**, 43–60.

Rutter, M., Korn, S., and Birch, H. Genetic and environmental factors in the development of primary reaction patterns. *British Journal of Social and Clinical Psychology*, 1963, **2**, 161–173.

Sainsbury, P. A method of measuring spontaneous movements by time-sampling motion pictures. *Journal of Mental Science*, 1954, **100**, 742–748.

Sanford, R. N., Adkins, M., Miller, R. B., and Cobb, E. A. Physique, personality, and scholarship. *Monograph of the Society for Research in Child Development*, 1943, whole No. 8.

Scarr, S. The origins of individual differences in adjective check list scores. *Journal of Consulting Psychology*, 1966a, **30**, 354–357.

Scarr, S. Genetic factors in activity and motivation. *Child Development,* 1966b, **37**, 663–673.

Scarr, S. Environmental bias in twin studies. *Eugenics Quarterly,* 1968, **15**, 34–40.

Scarr, S. Social introversion-extraversion as a heritable response. *Child Development,* 1969, **40**, 823–832.

Scarr, S. and Salapatek, P. Patterns of fear development during infancy. *Merrill-Palmer Quarterly,* 1970, **16**, 53–90.

Schachter, J. Pain, fear, and anger, in hypertensives and normotensives. *Psychosomatic Medicine*, 1957, **19**, 17–19.

Schachter, S. *The Psychology of Affiliation.* Palo Alto, Cal.: Stanford University Press, 1959.

Schachter, S. and Singer, J. E. Cognitive, social, and physiological determinants of emotional state. *Psychological Review*, 1962, **69**, 379–399.

Schaefer, E. S. A circumplex model for maternal behavior. *Journal of Abnormal and Social Psychology*, 1959, **59**, 226–335.

Schaefer, E. S. and Bell, R. Q. Development of a parental attitude research instrument. *Child Development,* 1958, **29**, 340–361.

Schaefer, E. and Bayley, N. Maternal behavior, child behavior, and their intercorrelations from infancy through adolescence. *Monographs of the Society for Research in Child Development*, 1963, **28**, whole No. 87.

Schaffer, H. R. and Emerson, P. E. Patterns of response to physical contact in early human development. *Journal of Child Psychology and Psychiatry*, 1964, **5**, 1–13.

Schneirla, T. C. An evolutionary and developmental theory of biphasic processes underlying approach and withdrawal. In M. R. Jones (Ed.), *Nebraska Symposium on Motivation.* Lincoln: University of Nebraska Press, 1959, 122–168.

Schoenfeldt, L. F. The hereditary components of the Project TALENT two-day test battery. *Measurement and Evaluation in Guidance*, 1968, **1**, 130–140.

Schooler, C. Birth order effects: Not here, not now. *Psychological Bulletin,* 1973, **78**, 161–175.

Schulman, J. and Reisman, J. An objective measure of hyperactivity. *American Journal of Mental Deficiency*, 1959, **64**, 455–456.

Sears, R. R., Maccoby, E. E., and Levin, H. *Patterns of Child Rearing*. Evanston, Illinois: Row and Peterson, 1957.

Sermat, V. and Smyth, M. Content analysis of verbal communication in the development of a relationship: Conditions influencing self-disclosure. *Journal of Personality and Social Psychology*, 1973, **26**, 332–347.

Sheldon, W. *The Varieties of Temperament: A Psychology of Constitutional Differences*. New York: Harper, 1942.

Sherman, M. The differentiation of emotional responses in infants: III. A proposed theory of the development of emotional responses in infants. *Journal of Comparative Psychology*, 1928, **8**, 385–394.

Sherman, R. and Poe, C. Factor-analytic scales of a normative form of the EPPS. *Measurement and Evaluation in Guidance*, 1970, **2**, 243–248.

Shields, J. Twins brought up apart. *The Eugenics Review*, 1958, **50**, 115–123.

Shields, J. *Monozygotic Twins Brought Up Together and Apart*. Oxford: Oxford University Press, 1962.

Shirley, M. *The First Two Years: A Study of Twenty-five Babies*. Volume III: *Personality Manifestations*. Minneapolis: University of Minnesota Press, 1933.

Sines, J., Pauker, J., Sines, L., and Owen, D. The identification of clinically relevant dimensions of children's behavior. *Journal of Consulting and Clinical Psychology*, 1969, **33**, 728–734.

Smith, J. M. The relative brightness values of three hues for newborn infants. *University of Iowa Studies in Child Welfare*, 1936, **12**, 91–104.

Spangler, D. P. and Thomas, C. W. The effects of age, sex, and physical disability upon manifest needs. *Journal of Counseling Psychology*, 1962, **9**, 313–319.

Sprague, R. and Toppe, E. Relationship between activity level and delay of reinforcement in the retarded. *Journal of Experimental Child Psychology*, 1966, **3**, 390–397.

Stern, G. G., Stein, M. I., and Bloom, B. S. *Methods in Personality Assessment*. Glencoe, Illinois: Free Press, 1956.

Sternbach, R. *Principles of Psychophysiology*. New York: Academic Press, 1966.

Strongman, K. T. *The Psychology of Emotion*. New York: Wiley, 1973.

Taylor, J. The relationship of anxiety to the conditioned eyelid response. *Journal of Experimental Psychology*, 1951, **41**, 81–92.

Thomas, A., Chess, S., Birch, H., Hertzig, M., Korn, S. *Behavioral Individuality in Early Childhood*. New York: New York University Press, 1963.

Thomas, A., Chess, S. and Birch, H. G. *Temperament and Behavior Disorders in Children*. New York: New York University Press, 1968.

Thomas, A., Chess, S. and Birch, H. The origin of personality. *Scientific American*, 1970, **223**, 102–109.

Thompson, W. R. Development and the biophysical bases of personality. In E. F. Borgatta and W. W. Lambert (Eds.), *Handbook of Personality Theory and Research*. Chicago: Rand McNally, 1968.

Thornton, G. R. A factor analysis of tests designed to measure persistence. *Psychological Monographs*, 1939, **51**, whole No. 229.

Thurstone, L. L. The dimensions of temperament. *Psychometrika,* 1951, **16,** 11–20.

Thurstone, L. L. *Examiner Manual for the Thurstone Temperament Schedule.* Chicago: Science Research Associates, 1953.

Tiger, L. and Fox, R. *The Imperial Animal.* New York: Holt, Rinehart & Winston, 1971.

Tinbergen, N. Derived activities: Their causation, biological significance, origin and.emancipation during evolution. *Quarterly Review of Biology,* 1952, **27,** 1–32.

Tuddenham, R. D. Studies in reputation: I. Sex and grade differences in school children's evaluations of their peers. *Psychological Monographs,* 1952, No. 333, 1–39.

Tuddenham, R. D. The constancy of personality ratings over two decades. *Genetic Psychology Monographs,* **1959,** 3–30.

Valins, S. Cognitive effects of false heart-rate feedback. *Journal of Personality and Social Psychology,* 1966, **4,** 400–408.

Van den Daele, L. Infant reactivity to redundant proprioceptive and auditory stimulation: A twin study. *Journal of Psychology,* 1971, **78,** 269–276.

Vandenberg, S. G. The hereditary abilities study: Hereditary components in a psychological test battery. *American Journal of Human Genetics,* 1962, **14,** 220–237.

Vandenberg, S. G. Hereditary factors in normal personality traits. In J. Wortis (Ed.), *Recent Advances in Biological Psychiatry,* Volume IX. New York: Plenum Press, 1967.

Vandenberg, S., Clark, P., and Samuels, I. Psychophysiological reactions of twins: Hereditary factors in galvanic skin resistance, heartbeat, and breathing rates. *Eugenics Quarterly,* 1965, **12,** 7–10.

Vandenberg, S. G., Stafford, R. E., and Brown, A. M. The Louisville twin study. In Vandenberg, S. (Ed.), *Progress in Human Behavior Genetics.* Baltimore: Johns Hopkins Press, 1968.

Walker, R. N. Body build and behavior in young children: I. Body build and nursery school teachers' ratings. *Monographs of the Society for Research in Child Development,* 1962, **27,** No. 3.

Walker, R. N. Some temperament traits in children as viewed by their peers, their teachers, and themselves. *Monographs of the Society for Research in Child Development,* 1967, **32,** whole No. 6.

Weiss, G., Minde, K., Werry, J., Douglas, V., and Nemeth, E. The hyperactive child: Five-year follow-up. *Archives of General Psychiatry,* 1971, **24,** 415–421.

Wellman, B. L. Sex differences. In C. Murchison (Ed.), *A Handbook of Child Psychology.* Worchester: Clark University Press, 1926.

Werry, J. S. and Sprague, R. L. Hyperactivity. In. C. G. Costello (Ed.), *Symptoms of Psychopathology: A Handbook,* New York: Wiley, 1970.

White, R. W. *The Enterprise of Living.* New York: Holt, Rinehart and Winston, 1972.

Wiggins, J. *Personality and Prediction: Principles of Personality Assessment.* Reading, Mass.: Addison-Wesley, 1973, Chapter 1.

Wilde, G. Inheritance of personality traits. *Acta Psychologica,* 1964, **22,** 37–51.

Willerman, L. Activity level and hyperactivity in twins. *Child Development,* 1973, **44,** 288–293.

Willerman, L. and Plomin, R. Activity level in children and their parents. *Child Development,* 1973, **44,** 854–858.

Wilson, R., Brown, A., and Matheny, A. Emergence and persistence of behavioral differences in twins. *Child Development,* 1971, **42,** 1381–1398.

Winker, J. B. Age trends and sex differences in the wishes, identifications, activities, and fears of children. *Child Development,* 1949, **20,** 191–200.

Wolfensberger, W., Miller, M., Foshee, J., and Cromwell, R. Rorschach correlates of activity level in high school children. *Journal of Consulting Psychology,* 1962, **26,** 269–272.

Zuckerman, M. Dimensions of sensation-seeking. *Journal of Consulting and Clinical Psychology,* 1971, **36,** 45–52.

Zuckerman, M., Kilin, E. A., Price, L., and Zoob, I. Development of a sensation-seeking scale. *Journal of Consulting Psychology,* 1964, **28,** 477–482.

Zuckerman, M. and Link, K. Construct validity for the sensation-seeking scale. *Journal of Consulting and Clinical Psychology,* 1968, **32,** 420–426.

Zuckerman, M. and Oltean, M. Some relationships between maternal attitude factors and authoritarianism, personality needs, psychopathy, and self-acceptance. *Child Development,* 1959, **30,** 27–36.

INDEX